# *Family* Evangelism

## Bringing Jesus to the Family Circle

# A Department of Family Ministries publication.

Prepared by Karen and Ron Flowers
Software formatting by Kathleen Sowards

Other Family Ministries Planbooks in this series:

*Passing on the Torch*
*Families Reaching Families*
*Empowering Families for Growth & Change*
*Making Families Whole*
*Family Seasons*
*Peace & Healing: Making Homes Abuse-free*
*Families Filled with Joy*
*Facing Family Crises: Supporting One Another with Love*
*New Beginnings*
*Understanding Families*
*Families of Faith*
*It Takes a Family*

**To order more copies of this book contact the General Conference Ministerial Association**
**12501 Old Columbia Pike, Silver Spring, MD 20904 • (301) 680-6499 • www.ministerialassociation.com**

# Preface
## An *Invitation* to Dialogue

The book you hold in your hands is more than the usual Family Ministries Planbook, in the genre of other such planbooks that have been forthcoming annually from the General Conference Department of Family Ministries for more than a decade. It is more than the usual resource for special family emphasis days on the world church calendar. In this special Year of Evangelism, as the myriad spotlights of church life are fused into one and tightly focused on mission, we feel the need for dialogue. We who are charged with responsibility for the health and well-being of the fundamental unit of the church—the family—need to listen and talk more with the people on the evangelistic front lines.

For starters, when we dialogue more, we remind ourselves often enough not to forget that we're all on the same team. As our world president, Dr. Jan Paulsen, has emphasized, there is no dichotomy between evangelism and nurture. We are all passionate about one thing—getting out the word of the Evangel that was first announced by the heavenly messengers who broke silence in unprecedented decibels that star-spangled night in Bethlehem, that glorious eve when God presented the world with the unspeakable gift of His Son. "Glory to God in the highest, and on earth peace to men on whom His favor rests."

We must foray more often into one another's worlds because there are things to be shared. There are things we long to share with you, and we're sure there are things you could share with us, to maximize our disciple-making efforts. For example, from our side, we see family as central to the disciple-making process. We read John 8:31 and John 13:35 as Jesus defining what it means to *be* a disciple, with obvious implications for what it will mean to *make* a disciple. Disciples are persons who live by the principles of Christ's kingdom and people who know how to enter into warm, loving relationships with God and others. Family, then, is at the heart of the disciple-making process—first because it is the primary place where values are caught, and second because it is in the family that the capacity for warm, close relationships with God and others is developed.

We who spend our days in the trenches with families need to talk with you about the hard realities of family life today. We want to talk with you about new understandings of the family as a dynamic system with complex connections and patterns of relating. We believe that within this understanding there are keys to better disciple-making practice. We want to bring what we know together with what you know, to empower us all to do evangelism in a way that draws whole families to Jesus Christ and intentionally strengthens the fabric of family in the church and in the community.

We need to talk about how the gospel radically transforms relationships. People, in every context, need practical help to put Christian principles into working clothes in their family relationships. We need to press to new levels of understanding and practice the question: What difference does the gospel make in human relationships? The words of Mary, the mother of Jesus, at the wedding feast at Cana poignantly sum the human condition and our ability to effect the transformation to which the gospel calls us, apart from Jesus. "They have no wine," she said. But in the presence of Jesus, the ordinary becomes extraordinary beyond belief. When this amazing makeover is worked in our families, nonbelievers will stand in awe. To make it happen, new believers will need both a miracle of grace and our encouragement and practical help for the growth journey on which they have embarked—a journey in faith toward the full restoration of all God had in mind when He created us relational creatures after His likeness in the beginning.

We need to talk more because the world has changed and Christianity is struggling to reach it. During the modern period, Christian theologians matched the philosophers idea for idea. Truth was an intellectual concept to be logically presented, discussed and debated. As Harry Lee Poe points out in his thought-provoking book *Christian Witness in a Postmodern World* (Abingdon Press, 2001) however, postmoderns "do not argue the same way. In fact, they do not want to argue at all." Summing up, he writes:

> The thirst for personal relationship and the dread of conflict and violence represent the driving themes of the postmodern generation. These two issues work themselves out in terms of the preference for personal rather than institutional involvement, a preference for acceptance of all differences rather than conflict over differences, and a desire for a sense of wholeness in a fragmented world. . . . The postmodern age is an anonymous age with a yearning for relationship. (p. 27)

If the Incarnation was incomprehensible to the modern age, it will be music to the ears of today's hearers. But for our children and our neighbors to dare to believe it is really true, Christians will first have to become great lovers for God. Our doctrines will make sense only in the context of their vital connection with the One who is Himself the Way, the Truth, and the Light. Even more important for the postmodern world is the good news that our Lord and Savior Jesus Christ is passionately in love with all His children and wants more than anything to enjoy a close relationship with them. What's more, He has broken down all the barriers that separate human beings and make relationships so difficult by becoming our Peace. This is the good news that ministry to families and evangelism must be all about if it is to meet the needs of postmodern human hearts.

Finally, we need to talk because talk is good. People engaged in healthy dialogue sharpen one another's thinking and multiply their wisdom. Extremes and rigidity give way to better balance and consensus. People who communicate usually grow on one another. Acquaintances often become friends. Associates become colleagues. Individuals become teammates. It sounds good to us! Will you join us in dialogue? This book is just the beginning.

Blessings as you lift up Jesus Christ in this Year of Evangelism 2003 and until He comes!

*Maranatha!*

**Karen and Ron Flowers**
*Directors, General Conference Department of Family Ministries*

end

# Contents

# Foreword

The family of Abraham was especially selected by God to be the first center of evangelism. Of him God said, "For I have chosen him, so that he will direct his children and his household after him to keep the way of the Lord by doing what is right and just, so that the Lord will bring about for Abraham what he has promised him" (Gen. 18:19).

God's testimony was a follow-up to the promise He had made to the patriarch, initially known as Abram, back in Genesis 12:3, "In you all the families of the earth shall be blessed."

Why Abraham's family? It is easy to figure out why from the Scriptures. The sacred writings reveal that Abraham led his family in regular worship wherever he pitched his tent (Gen. 12:7; cf. 13:4, 18). Also, Abraham's household was already a cosmopolitan group made up of hundreds of servants from a variety of nations (Gen.14:14), including "Eliezer of Damascus" whom he trusted very much (Gen. 15:2).

## NO GRANDCHILDREN

The impact of Abraham's spiritual life and God's covenant with him was felt far beyond his immediate family and generation. It reached even to his fugitive grandson, Jacob. Journeying north to find a wife among family relatives, Jacob was also desperately fleeing from his elder brother, Esau. One night, with a stone for a pillow, he slept and dreamed—of a ladder that stretched from the earth to the skies. At that time God repeated to Jacob the blessings which He originally bestowed on Abraham, concluding in a similar fashion, "All peoples on earth will be blessed through you and your offspring" (Gen. 28: 14). In that place Jacob set up a stone pillar and vowed to faithfully worship God and return his tithe if God would be with him and give him a peaceful return to his father's house (vss. 20-22).

Genealogically, Jacob was Abraham's grandson. But spiritually, Abraham has no grandchildren, only children. Gal. 3:29 clearly asserts, "If you are Christ's, then you are Abraham's seed, and heirs according to the promise." Today, Abraham is revered as the "father of faith" by three major world religions—Judaism, Christianity and Islam.

The messenger of God, Ellen G White, emphasizes the importance of making the home the first center for evangelism:

> Our work for Christ is to begin with the family, in the home. . . . There is no missionary field more important than this. . . . By many this home field has been shamefully neglected, and it is time that divine resources and remedies were presented, that this state of evil may be corrected. (*The Adventist Home*, p. 35)

This is an indictment on Christian families in her day and even more so in our day, isn't it? But let us also take it as a positive challenge, because we can redeem the time and regain lost ground!

## LASTING INFLUENCE OF EARLY TRAINING

The work of home evangelism should begin with children when they are still young. Someone has said, "It is easier to build a child than it is to mend a man." We can observe in the Scriptures that the people who made an appreciable impact on society got their basic discipline from homes where their parents taught them at an early age. Besides the noble job done by Abraham and Sarah, we can talk of the family of Jacob and Rachel in which Joseph was brought up. Joseph, of course, became the first foreigner to be the prime minister of the ancient superpower, Egypt. We can also mention the family of Amram and Jochebed which produced Moses, the first to commit the Holy Scriptures to a written form and the founder of the "church in the wilderness." "Train up a child in the way he should go," according to the advice of the wise man in Proverb 22:6, "and when he is old he will not depart from it."

Similarly, we read in the New Testament how parental influence impacted three successive generations. Said Paul to Timothy, "I have been reminded of your sincere faith, which first lived in your grandmother Lois and in your mother Eunice and, I am persuaded, now lives in you also" (2 Tim. 1:5). Timothy had grown up to be a useful leader in church administration. Paul reveals an important part of the secret to such a life: "From infancy you have known the holy

Scriptures, which are able to make you wise for salvation through faith in Christ Jesus" (2 Tim. 3:15).

Mrs. White makes a similar point in *The Adventist Home*, p. 32:

> One well-ordered, well-disciplined family tells more in behalf of Christianity than all the sermons that can be preached. Such a family gives evidence that the parents have been successful in following God's directions, and that their children will serve Him in the church. Their influence grows; for as they impart, they receive to impart again.

A Roman Catholic church leader once stated, "Give me a child before the age of seven, and I will make him a Catholic forever." I believe it is time for Adventist church leaders to make a similar declaration. I believe that if parents had been diligent in their first work of discipling their children for Christ, many more of our children would have remained Adventists when they were grown. Our world church would have twice its current membership or even more.

## OUTREACH, FAMILY TO FAMILY

As a center of evangelism, the family can also be involved in outreach activities. A good example of a family reaching out to others is that of Aquila and Priscilla. Their outreach touched Apollos, a Jewish orator who had accepted the gospel message and was proclaiming it in a powerful way. However, the couple noticed that his message was based only on the teachings of John the Baptist. So Aquila and Priscilla invited Apollos to their home "and explained to him the way of God more adequately" (Acts 18:26). From this time, Apollos grew even more powerful in preaching the whole gospel, so much so that Paul, in 1 Corinthians 3:1-31, had to rebuke the Corinthian believers for trying to trace their conversion to him or to Apollos rather than to the Spirit of God. Also, according to 1 Corinthians 16:19, the family of Aquila and Priscilla had a church that met in their home, a "house church." What a lesson for us all! Like Priscilla and Aquila, we can make our homes centers for small-group Bible studies. We can have "house churches," especially in places where it is not permitted by law to have a church building or in areas where church buildings are either too far away or too small to contain the growing number of new members joining the family of God.

Moreover, even though God saves each one as an individual, the value of corporate decision, especially in communities where the extended family system operates, cannot be overemphasized. The apostolic Church deliberately targeted whole families with the gospel. For instance, Peter's encounter with Cornelius, the centurion of Caesarea, led to the baptism of the entire family of the Roman army officer (Acts 10:1-43). Other biblical examples are no less dramatic. In Philippi, Paul and Silas met on the Sabbath day with a small group of women who were worshipping by the riverside at outskirts of the town. As a result, an influential lady named Lydia was baptized along with her family (Acts 16:15).

Even more remarkable is the story that next unfolds from Acts 16:16 onward. Through Paul's ministry in that place, devils were cast out of a slave girl. The miracle enraged her master, who was profiting from her witchcraft. So great was his influence on the civil authorities that Paul and Silas were beaten and imprisoned. That night in the prison, instead of complaining and cursing like other prisoners, these two prayed and sang. Then another miracle happened! Their chains broke loose! Thinking that his prisoners were going to escape, and with no credible explanation that he could give, the alarmed jailer contemplated suicide. The apostles assured him however, that no one had escaped. The stunned jailer's instant response to their incredible willingness to remain his captors is his heartfelt query, "Sirs, what must I do to be saved?" "Believe on the Lord Jesus Christ," came the immediate answer from the two apostles, "and you will be saved, you and your household" (Acts 16:30, 31). The story climaxes as the whole household became believers and were baptized.

Let us not shy away from targeting families in our evangelistic outreach.

Let us dare to try it even in the so-called "post-modern" secular societies. There is a lot of merit in it. We are aiming at more than one person. While we may end up winning one or a few initially, if we set our sights on sharing the good news with whole families, more may well respond. And if we win the entire family, not only will more share in the joy of salvation, but at the very least the degree of conflict that usually accompanies a change of religious persuasion in a given family will be lessened.

## FAMILY SALVATION

Finally, it must be noted that it is not just any family that can be a center for evangelism. Fractured family relationships do not create a winsome bridge to an understanding of God as a nurturing parent or a loving marriage partner in the minds of children. Families where there is unfaithfulness to the marriage vow, an unnatural liaison with a same-sex partners (cf. Romans 1:26, 27), or any of a variety of abuses and strife cannot speak eloquently of God as Creator and Re-creator. Such families must first seek and respond to the healing touch of God's grace in their own family circle before He can use them as His ambassadors to extended family and to the world. God is calling families into His mission service who are led by God-fearing husbands and wives, mothers and fathers whose commitment to God and the principles of His kingdom is evident in their everyday lives. He is looking for families whose lifestyle and quality of relationships are worthy of emulation.

Above all, each family who would share their faith with others must first make sure that its own faith remains firmly established on the solid rock, Jesus Christ, our Lord and Savior, "lest," as Paul warns in 1 Corinthians 9:27, "when I have preached to others, I myself should become disqualified." God forbid! I will be a happy husband and father when I see my entire family in heaven. My joy will be made complete when I see other families there who may be there partly because of the influence of our family and our decision to make our family circle the first center for evangelism. Amen!

**Luka T. Daniel**
*President, General Conference of Seventh-day Adventists, West-Central Africa Division*

# Sermons

# *Witness* in the Oneness

**by Karen and Ron Flowers**

*Christ prayed for unity among His followers. Where better could He look for such oneness than in the hearts of couples who have found their salvation in Him and demonstrate His grace toward each other in their married life?*

## INTRODUCTION

Is there anyone who doesn't enjoy attending a wedding? Everything about a wedding, the candles, the flowers, the music, the attire, especially the bride's gown, all are intended to make a glowing statement about marriage. Marriage is important to us. On their wedding day each couple is eager to find some way to give expression to their feelings, to get their marriage off to a good start!

Recently some friends of ours gave us the great honor of participating in their wedding ceremony. It was a day for making memories. Enraptured by the setting, the music, the inspiring words of the minister, and most of all the presence of his beautiful bride, the groom excitedly replied to the question, "Will you take this woman . . .?" with a resounding "I sure will!" His romantic flair overcame all inhibitions when, upon their introduction as husband and wife, he boldly scooped her into his arms and strode exuberantly off the rostrum down several steep steps to the sanctuary floor.

## THE UNIQUENESS OF MARRIAGE: "ONE FLESH"

Even more than it is to us, marriage is important to God. God intends that through the experience of becoming "one flesh" (Gen. 2:24), each couple will bear a special testimony to the world of the unifying effect of His love upon human hearts.

**From one flesh to "one flesh."** In Genesis 2 the Bible records the creation of the first human being. The narrative moves from the creation in Gen. 2:7 of the one "adam" (a designation for humankind) to the point (Gen. 2:18, 21, 22) where the one becomes two—the man (Heb. *ish*) and the woman (Heb. *isshah*). Finally, it moves to the climactic moment (Gen. 2:24) in which these two are reunited in mar-

riage as one. The Hebrew word for "flesh" in Gen. 2: 24 is the same as the word for "flesh" in Gen. 2:21.

Men and women have a common origin; they were fashioned by the Creator's hand. "Eve was created from a rib taken from the side of Adam, signifying that she was not to control him as the head, nor to be trampled under his feet as an inferior, but to stand by his side as an equal, to be loved and protected by him" (*Patriarchs and Prophets*, p. 46)

Originally one, they became two. They were created as complementary, harmonious parts of one humanity. Genesis 5:2, like Genesis 1:26, 27, indicates that this oneness was so complete "in the day when they were created" that they had one designation, "adam," given them by God. Together they were "adam." Only after the Fall do we read of the name "Eve" being given the woman and "Adam" being the common designation for the man.

**The deeper meaning of "one flesh."** "One flesh" in Gen. 2:24 has tremendous implications. It speaks of physical intimacy, yet much more. Emotional and spiritual bonding, mutual giving and receiving, exclusiveness, unswerving devotion, total commitment—all find themselves encompassed in this compact blueprint for marriage. Such oneness does not call for the surrender of personhood, of one becoming lost in the shadow of the other. Rather it represents a complete unity, mutuality, and harmony between two distinct persons who maintain full personhood and full equality.

## BARRIERS TO ONENESS

When sin altered human nature, the husband-wife relationship was changed. The curse of sin affected marriage (Gen. 3:16). Thereafter, under the reign of sin, marriage would suffer from selfishness, the quest for personal gratification, and the tendency to exploit or dominate one another. In their sinless state, neither of the sexes ruled the other. But with the entrance of sin, their masculinity and femininity were distorted and their delicate alignment in marriage was disturbed.

> When God created Eve, He designed that she should possess neither inferiority nor superiority to the man, but that in all things she should be his equal.... But after Eve's sin, as she was the first in the transgression, the Lord told her that Adam should rule over her. She was to be in subjection to her husband, and this was a part of the curse. (*Testimonies for the Church, vol. 3*, p. 484)

**Selfishness of human hearts.** Scripture points to the sinfulness of the heart as the source of difficulty in relationships between us as human beings as well as between us and God (Jer. 17:9). This heart condition is often acted out in relationships by withdrawal, by hiding feelings, by a lack of communication, or by fighting, blaming, or seeking to control others. Selfishness causes the normal human differences in age, race, gender, temperament, attitudes, habits, and experience to be exaggerated and aggravated. Disagreements, anger, and conflict often result. The closer together we try to bring our fallen hearts, as in marriage, the greater the potential for discord.

**Effects of the curse.** As both Scripture and human history bear witness, marriage has fallen far from the way of Eden. The curse has brought to marriage abuses and distortions of every kind imaginable. Many cultures have institutionalized models of marriage that give superiority to men (cf. Esther 1:19-22). The assault of the enemy upon marriage and its unique quality of oneness is comparable to the perversions and corruption brought upon the Sabbath truth.

Many couples today long to know an experience of equality and mutuality in marriage. When interviewed, husbands have often indicated that they would prefer this. Counselors find couples struggling over equality and mutuality issues, not knowing how to implement in their own lives a pattern that frequently runs counter to cultural or social norms. Many are not aware that such equality and mutuality was God's plan from the beginning and that, through Christ, He has made it possible for couples to experience an equality and mutuality reminiscent of Eden.

## ONE AGAIN IN CHRIST

God did not abandon His original plan for men and women to experience oneness in marriage. Jesus reaffirmed the Edenic ideal (Matt. 19:5, 6), knowing

that His gospel redeemed marriage, redeemed men and women, and provided the means whereby couples could experience this sacred institution as God planned. "Like every other one of God's good gifts entrusted to the keeping of humanity, marriage has been perverted by sin; but it is the purpose of the gospel to restore its purity and beauty" (*Thoughts from the Mount of Blessing*, p. 64). Writes well-known Bible teacher and author John Stott, "Without any fuss or publicity, Jesus terminated the curse of the Fall, reinvested woman with her partially lost nobility, and reclaimed for his new kingdom community the original creation blessing of sexual equality (Stott, 1984, p. 136).

**Reconciliation in the cross.** Genuine Christianity abolishes all religious, cultural, social, or gender barriers which separate people from each other (cf. Gal. 3:28). The cross of Christ is the source of reconciliation (cf. Eph. 2:14-18). The curse involved the wife's subjection. When the gospel concept of mutual submission (Eph. 5:21-28) is believed and practiced, it has the practical effect of neutralizing the curse and its effects by emphasizing instead the love and service of husband and wife to each other. Christ makes a difference in the marriage of Christians. A new mutuality prevails. Husbands and wives are "heirs together of the grace of life" (1 Peter 3:1-7).

> It is because of our commitment to Christ that we are able to grant one another in marriage full equality, personhood, and freedom. It is in Christ that the brokenness of the relationship between male and female is overcome, and the possibility of joyful equality and unity between husband and wife is restored. (Achtemeier, 1976, p. 104)

## MARRIAGE AS MINISTRY

**The witness of the oneness.** Jesus was concerned for the witness of His disciples before others: "By this all men will know that you are my disciples, if you love one another" (John 13:35). Where better to find a love for one another that would testify to the world about Him than in Christian marriage? He longed for oneness among His followers which likewise would be a testimony for God in the world: "I pray ... that all of them may be one, Father, just as you are in me and I am in you" (John 17:20-23). Where better could He look for such oneness than in the hearts of couples who have found their salvation in Him and demonstrate His grace toward each other in their married life?

Jesus once told His disciples that we are the "light of the world," and that we should not try to be like other people, hiding our light under convention's bushels, but rather that we should put our lamp on a stand and let it give "light to all in the house" (Matt. 5:14-15). Could it be that that is finally the task of Christian marriage? Is it not only a lifelong vocation in which we wrestle and grow and learn and fight for our commitment to God and to each other, but is it also to be a light shining into the darkness of our society's homes? . . .

By the way we spouses get along with each other and with our children, we tell our agonized society that there is hope of healing for its grievous wounds, or we announce that the patient has the "sickness unto death" and that there is no possibility of recovery. By the way we conduct our marriages, we proclaim that Jesus Christ has won the victory over sin in the marital sphere too, or we confess that He is powerless to reconcile husband and wife, parents and children, old folks and youth. (Achtemeier, 1976, pp. 107, 108)

**Setting the home atmosphere.** The first setting in which marriage ministers is to those who dwell in our homes with us. The health of the whole family depends heavily on the health of the marriage relationship.

Mutual affection between husband and wife will be to the family what the heating system is to a house. It will maintain the relationship of all family members in a pleasant and comfortable atmosphere. That does not mean, however, that the peace of the family will never be disturbed. Striving to maintain a superficial peace may actually create a less happy home than allowing hostility, when it arises, to express itself and be resolved. The point is that a family in which there is true affection can meet disturbance of this kind without suffering harm. It is not the absence of problems that marks the truly happy family, but the confident assurance that relationships in the home are so basically sound that family members can deal with any problems which may arise" (Mace & Mace, 1985, p. 109)

**Beyond the sphere of our homes.** Each Christian married couple is a ministering unit which can be highly effective in reaching out to strengthen and encourage other couples and individuals. Needs exist today for couples to minister to other couples within and outside the church. A great need is present in the lives of countless husbands and wives for guidance and encouragement in their marriages. Fewer and fewer couples have models of lasting, committed, satisfying marriages. Fewer and fewer have any genuine friends. We, as Christian couples, could be those friends.

Our sympathies are to overflow the boundaries of self and the enclosure of family walls. There are precious opportunities for those who will make their homes a blessing to others. Social influence is a wonderful power. We can use it if we will as a means of helping those about us. (*The Ministry of Healing*, p. 354)

## CONCLUSION

The nurture and outreach potential of marriage to marriage ministry is enormous. Christian marriage enrichment programs and marital growth groups have given Christian couples opportunity to fellowship and bear testimony to the effect of the love of God upon their lives. One wife wrote of the effect the meeting of Christian couples had upon their couple life:

It has been almost two years since we went through the Marriage Enrichment Seminar. There has been a dramatic change in our home. The hours we used to spend watching television are now spent reading and studying. The tapes on righteousness by faith that had been in the desk drawer for a year have been taken out and listened to. The Lord has led us step by step in our Christian growth. Our communication skills have improved as a result of the things we learned at Marriage Enrichment. We find it much easier to communicate our deep feelings to each other and to talk over our problems. Our relationship with our teen-agers has also improved.

I used to worry about not being able to witness to those around me. After Marriage Enrichment that was no longer a problem. When Jesus has changed your life the way He did mine, you can't help but share it with others. (Arlene Jenkins, quoted in Dudley, 1980, pp. 138, 139).

Today God calls married couples to drink deeply from the fountain of His love, letting that love call forth respect and caring and forgiveness for one another. When a couple realizes the healing, enriching implications of Christian faith for marriage, they will find opportunities to reach out in dynamic relational evangelism. They will build bridges of friendship to other couples, putting them in touch with the One who cares infinitely about them personally and about their marriage.

## References

Achtemeier, E. (1976). *The committed marriage*. Philadelphia: The Westminster Press.

Dudley, R., & P. (1980). *Married and glad of it*. Hagerstown, MD: Review and Herald Publishing Association.

Mace, D., & V. (1985). *In the presence of God*. Philadelphia: The Westminster Press.

Stott, J. (1984). *Involvement: Social and sexual relationships in the modern world*. Old Tappan, NJ: Fleming H. Revell Co.

White, E. G. (1958). *Patriarchs and prophets*. Nampa, ID: Pacific Press Publishing Association.

White, E. G. (1948). *Testimonies for the church, vol.3*. Nampa, ID: Pacific Press Publishing Association.

White, E. G. (1942). *The ministry of healing*. Nampa, ID: Pacific Press Publishing Association.

White, E. G. (1946). *Thoughts from the mount of blessing*. Nampa, ID: Pacific Press Publishing Association

# The *Holiest* of Callings

**by Alicia Patterson**

*"Living portraits" of three women in the New Testament poignantly portray the warmth of a mother's love and their passion for bringing their children to Jesus.*

## ABOUT THIS RESOURCE

The following is suggested for a special Sabbath worship honoring mothers. [You will find a sermon resource on fathering—"Father Power" by John and Millie Youngberg—in the Leadership Resources section.] The program consists of three "living portraits" of women, from the perspective of daughter, mother and grandmother from the Bible. Just before each portrait, a narrator reads the passage of Scripture from which the monologue that follows can be imagined. Three women may be chosen from the congregation to present these portraits, or several pastor's wives may wish to develop this program and present it in one another's churches. The portraits may be used during the usual time given to the sermon, or the entire program may be featured at another time.

**SCRIPTURE READING: Mark 10:13, 14.**

**MORNING PRAYER:** You may wish to invite the mothers to bring their children to the front for the morning prayer and make your prayer a prayer of blessing on them as they support and nurture these children and lead them to Jesus.

## Testimony of the Syro-Phoenician Woman's Daughter

**THE WORD: Matt. 15:21-28.**

## LIVING PORTRAIT:

"I am a mother now. And it is only in the years since my 'change in status' that I have come to fully understand my own story.

"I am alive today because of two remarkable people: my mother, a Syro-Phonecian woman named Anath, and a Jewish rabbi named Jesus. He was much more than a Jewish rabbi, but I will tell you about that later. And really, if it weren't for me, these two may never have met. It is true that my father and mother brought me into the world. It is through them that I was given life. And Jesus gave me new life—a re-birth. But without my mother's audacious courage I would most certainly be dead by now. At least that is what the voices told me. 'Die, you will die!' they would hiss, those voices that finally convinced my mother that it was something more than a strange illness that would cause my body to convulse and leave me screaming helplessly for her.

"The first time it happened I was so young I can hardly remember it. My mother and I were in the marketplace buying spices. It was the day after my parents had come home from a short trip. I had spent the weekend with my aunt and uncle. I have no recollection of the actual events of that weekend, however. I have only terror and a vivid memory of an evil presence and the coming of a cold fear that never left me . . . until the day my mother met Jesus.

"I don't know how many doctors and charlatans my mother took me to, how many hours she held me as I thrashed and clawed and bit until the anger turned to sobbing. I couldn't keep track of how many days she brought me meals and coaxed me to eat as I stared blankly at the walls in my room.

"When it became clear that I was possessed by a demon, my father completely withdrew from me. He was embarrassed by my behavior and completely frustrated by their inability to find a cure. 'See, not even your own father loves you!' the voices inside my head mocked me. 'You are worthless! You'd be better off dead.'

"My mother was the only one who never gave up on me. At least weekly she brought me to the temple of Baal and paid the priests handsomely to chant incantations over me, using the money she made weaving the expensive purple cloth that was the trademark of our region. As she tirelessly made the rounds of the many shrines and sanctuaries of Asherah, she left small votive figures of the goddess as offerings on my behalf. But despite her faithfulness, my condition worsened.

"I remember the first time I heard Jesus' name. A friend of my mother's came to visit and casually mentioned there was news of a Jewish magician, Jesus of Nazareth, who was a very powerful healer. My mother hated Jews and showed no interest. Finally her friend came straight to the point: 'I think you should take Tallay to see him.' It's hard to explain, but at the sound of Jesus' name, I felt a warmth spread throughout my body, as if I had been bathed in sunlight. With it came a feeling of hope. It was to be short-lived.

"'I can't believe you would even suggest such a thing, Donasherah,' my mother began. 'Do you think we were born in purple? Are there not enough greedy charlatans in the region of Tyre and Sidon that I must go and look for one in Israel? Our money is quickly running out, and I will most certainly not waste what is left on a Jew!' Her voice was cold and angry, and with those words the dark coldness to which I had become accustomed returned.

"I vaguely remember her friend's gentle reply: 'You've worked so hard to find a cure, Anath. I would hate to see you miss a possibility because of your pri . . . .'

"My mother's voice cut her off. 'Thank you for your concern, but I have not yet exhausted the possibilities here,' she said in a tightly-controlled voice. Then she stood up and escorted her friend to the door.

"The attacks increased in frequency and severity. For a year I lived in an almost unbroken nightmare. I know now that there is nothing that makes a mother feel more helpless than watching her little one writhe in pain and being unable to alleviate it. I don't know how she stood it! Night after night, my eyes open but staring blankly, my little hands stiff like claws, my normally soft and round little face contorted into an evil grimace. 'It hurts, Mommy, it hurts!' I would cry when I could make any sound at all. Then my screams would be interrupted by the hateful voices hissing, 'Die, you will die!'

"I don't know how Mother heard the news that Jesus was in our region, but I doubt her friend Donasherah had the courage to bring it up again. Desperate for help, my mother left me with a servant—the only one we had left by now—and went out.

"It was about the tenth hour. I remember nothing but the cold, dark fear all afternoon, and the voices chanting their usual refrain. My heartbeat slowed in self-protection. I was shivering with cold and wishing I could just *be* dead, when suddenly every-

thing changed. Warmth and light flooded my room. The evil presences with whom I had lived for so long shrieked as I had never heard them shriek before, and then fled. I became aware of a sweet fragrance. Then I felt a loving but powerful presence, bathed in light and standing by my bed: 'Live, my daughter, LIVE!' the Being said. And at once, I was more fully alive than I had ever been. Warmth flowed through my whole body as I sat up. My head was clear; my body was strong. I felt joy! I was alive! And hungry!

"What a story I had to tell my mother when she returned—from seeing Jesus, of course! I will never forget the joy on her face when she saw the peace in mine. She told me only briefly of her encounter with the Savior, of His commanding presence, His kind merry eyes, and of His promise to heal me. Then she wanted to know everything that had happened to me and exactly when it had happened. . . . It was only many years later when I heard the full story of her encounter with Jesus that I fully realized the desperation she must have felt and the love that compelled her to flout all the rules of her race, religion, gender, custom, and good manners to approach Jesus alone. This happened over 40 years ago now, but I will never tire of telling about it. There is a written account of my mother's quick-witted interaction with Jesus that is now circulating within the Christian churches. It was written by a certain John Mark, the one to whom the Apostle Peter told of his experiences with Jesus.

"My mother and I talked many times about her encounter with Jesus as I got older. She spoke again and again of the incongruity of Jesus' words with the caring expression on His face, or with my healing, or with His kindness toward us in our further interactions with Him. 'The fabric of life is complex,' she would say. 'You and I are only two strands, and God's design is intricate. He can weave many disparate strands together into a beautiful seamless whole.'

"In retrospect, I think Jesus' words to my mother tested the pride and prejudice of both my mother and the disciples. She was toward the end of her lesson; they were at the beginning of theirs. I don't think they realized it yet, those early disciples of Jesus, that their Messiah was not sent only to the lost sheep of Israel, but to those in Tyre and Sidon, and the whole world. . . . And just think! I was the first little lamb of the many to come.

"So the Jews finally brought something worthwhile into our world after all—a knowledge of the true God and the incredible offer of a personal relationship with Him through Jesus. Even my father has had to admit it after seeing the freedom Jesus brought me. He was skeptical for about a week, but then gave in to pure joy over the transformation in me. He was the one who changed my name from Tallay, daughter of the rain, to Pidray, daughter of Light.

"And that is my prayer for my life, to bring the Light wherever I go. I want whoever sees me to see a shining star, holding out the offer of life in Jesus to a dark and depraved world. I want to hear the plea of the helpless. I want to love like Jesus, to help the world overcome fear and prejudice and pride. I want to exchange exclusiveness and separation for inclusiveness and acceptance. I want to invite all who will come into the circle of God's grace.

"And I want to be a mother like my mother. I want to work unselfishly, persistently for the good of my children, caring more for them than for public acclaim. As I have often heard my mother say, 'God's purpose in giving us children was not to make us look good.' I pray that the Lord will give *me* the courage to flout tradition and cultural expectations where I need to, in order to get my children to Jesus for forgiveness, healing, love and life. And who would have guessed it! As I bring my children to Jesus, I find myself blessed over and over and over again! He's ready and waiting to do the same for you.

"'I am the Way, the Truth, and the Life,' Jesus said. John testified: 'In Him was life, and the life was the light of men. The light shines in the darkness, but the darkness has not understood it. [He] was the true light that gives light to every man. He was in the world, and though the world was made through Him, the world did not recognize Him. He came to His own, but His own did not receive Him. Yet to all who received him, to those who believed in his name, he gave the right to become children of God—children born not of natural descent, nor of human decision or a husband's will, but born of God.'"

# Prayer of the Prodigal Son's Mother

**THE WORD: Luke 15:11-31**

**LIVING PORTRAIT:**

"He's gone, Lord. My baby's gone. My little, curly-haired Jonathan. And part of my heart is gone with him. I know, he's a young man now, but since he's

been gone all I can think of is my little rosy-cheeked boy toddling along after the sheep and chasing the calves as soon as he could run fast enough. I miss him so much. He was the delight of my eye and he's gone! . . . . What's that You say? Do I trust You?

"I don't even know where he's gone to. I just know it's a city. That's all he could talk about the last couple of months he was at home. He wanted excitement, adventure. He said he was bored on the farm. He wanted to see the world, 'really live,' he said. I hope he's just *living*. Oh God, let him be alive! I can't erase my imaginary images of him wounded by the side of the road, bucked off his horse, or robbed and beaten and left to die. What if he's gotten in the wrong company, spent all his money on a pretty girl, or started drinking or worse. He's not wise, Lord. He's impetuous . . . . What's that again? Do I trust You?

"Why has he gone, Lord? You promised in Your word, 'Train up a child in the way he should go, and . . . he will not depart from it.' We tried to teach him Your ways, but he's gone. He's departed—not only from home, but from You. I fear for him—for his life, for his soul. We want him home again. Day after day his father waits by the gate. In the early morning, when the daylight is fading, still he waits. As if waiting and watching will bring Jon back! It's so foolish. I just wish he would *do* something! Why doesn't he go and look for him? But he says, 'Jonathan is not a child anymore. He'll come home when he's ready.' He says that Jonathan is in Your hands, Lord, that he has some lessons to learn. But until Jon comes, he will watch and wait. I wish I had his faith.

"What did I do wrong? Oh, what did I do wrong? I know I gave in to him too easily, too many times. Jonathan has always had such a pleasant manner. It was always so easy for him to get his way. I should have been stricter with him, Lord. Please make up for my failings; You know I wasn't a perfect mother. Just bring him home safely, Lord. I can't stand it much longer. I know I need to be brave for James. He says I must remember I still have a son. But I want both of them home again. It doesn't seem like home without him here. I can't sleep at night and my food tastes like dust. A part of mind is always thinking about him. You know I've repented of my failings a million times. Why haven't You brought him back? It's so hard to trust. Oh, I know You won't force a person's will. I just sometimes wish You would!

"What's that, Lord? Of course I remember the night he was born. He was so beautiful. Holding him made me forget the pain of birthing him. All night he slept beside me. My heart was in constant praise! I couldn't think of any way to adequately thank You. What could I give You that was even close to as precious as what You had given me? And then it came to me. I could give You the baby himself. I held him up to You, remember? Do I remember what I said? Yes, Lord, I remember. I gave him back to You, dedicated his life to You for safe-keeping. . . .

"Do I trust You? Yes, I choose to put my trust in You. I have nowhere else to turn. I can love him and keep him in prayer, but only You can save him. I will arise now and take care of the dear ones who are still here with me. Thank you for my husband James and my son Robert. I leave Jonathan in Your hands.

"Blessed be the name of the Lord."

(*She gets off her knees and calls out, as if calling out of the door of the house.*)

"Robert . . . ? Oh, no, I don't need you for anything. I just wondered how you were doing. Do you want to take a walk tonight when it's not so hot, like we used to? I'd like to hear about how the crops are doing and your plans for developing the place. . . ."

# Letter from Lois to Eunice Concerning Timothy

**THE WORD: 2 Timothy 1:3-5**

**MY DEAR EUNICE,**

I thank God for you every day. What a blessing you have been to me, from the time you were a little girl. Despite your strong will, you have always had a sweet spirit, and both your strength and your sweetness are a great comfort to me in my old age. Perhaps it's my old age that sparks this letter. . . .

I am enjoying this stay with my sister, but I think, perhaps, that this will be the last time I will see her in this life. I feel the end of my days approaching, and quickly. Right now I am missing Lystra—the view of our beloved mountains, and the expansive plain—and my mind turns frequently to you and Timothy. I stop then to remember you both in prayer.

I know you were aware of my concerns when you married Dinekis. I just couldn't imagine you married to a Greek! But don't worry, dear. That is not why I'm writing you today. I just want you to know what a joy it has been for me to watch you bring up young Timothy in the faith. What a good mother you have

been to him! Dinekis is a good man, but I know it has been doubly hard for you to instill the teachings of Jesus in Timothy without your husband's support. I don't know how you have managed in the presence of his unbelief. You have been a good wife to him, Eunice. I admire you for it.

Watching you with Timothy has brought me pleasure I could not have anticipated. I had no idea how wonderful it would be to be a grandmother—being filled with such love for a child, and so thoroughly enjoying the interaction, without the heaviness of the responsibility of parenting. I know being a mother isn't easy, and neither of us has been perfect! But I want to affirm you for living out the instruction of Deuteronomy. You have put God first in your life, and you have made the Christian values I taught you your own. And you have taught the words of our Lord to your son, talking about them when you snuggled in a chair, as you walked with him to the market, and as you tucked him into bed at night and awakened him in the morning. You have so tightly braided the elements of everyday life with the Holy Scriptures and the Good News about Jesus that Timothy would have to rip at the very fabric of his life to separate them. You have made me proud.

I will have to admit, there have been times when I was worried. I wondered how you would foster a good relationship between Tim and his father without compromising his belief in God. Hasn't God been good to bring Paul into Timothy's life, just when a Christian male role model was most important? Think of all the times we have prayed for a godly father figure in Tim's life. As usual, God has abundantly provided more than we could ask or think! Paul truly treats Timothy like a son. And I believe Timothy has been an encouragement to Paul as well, as they have traveled together, and now that Paul is in prison. How I miss Paul . . . .

But speaking of Paul, I am so proud of the way Timothy has taken over his work in the church in Ephesus. How I have enjoyed watching him grow in his ministry. But he's still young and inexperienced. Paul's shoes are difficult to fill, and I am concerned that the sophisticated congregation in Ephesus will be a test of all his pastoral skills! I pray that Timothy will remain teachable and learn everything he can from Paul. I'm not saying that Timothy isn't a gifted apostle in his own right. He's just different from Paul, and that difference is needed. I pray that he, like David, will have the wisdom to fight with the weapons he has been given. I have felt strongly impressed to pray for courage for him, courage to take up the mantle of ministry God has given him, and courage to fully become the strong man of God that he has the potential to be. In some ways it is a hard prayer to pray, knowing that the more successful he is at proclaiming the Good News about Jesus, the more likely he will have enemies and maybe even follow in Paul's footsteps to prison, and perhaps to death.

I know Tim is greatly on your heart, too, Eunice. Ephesus must seem a million miles from Lystra to you. And these are such troubled times. And so I pray for you as well, that the Spirit of courage and loving self-sacrifice that was so evidenced in the life and death of our precious Lord Jesus will come upon you in full strength. For I am more and more convinced that the afflictions that we face presently will so pale in contrast to the glory that will be ours, that we will hardly be able to recall them.

I love you, my dear daughter. Rely not only on your considerable inner strength, but on the power of God to see you through every trial. May the awareness of His presence bring you comfort and hope. And may the grace, mercy and peace of our Lord Jesus Christ be with you now and forever. I hope to see you soon!

With love,
Mother

---

Alicia Patterson is a Seventh-day Adventist pastor by calling, wife and mother of three in Yakima, Washington

## CLOSING PRAYER

Provide everyone with a blank sheet of paper, either as a bulletin insert or handed to them as they enter the sanctuary. In preparation for the closing prayer, allow time for people to write prayer requests for their own children and children in the wider circle of the congregation, community, and the world. Provide two attractive containers at the front, one labeled "For God's Eyes Only" and the other "For Prayer Support." Invite the congregation to bring their requests and place them in the appropriate box. Explain that requests placed in the "For God's Eyes Only" container will be destroyed by yourself or the pastor immediately following the service, while the ones placed in the "For Prayer Support" will be included in the prayers of the congregation's prayer support team, in the pastor's prayers, etc. Be sure to follow through on your promise to protect the confidentiality of those placing requests in the "For God's Eyes Only" container by shredding or burning these requests.

*end*

# How to *Enjoy* your. Imperfect Family

### by John McVay

*God loves your imperfect family and every imperfect family. He longs that each family might acknowledge Him as the Father of all and lay hold of the resources that He has to help them live life as a family of faith.*

## INTRODUCTION

In planning for your wedding, you decide you're going to follow all 107 wedding tips that you find in *Modern Bride*. Actually, you discover that these tips provide an invaluable time-line—107 tasks to accomplish before that blissful, perfect, joyous, choice day. Under the heading "12 to 24 Months before the Wedding" you find tip # 1: "Together visit your clergy and set the date for the ceremony." Ah, that's good advice, as far as it goes. You move on down the list. You especially attend to wedding tip # 34. Now please remember, this is in a journal called *Modern Bride*. These words are addressed to brides-to-be. "Decide on your honeymoon destination. Consult a travel agent." "Traditionally," the journal goes on, "the groom makes these arrangements, but if you are better at that, don't hesitate to offer." Gentlemen, the world is changing. Under the heading "Wedding Day" come the last three tips. Number 105: "Rest and thoroughly relax in a nice warm bath." Oh sure! Number 106: "Allow at least 2 hours before the wedding to dress." And # 107: "Have a wonderful day and enjoy every moment." And you do.

Of the 500 gowns in *Modern Bride* you choose the one on p. 328, the one labeled "Pure Perfection," the one with the elaborate hand-beading, the one your father has to drive to a small boutique in New York to purchase. But it is worth it. That's what you want your wedding day to be; that's what you want your marriage to be; that's what you want your family to be—"Pure Perfection". And as you take flight for a honeymoon in the Greek isles, you and your brand new husband imagine that your marriage, your family, will be pure perfection, one joyous port-of-call after another in an unending blissful cruise through life.

Incidentally men, *Modern Bride* doesn't fail you. They give grooms some help also. A section entitled "Planning Your Life Together," has two short articles.

It is interesting that they amount to less than 4 of the journal's 518 pages!

## LOOKING FOR PURE PERFECTION, BUT . . .

Despite the notion of "*life* together" in *Modern Bride*, married couples today cruise straight into a statistical storm. You know the marriage/divorce statistics. Annually, in the U. S. A. there are some 2.4 million marriages and 1.2 million divorces. So, about 5 million Americans will make commitments for *life* this year. Most of those who mumble the words "I do" expect to keep the commitment. Almost every bride and every groom look forward to pure perfection. However, about half of the marriages will break apart before 15 years have passed. The percentage of first marriages that end in divorce stands at about 50 percent, while the percentage of second marriages—or third or fourth marriages—that end in divorce is about 60 percent. The average duration of marriages is 7.2 years.

If your idea of a perfect home includes a mom, dad and 2.1 kids, your chances of perfection are diminishing quickly. In 1970, 40 percent of households had a mom, dad and at least one child living together. In 1990, only 26 percent of households in the United States fit that model. By the year 2000, the figure had slipped further to 24 percent.

In 2 Timothy 3:1-5 God's word predicted some rough waters in our time: "You must understand this" the apostle writes. "This has got to be part of your curriculum."

In the last days distressing times will come. For people will be lovers of themselves, lovers of money, boasters, arrogant, abusive, disobedient to their parents, ungrateful, unholy, inhuman, implacable, slanderers, profligate brutes, haters of good, treacherous, reckless, swollen with conceit, lovers of pleasure rather than lovers of God—holding to the outward form of godliness but denying its power (NRSV).

What a setting in which to try to maintain a commitment! What a setting in which to raise children who love God and find joy in serving others! What a mess! And, by the way, what a challenge for all who seek to minister to families. If you want a real challenge in life, become a Family Ministry professional.

**Every family is imperfect.** Sooner or later in the midst of the statistical and moral storm of these last days, you and I will discover this simple truth: Every family is imperfect. The family to which you belong, the family to which I belong, is imperfect. Worse yet, you are likely to discover that at least part of the problem with your family is with *you*. Once you have discovered those sad facts, what is to be done? Can nothing be done? Is it all over? If your family is not going to be the pure perfection you had imagined it would be, is there any point to it all?

## BEARERS OF THE DIVINE NAME

Ephesians 3 is one of the most important passages in Scripture for family ministry. Beginning with vs. 14 (NRSV) the apostle writes, "For this reason I bow my knees before the Father, from whom every family in heaven and on earth takes its name." Do you like that? There is a little word play going on in the original Greek language that isn't obvious in translation. The word for "father" in Greek is "*pater.*" You hear it in words like "patriarch," don't you? *Pater.* The term for "family" is "*patria.*" So Paul is saying, "For this reason I bow my knees before the *Pater* from whom every *patria* in heaven and on earth takes its name." He employs the phonetics of the language. Every family (*patria)* in heaven and on earth takes its name from the Father (*Pater*).

**Your family belongs to God.** Your family with all of its imperfections belongs to God. That's what the apostle is telling us. By the way, he is also telling us, I think, that all human beings are children of the Father. Our winsome task as Christians is not so much to twist arms to pressure people to come into the Father's family, but to announce to them the winsome message that *they are already members now.* Your family with all of its imperfections belongs to God; your family with all of its imperfections is not in the cruel grip of fate, but in the caring hands of God. That is the apostle's message: God loves imperfect families. They bear the divine name; they carry the mark of God's ownership.

God loves your imperfect family and every imperfect family. He longs that every family might acknowledge Him as the Father of all and become a family of faith. When the dishes are stacked high in the kitchen sink, when the kids are screaming at each other and there is no one to help pull them apart, when the mail box is full of bills, when the relationship is devoid of thrills, when the behavior of the teenagers causes you chills—when all of this is happening—it's easy to see the problems and the impossibilities. But your family, your imperfect family and every family to which you minister is God's family. And God doesn't just hear the screams; God hears the laughter. God doesn't just listen in on the arguments; He hears the words of affirmation. God doesn't just watch the tears that fall; He sees the ones that are wiped away.

## ACCESSING DIVINE RESOURCES

Amid the problems and the impossibilities God invites you to consider all the possibilities and the opportunities. God longs to provide an inner strength that will give you resources to match the outward turmoil. God longs to provide you with a divine love that will help you grow. Listen as we continue to trace the thought begun in Ephesians 3:14 (NRSV):

For this reason I bow my knees before the Father, from whom every family in heaven and on earth takes its name. I pray that, according to the riches of His glory, he may grant that you may be strengthened in your inner being with power through his Spirit, and that Christ may dwell in your hearts through faith, as you are being rooted and grounded in love.

**Understanding growth and commitment.** In his book *Caring and Commitment* (1988), Lewis Smedes tells the story of his friend Ralph. Two months after Ralph's divorce, he was overwhelmed with remorse for having failed to keep his commitment. He sought relief in counseling.

"You should be grateful," this particular therapist told him, "You've concluded an important stage in the journey of self discovery. Your ex-wife has traveled with you up to this point. She's helped you along as far as she could. True, she didn't bring the perfection you seek, so you must move on. But be thankful for her gift and take it with you as you leave." (p. 73)

You see, for the therapist Ralph chose, a person's commitment to marriage is an investment in his or her own growth. According to this view, when a person's investment has not yielded any growth for a while, it's time to get out of that relationship and to seek another with greater potential for personal profit. Smedes comments about this kind of "personal-investment" commitment and then offers insight into a kind of commitment that truly leads to growth:

> Real growth is healthiest when we put commitment to another person ahead of growth for ourself. . . .
>
> We don't grow into mature persons by chasing fantasies. And one fact about marriage in general is that every marriage in particular is imperfect. No one marries exactly the right person; we all marry someone who is only more or less right for us. We are all flawed partners. And if we accept this regrettable but invigorating fact of life, we may be ready for real growth.
>
> We do not give ourself a good chance for growing personally if we keep hankering after our fantasy of the ideal woman. Or man. We grow when we keep renewing our commitment to the only spouse we've got. We grow when we stop dreaming of a perfect marriage and adjust caringly to the one we have. Our best growth comes when we forget about our own growth and focus on caring instead. (p. 73)

"Here is a nice twist," Smedes concludes, "instead of giving us a good reason for giving up a lifetime commitment, our need to grow is a prime reason for keeping it" (p. 74). Smedes' words are true not only in the husband-wife relationship, but also in the commitment each family member makes to another.

Returning to Ephesians 3, "I pray that, according to the riches of his glory, he may grant that you may be strengthened in your inner being with power through his Spirit, and that Christ may dwell in your hearts through faith, as you are being rooted and grounded in love. I pray that you may have power to comprehend, with all the saints, what is the breadth and length and height and depth, and to know the love of Christ that surpasses knowledge, so that you may be filled with all the fullness of God" (vv. 16-19 NRSV).

**Growing in love.** The age in which we live is not one that's kind to families. Love tends to get drained out of families. But, says the apostle, "I am praying that you might know something of the grand dimension of Gods love; I'm praying that you might have a transfusion of love, of divine love that will be more than a match for the turmoil and the temptations of

the times. God loves imperfect families like yours, like mine, like the ones to which we minister. So the apostle says, "I'm praying that you will be able to establish a family of love, a family of faith. I'm praying that you will be able to nurture families of faith."

Verse 20 (NRSV), "Now to him who by the power at work within us is able to accomplish abundantly far more than all that we can ask or imagine, to him be glory in the church and in Christ Jesus to all generations, forever and ever. Amen."

## JAY AND HIS IMPERFECT FAMILY

Consider the case of a man whom I will call Jay. I don't know when Jay first sensed that his family was less than perfect, but it must have been quite early. The family recording tapes had rather faithfully captured past events and, though perhaps no one had intended to deliberately do so, those tapes frequently played and replayed.

Little by little Jay as a growing child picks up sound bites—a sigh of disgust hurriedly stifled, or a smirk on an older sibling's face that is quickly erased when parents enter the room. Slowly, but surely, Jay begins to piece together the story of his family and his own part in it.

Clearly his older siblings regard him as inferior. At a rather tender age he discovers the reason: his mother is not their mother. Though it takes him a little longer to catch this part of the story, the date of his conception apparently precedes the date of his parents' wedding. (This happened years ago when the sense of morality about inappropriate relationships ran deeper. Yet, despite this sense of morality, people did not understand that, though there maybe an illegitimate relationship of a child's parents, there is no such thing as an illegitimate child.) His older siblings looked down on his mother for seducing their father. They also looked down on her son.

**Bearing family pain.** Things did not go well in the family. Relationships were not what they should have been. All the family members now sense how imperfect the family is and they begin to provide a classic example of what is commonly called "scapegoating," making one person bear the burden of the family's dysfunction. Our family's having problems, they conclude. There must be reasons for the problems. They focus on Jay. Jay, he's the reason. If only Jay would shape up, or if only Jay were out of the picture, everything would be all right. In families like this, there is no attention to the family as a system, no treatment of the family as a unit, no attention to an unhealthy complex of relationships, only blame heaped again and again upon one who has been designated the scapegoat.

One incident in his early adolescence shaped, or perhaps misshaped, Jay's self concept. He and his family are on vacation at a favorite spot. When it comes time to go, the family packs up and leaves, but something is left behind. It's not just their favorite vacation spot. It's something more than the family cat or the old portable ice-chest cooler. They leave Jay! The experience serves as a kind of metaphor for this family's dysfunction and Jay's place in it: Things would probably be happier if he were not around. If he would just get lost, maybe this family would be, could be, a perfect family.

**Grasping a sense of one's specialness.** Things only worsen when the father dies. But Jay is quite an incredible person. You know the human spirit can be indomitable. Amidst it all—the tapes of a sordid past, the scapegoating, the conglomerate family, the sneers and smirks, the condescending gestures, Jay manages somehow to grab on to the idea that, no matter what the others believe, he is special. He has a place in life, he has a destiny, a mission, and eventually he founds his own enterprise that meets with amazing success.

His brothers won't let the old stories die though; they jeer at his achievements. They try to get him to over extend his resources to prove his worth to them, but he refuses. In the midst of his accomplishments, they are able to turn his own mother against him. They manage to get her to support their plot to identify his genius as lunacy. This must have hurt him deeply.

Eventually, the family tapes play again. This time, the sound is loud—at concert levels on a grand scale. Jay becomes the scapegoat, not just for his family but for his nation. He dies an ugly death—on a Roman cross.

## HOW JAY'S FAMILY CHANGED

Something happens, however, at the foot of that old rugged cross. Something happens to the family of Jesus. Have you noticed it? In the Book of Acts, in the introduction to this glorious story about a period in the life of the church following Jesus' ascension, Scripture says, "All these were constantly devoting themselves to prayer" (Acts 1:14 NRSV). All these people were doing what? Devoting themselves to prayer. And the passage

continues, ". . . together with certain women, including Mary the mother of Jesus, as well as his brothers."

Moving on through the New Testament we come to a couple of little books that are often thought to have been written by two of Jesus' brothers, James and Jude. Notice James' introduction in his letter: "James a servant of God and of the Lord Jesus Christ." James, a servant of Jesus! And in James 2:1 (NRSV), "My brothers and sisters, do you . . . really believe in our glorious Lord Jesus Christ?" Wow! Then we come to that little letter of Jude. Verses 1, 2 read, "Jude, a servant of Jesus Christ and brother of James." Don't you like that? "To those who are called, who are beloved in God the Father and kept safe for Jesus Christ: May mercy, peace and love be yours in abundance." Verse 4 refers to Jesus as "our only Master and Lord, Jesus Christ."

Something happens at the foot of the old rugged cross that transforms some well-worn footage in the family tapes. Something happens that converts the scapegoating into worshiping. The family of Jesus, imperfect as it is, becomes a family of faith.

## CONCLUSION

The message of the story—the gospel story—is this: the change in Jesus' family is not an isolated case. The same transformation can occur in your family and in mine and in each family to whom we minister.

> For this reason I bow my knees before the Father, from whom every family in heaven and on earth takes its name. I pray that, according to the riches of his glory, he may grant that you may be strengthened in your inner being with power through his Spirit, and that Christ may dwell in your hearts through faith, as you are being rooted and grounded in love. I pray that you may have the power to comprehend, with all the saints, what is the breadth and length and height and depth, and to know the love of Christ that surpasses knowledge, so that you may be filled with all the fullness of God. Now to him who by the power at work within us is able to accomplish abundantly far more than all we can ask or imagine, to him be glory in the church and in Christ Jesus to all generations, forever and ever. Amen. (Eph. 3:14-21 NRSV)

John McVay is Dean of the Seventh-day Adventist Theological Seminary, Berrien Springs, Michigan. Transcribed and edited from a sermon presented at the 2002 Adventist Family Conference on the campus of Andrews University, Berrien Springs, Michigan. Used by permission.

## References

Smedes, L. B. (1988). *Caring and commitment.* San Francisico: Harper & Row Publishers.

———— end ————

# Mini-Seminars

# Let *Love's* Light Shine

**by Karen and Ron Flowers with Peggy and Roger Dudley, authors of *Maximum Marriage***

*In this program resource, seven couples provide windows into their marital journeys that fellow travelers may be encouraged.*

## INTRODUCTION

In the strengthening of personal faith, Christians have long known the benefits of meeting with fellow believers, talking together about their various experiences, praying together, and gathering valuable insights as well as courage from one another. Through this kind of fellowship, Christians help each other grow in the community of faith. In the crucible of such real, genuine living and sharing, where Christians are willing to make themselves vulnerable by authentic sharing, unbelievers may be brought to belief in Jesus, the doubting may find faith, and the discouraged may be filled with hope.

All have not the same experience in their religious life. But those of diverse exercises come together and with simplicity and humbleness of mind talk out their experience. All who are pursuing the onward Christian course should have, and will have, an experience that is living, that is new and interesting. A living experience is made up of daily trials, conflicts, and temptations, strong efforts and victories, and great peace and joy gained through Jesus. A simple relation [telling] of such experiences gives light, strength, and knowledge that will aid others in their advancement in the divine life. (*Testimonies for the Church*, vol. 2, p. 579).

Just as individuals are refreshed and encouraged by meeting and sharing together, there are great blessings to be gained as husbands and wives come together with other couples for periodic refreshment, encouragement and renewal in their marriages. A marriage is more than just a man and a woman. It is a dynamic entity, a couple unit, with a life of its own. Couple units in their oneness also need fellowship and social, emotional, intellectual, and spiritual support from other couple units with common needs and desires and a willingness to commit to nurturing and supporting one another in the journey of married life. As they pray together, open themselves to fresh understandings of the marriage relationship from the Word, share common experiences, and work together to develop their relational skills, many find themselves rekindling their faith in God—the Creator of marriage—and recommitting themselves to the sacred institution itself. Marriage for such couples is radically different from the marriages of couples around them, as they grow in grace and in their understanding of how to practically apply the teachings of Jesus to their relationship.

This is not to overlook the reality that around every marriage a sacred circle exists which should be carefully guarded and preserved. "No other one has any right in that sacred circle" (*The Adventist Home*, p. 177). The sacred circle that gives a couple individuality and privacy must remain in place, even as they fellowship with other couples. In bearing their testimony and sharing from their marital experience, each should be attentive to one another's wishes, protective of each other and the uniqueness that is theirs as a couple, and careful to maintain an appropriate boundary around their relationship.

The circle around a marriage is not unlike the membrane around a human cell. The cellular membrane provides distinctiveness and integrity for the single cell, but it also allows for communication among surrounding cells and the transfer of information and resources between them. Likewise, the sacred circle surrounding a marriage was not intended by God to become an impenetrable wall that inhibits the flow of fellowship and encouragement into and out of the relationship. In the presence of other caring couples, husbands and wives may witness practical demonstrations of love and find affirmation for their own coupleness, comfort in the midst of difficulty, hope to carry them forward, and inspiration to work together for God.

## ABOUT THIS RESOURCE

This resource is intended for use in small groups of married couples, where opportunity is given for individual couple dialogue as well as group discussion. The seven stories of fellow pilgrims on the marriage journey, upon which these marriage-building dialogue starters are built, are excerpted from *Maximum Marriage* by Peggy and Roger Dudley.\* (For many more stories and inspiration, you may wish to make available a copy of the book for each couple in the group.)

Peggy and Roger Dudley, on the faculty of Andrews University, have spent most of their professional life serving Adventist youth and families. Both hold degrees in counseling and have also made their mark in education and research. Of particular importance here, they are a happily married couple who have worked tirelessly for three decades to strengthen their own and the marriages of others. In their own words:

> We wanted to share positive examples from real life that demonstrate problem-solving skills. We wanted to write a book about successful, actual life experiences that would illustrate that good marriages don't just happen—they represent hard work. But the effort is so very worthwhile. (Dudley, 2003, p. 8)

**USING THE STORIES IN A SMALL GROUP.** It is suggested that one couple in the small group be recruited to read aloud each of the stories. This same couple may lead the group in discussion, and this will be followed by a time devoted to personal couple dialogue. Personal couple dialogue can occur with couples in the same room, but with enough distance between them to allow for a reasonable amount of privacy.

**GUIDELINES FOR GROUPS.** For group discussion, several very important guidelines help to set appropriate boundaries on sharing. These should be discussed with the participants beforehand, so that discussion within a group is kept at an appropriate level and embarrassment on the part of spouses or others in the group is avoided.

• *Speak for yourself.* Take ownership of your feelings and ideas. Do not speak for your spouse or others. Give others the responsibility to do the same.

• *Share your own experience.* Let others draw whatever lessons are meaningful to them from your experience and make the application to their lives for themselves.

• *Share voluntarily.* No one is ever under pressure to talk.

• *Respect your sacred circle.* Share only those things that both of you feel comfortable sharing and only about issues that are common to all couples and which you feel you are well on your way to resolving in a way that is acceptable to both of you.

**COUPLE DIALOGUE.** You may wish to provide couples with the dialogue starters pre-printed, or provide them with paper and pencils to write down the dialogue starters along with brief responses that they can then share with each other.

# Roger and Peggy's Story

**ROGER:** As a young college student studying for the ministry, I was strongly impressed with the sacredness and importance of God's calling. I emerged from college with high ideals and a lofty concept of ministry. Somehow, though, I failed to balance this zeal with the importance of family. For a number of years (I'm ashamed to tell you how many) I operated on the principle that "the work" must always come first.

I loved Peggy very much, but I expected her to understand that as a minister's wife she must make sacrifices. What's more, she should make them willingly and cheerfully. Then came the awakening. As a conference director of youth ministries, I was working with a group of teenagers and young adults in a series of Voice of Youth meetings. One morning I received an urgent phone call. Peggy was calling from the hospital. She had developed a problem that would require surgery. While the condition was not serious, she would have to undergo general anesthesia. She was frightened and alone.

But we had a crucial meeting scheduled for that evening. "If you need me, I'll come now and skip the meeting," I offered.

In her fear and uncertainty she needed me, all right—desperately. But good Christian girl that she was, she knew the appropriate answer. "No, I'll be OK. You stay for the meeting; I know it's important. But please pray for me."

Of course she was hoping against hope that I would say, "No, you are more important," and that I would jump into my car and race to her side as quickly as possible. That's what I should have done—but I didn't. My training and mind-set allowed me to accept the spoken message and ignore the heart cry that I was too insensitive to hear.

\*Dudley, P., & Dudley, R. (2003). Maximum marriage. Hagerstown, MD: Review and Herald. Selections used by permission.

It wasn't until later that she found a way to tell me about how afraid and lonely she had been. I began to realize for the first time just how far I had drifted from an understanding of what really mattered most to me. I knew that I had to make some changes in my life. I decided that I needed to block out significant quality time for her and for our daughter. We began to schedule times to do things together, and to nourish our relationship.

I wish I could report that my "conversion" was permanent, and that I never lost sight of my priorities after that. However, human growth does not take place in a single bound. With new insights we tend to make gradual—and sometimes slow—progress, with slip-backs along the way. How wonderful that the good Lord is patient with us! I needed a few more experiences to bring me back to those priorities that would eventually come to mean the most.

**PEGGY:** The last thing I wanted to create was conflict. I had seen enough of that in my childhood. There had been no models in my growing-up years from whom to learn the right way. But praise the Lord, we learned those skills while attending marriage seminars and reading books about marriage. These did not become available until we were in midlife. Before that, rarely did anyone talk or write about such deeply private things as one's marriage.

Once we learned these skills I was able to talk with Roger about our relationship in a way that was not an attack or blaming. And Roger learned to listen and accept my feelings without trying to convince me that they were illogical. I realized that I also had responsibility for the way we lived our lives. There were times I fell into the same trap of skewed priorities. Indeed, there were times Roger felt less important than my doctoral studies or work demands. But with improved communication skills it was not so difficult to make the adjustments when priorities became skewed. We learned that life is constantly changing, and so must our adjustments to these changes. I now truly feel that I am Roger's highest priority, next to God, and I work on letting Roger know that in the same way he is mine.

## GROUP DISCUSSION OPENERS

It may be appropriate to review the guidelines for group discussion.

• What parts of Peggy and Roger's story stood out for you?

• What do you think made it so difficult for them?

• What brought Roger to new commitments to his wife and family?

• What do you think Roger meant when he described relational growth as "gradual and slow," "progress with slip-backs along the way?"

• What does Peggy say made it hard for her to tell Roger how she really felt?

• What skills were they able to develop that made it easier for them to communicate authentically?

## COUPLE DIALOGUE STARTERS

• Times when I have let my work and my own personal agenda take priority over my relationship with you . . .

• Feelings I have when I feel our relationship seems to be far down on the "to do" list . . .

• Ways I can adjust my life to allow more time and energy for our relationship . . .

• My pledge of commitment and love to you . . .

# Margaret and Larry's Story

**MARGARET:** Our dog, Kori, loves to "go along." Larry didn't think that I should take her with me to buy a few groceries, as it would be very hot in South Carolina's summer temperatures. I assured him that I would take only a few minutes and that I would open all the car windows while I was in the store.

When I came out of the store, I saw a police car blocking my car. I had not displayed my "handicapped" card. After I showed the police officer my card she said, "You will need to wait. You have two violations. You left your dog unattended. The animal control officer is on the way."

Both officers were very kind as I readily admitted that I was wrong on two counts. They very graciously forgave me for both offenses but reminded me that I could have been fined $200 for each one.

I was elated as I related my adventure to Larry, but was totally unprepared for his angry response. Such things don't usually upset him. Larry's unexpected anger about my police encounters made me angry, and I retorted, "The police were far more understanding than you are." I banged the door loudly and went outside to lick my wounds. After a few minutes I came back in and said, "I'm sorry."

"I'm sorry, too," Larry said.

Even though we had made things right, I was still feeling hurt. Larry left for school, and I sat down with my Bible. I needed to find something that would tell Larry how deeply I was hurt, something that would encourage him to be more understanding. Nothing helpful came to my mind. I reached for a Bible promise box, asking God to give me a text that would help me. I could hardly believe the printed answer He gave me: "Now instead, you ought to forgive and comfort him, so that he will not be overwhelmed by excessive sorrow. I urge you, therefore, to reaffirm your love for him." In the margin of 2 Corinthians 2:7, 8, NIV, I wrote: "Police-Kori-Larry 7-11-01."

**LARRY:** There are several things that we believe strengthen our marriage beyond normal expectations. By far the most important is that we are firmly committed to the Lord and to our church. We spend 30 to 40 minutes each day in morning and evening worship and prayer together. We also spend additional time in our private devotions.

Both of us paid tithe and gave additional offerings before we were married and continued that pattern after we were married. We love our church, support it financially, and invest our time in it. Both of us believe in regular church attendance and in attending the mid-week service, as we both had done before we were married.

[We believe] the couple should pray together and for each other every day. God at the center of a home is a unifying force.

## GROUP DISCUSSION OPENERS

• What parts of Margaret and Larry's story stood out for you?

• Why do you think the experts call anger a "secondary emotion," that is, an emotion that erupts when other feelings go unexpressed?

• What hidden feelings do you think gave rise to Larry's unexpected anger? To Margaret's response-in-kind?

• What connection do you think there might be between Margaret and Larry's ability to work through this problem and their spiritual life together as a couple?

• What evidence can you cite from your own experience that Larry is right when he says, "God at the center of a home is a unifying force"?

## COUPLE DIALOGUE STARTERS

• A time when your forgiveness powerfully communicated your love for me . . .

• Hidden feelings I sometimes experience which give rise to anger . . .

• Things I can do to open the way for us to communicate our feelings openly. . .

• Ways I can contribute to our spiritual growth together as a couple . . .

# Tena and George's Story

**TENA TELLS A PIECE OF THEIR STORY:**

We will never forget that day 38 years ago when we first met. It was at a Little Peoples' Conference (for short-statured people four feet, 10 inches and under) in Asheville, North Carolina. Both in our late 20s, we each wanted a life companion whose beliefs were centered on God. Also, we each wanted a mate who had similar physical conditions—dwarfism. Eye-to-eye contact can't happen when one person is six feet tall and the other is four feet tall. We were both praying that a miracle would happen. And it was a dream that God fulfilled. . . .

During the past six years we have become involved with Maranatha Volunteers International. We have traveled to many places of the world—India, Nepal, Argentina, Africa, Australia, Venezuela, Honduras, Panama, etc.—to use our small hands for God in the building of churches, schools, orphanages, and health clinics.

Most of these trips have been to developing countries, where they had shacks in which to worship. When we left, they had beautiful buildings, filled to capacity. In helping others we have received such blessings! We know God has a purpose for us to fulfill in life. Meeting other couples who enjoy engaging in this same type of effort, as well as sharing stories of how God has enriched their lives and their marriages, has helped us grow.

What a thrill to make a difference in someone else's life! To have that opportunity to witness and to work with others of another culture can indeed be a joyful experience. We come home truly blessed. We have been on 30 projects and want to keep going as long as we can.

Today we are stronger than ever in the Lord's love and in our love for each other and for others.

## GROUP DISCUSSION OPENERS

• What picture of a couple was conjured up in your mind when you learned that Tena and George had dwarfism? What limitations did you expect them to have?

• In what ways were your preconceptions of them changed by their story?

• What does this tell you about the potential of every couple for blessing others in the name of Christ?

• What experiences have you had that confirm the truth of their conviction that finding joy in service together is a great marriage builder?

## COUPLE DIALOGUE STARTERS

• A memory I have of a time when helping someone else brought us close together . . .

• Things that sometimes get in the way of our committing more of ourselves and our resources in service to others . . .

• Things I wish we could do together to keep us counting our blessings and sharing them . . .

# Melissa and Ken's Story

**IN MELISSA'S VOICE:** After 13 years of marriage I have discovered that happiness in a relationship can be as unpredictable as a flip of a coin. Heads, our marriage is great; tails, it's rotten. I'm sure that God never intended any relationship to be tossed to and fro by mere luck. So for years I struggled to determine the secrets of true contentment in my marriage, fearing my chances were about as good as winning the lottery.

On one particular "tails" day, I asked Ken how he felt our marriage was going. He looked me straight in the eye and replied, "Our relationship seems to revolve around the mood you are in." For some reason his response haunted me like an overdue bill. The more I tried to ignore it, the more urgent it became. I felt God tugging at my angry heart, but stubbornly I resisted. After all, I had plenty to resent.

For instance, Ken was supposed to finish building a fence for our backyard. With two small children

a fence was more than just a casual want; it was a safety issue. However, Ken always came up with some excuse to work on something that I felt was less pressing. After I had [waited] several months for its completion, my patience expired and my anger boiled. As I sat down for my worship I began emptying out my frustrations on God. Why didn't He change Ken? I knew He had the power. I had certainly prayed hard enough that He would. So why wasn't He answering my prayers? If only Ken wasn't so unreliable. When *I* said that I would do something, I always did it. Why couldn't he be more like me? *More like me?*

And then it hit me. The cold hard truth. I was dependable, all right, but rather monotonous. In all honesty, one of the things I admired most about Ken was his spontaneity. For example, when we got engaged we hopped in the car and drove all night to tell his folks in person. Ken's idea, of course. And then there were the flowers. They came when I least expected them, even when no birthday or anniversary was in sight. If he were more "dependable," like me, would he be as fun-loving? Could it be that the character "faults" that irritated me most about Ken were the flipside of the ones I loved the most?

As the reality of this truth stacked up in my mind, I stored it away as one of my priceless treasures. God accepted my weaknesses as well as my strengths and loved me with an "everlasting love." Perhaps I could apply His strategy on my husband. Then our marital happiness would no longer be dependent on a mere toss of the coin. It would be safe in God's bank account.

## GROUP DISCUSSION OPENERS

• There is an old adage that says "opposites attract." How did that seem to be true of Melissa and Ken?

• What does Melissa say is the natural response of the human heart to differentness in another?

• Why do you think their attempts to change one another didn't work very well?

• Why is Melissa's moment of insight such an important lesson for Christian married couples?

## COUPLE DIALOGUE STARTERS

• Times when I have felt fully known, fully accepted, fully loved by you . . .

• Ways in which we are so different . . .

- A funny experience we have had trying to change one another, without success . . .

- My affirmation of you as the different but treasured person whom I want to cherish for the rest of my life . . .

# Teri and Richard's Story

**RICHARD:** As the first Christmas of our marriage approached, Teri and I were teaching at Hylandale Academy in Wisconsin. We were making so little money that when I got drafted into the Army a few months later, I got a raise.

There was no money for Christmas gifts, let alone for a tree or decorations. In the woods we were able to cut down a large Christmas tree that we dragged home in the snow. The branches were so full at the bottom that it held itself up without any base on it. The tree took up a big space in our sparsely furnished living room.

**TERI:** I was so excited about our first Christmas, and I had never imagined that we would have a tree so big it reached the ceiling! I made real cookies for tree ornaments.

**RICHARD:** A few days before Christmas, Teri asked me to move a dresser into the extra bedroom on a Saturday night. I didn't want to do it, but she kept after me. Finally I relented, but I was exasperated with Teri. I enlisted my brother-in-law, Gerald, to help me move the dresser. I chose to take it through the living room, much to my later regret. As we went through the living room, we brushed the dresser against the Christmas tree. Gerald wondered if we should stop, but I was impatient with Teri and just wanted to get the job done. As we pressed on by the tree, we jostled the branches so much that the cookies fell to the floor.

**TERI:** I heard the crash and went into the living room, where I saw the tree had fallen. No problem. I could just pick it up and right it again. But there, on the floor, was a pile of broken cookies. All my hard work was destroyed. I ran to the bedroom and flung myself over the bed, trying hard not to be heard crying.

**RICHARD:** When I came back into the living room after moving the dresser, I knew that something was seriously wrong. I went into the bedroom, and there was Teri, lying on the bed, crying very hard. I sat down beside her and asked her what was the matter. She was crying so hard she couldn't say anything at first.

**TERI:** Between sobs I finally choked out, "You . . . you . . . you broke . . . my . . . cookies!"

**RICHARD:** When Teri told me why she was crying, I immediately felt remorse. I told her we could make more cookies, and other soothing things, but nothing I said seemed to comfort her.

**TERI:** Richard patted me and said he was sorry. He seemed to really care and, of course, I forgave him. I never had time to make more cookies.

**RICHARD:** I think the fact that Teri wasn't able to make any more cookies reinforced for me an important lesson from that Christmas experience. After acting impulsively, it is not always possible to make everything completely right in a marriage. Better to give some thought first. But the experience also proved to have positive lessons for our marriage as well.

**TERI:** Today, 30 short years later, we don't agree on every detail as to why or how the "cookie tragedy" happened, or why Richard was peeved about moving the dresser. Those details are forgiven and forgotten. The important thing is that we have been using this experience to better communicate an understanding of each other's hopes and dreams.

Whenever we come to a situation that one of us cares a lot about, we will just say, "Don't break my cookies." That is a gentle reminder that conveys a great deal of experience and emotion and helps us recognize when there is a need not to press too hard and to be more supportive. "Don't break my cookies" is a way of speaking our own language. We used it often in the early years of our marriage. Our relationship eventually grew past the point of needing to employ that phrase very often.

Christmas trees and cookies no longer seem so important. I learned that *things* in life are not nearly as valuable as our relationship.

## GROUP DISCUSSION OPENERS

- What truth is there in Richard's conclusion that "After acting impulsively, it is not always possible to make everything completely right in a marriage."

- No one cries that hard about broken cookies. What did the broken cookies symbolize for Teri that Christmas that made her sob uncontrollably?

- Teri says they have been using this experience ever since it happened "to better communicate an understanding of each other's hopes and dreams." Why is it so important to understand and help one another hang on to hopes and dreams in marriage?

- What did the shorthand communication "Don't break my cookies!" come to mean between them?

- Why is this such an important lesson for couples today?

## COUPLE DIALOGUE STARTERS

- A "broken cookie" experience we have survived together . . .

- Times when we could use a shorthand reminder of how important it is to listen to one another and to hear the deeper feelings and concerns . . .

- Things I can do to help our marriage ride out the difficult moments when we have hurt each other and are having difficulty hearing one another's hearts . . .

- Dreams and hopes I would like to share with you . . .

# Shelly and Wayne's Story

**AS SHELLY TELLS IT:** We got married when we were young (21 and 23 years old). I was in the middle of college, and Wayne was to start his degree when I finished. When I completed my master's degree, we decided it was in our best interest to purchase a house. My parents were willing to let us borrow the down payment, but this rapidly added to our school loans and "other" bills, so we found ourselves deep in debt.

I, by nature, tend to be an extrovert. I like being around people and having fun. The down side of my personality is that I have a hard time staying focused on a goal, such as paying off bills and loans, because I don't see anything happening, yet I never seem to have money to spend. Fortunately, opposites attracted, and I married a man who is more introverted and goal-oriented. He realized that for us both to be focused on the goal of getting out of debt he had to make it real for me.

One day Wayne was "in the back room" paying the bills when he called me. He proceeded to show me a chart he had made on a large poster board. (I prefer things that are visually stimulating and interactive. A piece of paper would not have worked as well.) He had listed the loans we owed across the top, and the months down the side. The amounts with the highest interest were listed first.

Every month thereafter, while he was paying bills, he would call and give me a big red marker to put an X in one of the spaces provided. When the first account was paid off, the money set aside for that debt went toward the next bill on the list (yes, this was already figured in when he created the chart) and on down the table. We also would have a special celebration when a bill was paid off.

Our final loan was to my parents for the down payment on our house. We ended up being able to pay them $1,000 per month until our $10,000 bill was paid—an accomplishment I would have never dreamed possible. It was only by not elevating our pattern of living (we continued to live like students, even though I had a professional job), and having the "bill" money accumulate, that we were able to do it.

This method really helped me. We could see the end in sight. We became a team as we focused on our end goal. We celebrated our successes. We could discuss what we wanted to do with our money after a specific date instead of saying "once our bills are paid." I could *see* where my hard-earned money was going. It didn't just disappear with the explanation "I had to pay bills."

## GROUP DISCUSSION OPENERS

- Why are finances always high on the list of issues that create marital conflict?

- How was Wayne able to help Shelly understand and cooperate with him in reaching their goal of being debt-free?

- Why is goal-setting so important in a marriage?

- What were the rewards Wayne and Shelly experienced for having accomplished a goal together?

## COUPLE DIALOGUE STARTERS

- Things I want for me (think about your most important personal and relational goals) . . .

- Things I want for you . . .

- Things I want for us . . .

# Elaine and Willie's Story

**ELAINE:** A few days after we had unloaded the moving truck at our new home, with many boxes still unpacked, Willie had to leave for a four-day trip to Alberta, Canada. As his job required ever more travel, our previously well-orchestrated system [for sharing home responsibilities] began to unravel.

I missed having Willie at home on a daily basis and began harboring feelings of anger and resentment. I spent much time worrying and thinking about the "what ifs." I was irritated by the fact that because I was the one left to manage the household and the kids by myself, with no family or close friendships established yet, there was little time left for me to find a job. I wanted to be supportive of Willie's ministry but resented the disruption to our family life and to my career. I became very defensive and bitter in my interactions with Willie. The tension in our relationship began to escalate.

**WILLIE:** For my part, I was feeling the pressure of the need to adapt to the multiple demands of my new position yet remain connected to my family. I began to feel that Elaine was being unsupportive of me and was feeling frustrated at having to deal with so much tension at home while dealing with my most demanding job ever. Our financial picture was also very bleak because of changing from two-incomes to a single-paycheck budget. That added even more pressure to the situation.

Unfortunately, we didn't spend a lot of time sharing our feelings with each other. We found ourselves miscommunicating and arguing a great deal of our time.

**ELAINE:** The more resentful and bitter I became toward Willie, the easier it was for him to work late and stay away from home.

**WILLIE:** The more I was away from home, the more angry Elaine became. It became a vicious cycle for us, one that could have been very destructive had we not allowed God to intervene.

**ELAINE:** It all suddenly changed one day as Willie was preparing to leave for a trip. I found myself feeling very weak and unable to get out of bed. Willie asked if I was OK. I answered an honest no and managed to confess to him how lonely and sad I

was feeling. He became very concerned and asked if I wanted him to stay with me, and I said yes.

**WILLIE:** It suddenly hit me hard that something was very wrong with Elaine and that attending to her was more important than anything else in the world that "needed" my attention. I immediately canceled my trip and told Elaine that I would stay for as long as she needed me, and until she was well enough to function properly—even if it meant canceling a few more trips.

We spent the day talking and praying together. We shared our true feelings with each other and really tried to understand each other's viewpoint. We also agreed that we would need to find outside help—other people whom we could trust and who could hold us accountable. It was very difficult for us to share our problems with others, but we knew it would be necessary in order for us to get past this hurdle.

**ELAINE:** I decided to see a Christian counselor, and Willie shared with a trusted colleague. The first change we made was to get back into the habit of praying together each morning. The one-minute hug was reincorporated into our daily routine when we arrived at home in the evening, or at anytime, for that matter.

**WILLIE:** As for the traveling, I established a policy that I would accept appointments to be away from home only two weekends out of every month. The other two weekends I would spend at home.

**ELAINE:** I agreed that I would try not to schedule any appointments or activities for myself or our children on the days that Willie would be returning from a trip or during the time he was home. This way he wouldn't feel as if he were being left out of our lives. We also established more intentional conversation times while Willie was traveling. Instead of simply talking about the kids and the events of the day, we began asking about each other's feelings, thoughts, and concerns.

We finally began to operate as a team again. We recognized that we had been fighting against each other instead of fighting as allies against the evil forces that were threatening our relationship. Yes, things are drastically different than they were with our well-oiled machinery of those earlier years, and we know that many hurdles lie ahead. Nevertheless, each challenge gives us opportunity to grow much closer to each other and to have a much clearer picture of the oneness that God intends for us to have as married people. We know that no matter what circumstances change in our lives or what challenges we may face in the future we are allies—intimate allies.

## GROUP DISCUSSION OPENERS

- In what ways can the demands of work threaten marital intimacy?

- With what feelings expressed by Willie and Elaine can you identify?

- Why do you think this couple found confiding in a counselor and trusted colleague helpful?

- What do you think Willie meant when he said they needed someone who could hold them accountable?

- What do you admire most about the way Elaine and Willie resolved this problem?

## COUPLE DIALOGUE STARTERS

- Seasons in our lives when we have been the most balanced in our living . . .

- Times when the demands of work have threatened our marital intimacy . . .

- Feelings and concerns I need to share with you right now . . .

- Things I can do to help us establish appropriate boundaries between our responsibility to others and our responsibility to ourselves . . .

### References

Dudley, P., & Dudley, R. (2003). *Maximum marriage.* Hagerstown, MD: Review and Herald.

White, E. G. (1948). *Testimonies for the church, Vol. 2.* Nampa, ID: Pacific Press Publishing Association

White, E. G. (1952). *The Adventist home.* Hagerstown, MD: Review and Herald Publishing Association.

# From The *Window* Ledge

**by Karen and Ron Flowers**

*A program of dialogue for parents and church folk who care passionately about the spiritual well-being of children and youth.*

## INTRODUCTION

The educators whose experience and research inspired this seminar know what they are talking about when it comes to understanding Adventist youth. Ivan Goes is the Education and Family Ministries Director for the Northeast Brazil Union. He is in daily contact with young people at home and in his ministry. They keep him in close touch with their world, and he is passionately concerned for their spiritual well-being. He finds in the New Testament story of Eutychus (Acts 20:7-12) a springboard for contemplating the real-life experience and perspectives of today's youth and the challenges facing parents, teachers, youth leaders, and the church at large if we are to hold our young people close to the church for a lifetime.

Roger Dudley is the director of the Institute of Church Ministry at Andrews University. The stories that have eaten their way into his heart are the stories of young Adventists of the post-modern era, many of whom struggle to find meaning and fulfillment in the church of their childhood. For more than 10 years he traced the lives of 1,500 teenagers as they moved through the transition periods of adolescence and young adulthood, often growing disillusioned with the Adventist church. His recent book, *Why Our Teenagers Leave the Church* (2000), chronicles in their own words the journey he and these young people took together.

Goes' and Dudley's reports from the front lines and their reflections on what they have seen and heard raise significant issues which must be urgently addressed by parents, teachers, church leaders, and other caring adults if the church is to be perceived as relevant and inviting to this generation. We must confront ourselves with the hard questions: Are we willing to listen carefully to youthful voices? Are we really hearing what they are telling us about why they leave, why they stay, and why working for change is for so many discouraging and hard? What are the implications of their perceptions for the way we do church? What will we actually do with what they have said, now that they have cared enough to risk speaking from the heart? How can we share Christ and the principles of His kingdom in language and action that they find winsome? Grappling with these issues is what this seminar is all about.

## ABOUT THESE SEMINAR MATERIALS*

The seminar is presented in four parts:

• **PART I** - The Story of Eutychus through Contemporary Eyes

• **PART II** - Facing the Numbers

• **PART III** - In Their Own Voices

• **PART IV** - Why Adventist Teenagers Stay in the Church

Each part has a presentation followed by group discussion. The seminar parts are designed to flow together in sequence. Approximate time for the seminar: 1½ to 2 hours. Be sure to provide sufficient quantities of Handout 1 • *Why Adventist Youth Leave the Church: In Their Own Voices* (used in Part III) and Handout 2 • *What My Church Did Right* (used in Part IV).

## PART I - The Story of Eutychus through Contemporary Eyes

A simple reading of the story of the young lad Eutychus in Acts 20:7-12, or the dramatization of this story through contemporary eyes as in the skit below, can be used to create the setting for this dialogue among parents and other adults who care passionately about the spiritual well-being of children and youth. Very simple props can be used, or word pictures painted, to help the participants visualize the scenes in their minds. The cast for the skit are:

**Eutychus** - a typical teenager in the church

**Lydia** - Eutychus' mother

**Theo** - Eutychus' father, head elder in the church at Troas

**Chloe, Ty, and Lois** - Teenagers in Eutychus' cohort

**Town folk** - people doing business in the village square

**Church folk** - members of the Troas Christian Church

**Paul** - an apostle of our Lord Jesus Christ

## SCENE 1

The home of Lydia and Theo (pronounced Tay-oh) and their son Eutychus. Lydia is in the kitchen preparing dinner and Eutychus is doing homework in the next room when Theo comes in excitedly from work.

**Theo:** Guess what Lydia! I just found out that our beloved friend, Paul, is here–in Troas! I bumped into Timothy and a couple other men who have been traveling with him in the market. He just arrived this morning.

**Lydia:** Oh, that's wonderful! I have missed him and the others so much. Somehow the church just seems stronger, more vibrant, when they're here. And the preaching! Oh, how I have missed Paul's preaching!

**Theo:** (*Starting to set the table as Lydia continues meal preparations.*) And why is it that the troublemakers all show themselves after he leaves?

**Lydia:** Hmmph! They never would have had the courage to confront Paul!

**Theo:** I do wish Paul had more time for counsel. There are several serious matters that I wish he could settle once and for all! But I hear he may only be around for a week or so. Anyway, we're trying to organize a big meeting for all the believers in this region on Sunday night.

**Eutychus:** (*Calling from the adjoining room, sounding frustrated.*) Does this mean the youth campout is off for this weekend?

**Lydia:** (*Trying to be understanding.*) Eutychus, you can always go camping. We don't always have Paul with us!

**Eutychus:** Well, his timing is really great! (*Heaving a long heavy sigh.*) And I suppose you'll make me go to this meeting too!

**Theo:** Of course. How would it look with me there as the head elder of the congregation and my family not present? (*In disbelief.*) What's wrong with you? Believers will walk miles to hear this!

**Eutychus:** But Paul's sermons are so long! Just when you think he's winding down, he thinks of another 20 points he just has to make. And then he wants to sing all nine verses of the closing hymn! Oh, why does he have to turn up on the weekend we were going camping!

**Theo:** That'll be enough criticism of God's anointed from you, young man. And see to it that you get a haircut before the weekend too. (*Theo turns his full attention back to his wife.*) Now, Lydia. Do you think we could have something to eat for Paul and all the leaders of the church at our house after the meeting? That may be the only time we have to ask the questions we need his guidance on. . . .

## SCENE 2

Sunday evening, the balcony of the Troas Christian Church. Eutychus and his teenage cohort are sitting in a row, chatting animatedly amidst the din of meeting preparations.

**Eutychus:** What a bummer! We should be sitting around a campfire about now!

**Ty:** You got that right! I still can't believe that out of all the weekends in the year, old Paul had to pick this one to turn up in Troas!

**Chloe:** If you ask me, I'd have been better off if he'd never shown up in Troas at all. Ever since my folks joined this church, I've been nothing but restricted! Can't wear this, can't go there, can't do that, can't listen to my music . . .

**Eutychus:** Some of the rules don't seem to make much sense. It's like the church majors in minors. But I could deal with the rules and stuff if church just wasn't so boring. All we ever do is sit. They don't seem to need us for anything.

**Lois:** Yeah, well, look on the bright side. If it wasn't for church, we wouldn't be friends.

**Eutychus:** True. And this place does have the best potlucks! Remember that rice dish Anna's mother made last time? It was awesome. I think I had thirds!

**Ty:** Eutychus, man, all you think about is your stomach. (*Eutychus just rolls his eyes.*)

**Chloe:** That was the potluck when none of you bothered to save me a seat! (*She pretends to be upset with them for a brief moment, then goes on talking.*) Well, the only seat left was with this bunch of old ladies. I didn't think they could get two brain cells to work together, but it was the most amazing thing. They were genuinely interested in me! They wanted to know how school was going, and whether I had thought yet about college and what I want to do with my life. . . . The next week one of them even came up to me in the hall and called me by name and said she'd looked up on the Internet and discovered that the University of Reading has a really good International Relations program. I still can't get over it that she remembered my name and what I'm interested in! And who would have guessed she even knew how to get on the Internet!

**Lois:** Hey, speaking of potlucks, did anyone see Christy last Sabbath? She usually stays for lunch if she's here.

**Chloe:** Come to think of it, I haven't seen her in several weeks. It doesn't surprise me really. Since her dad lost his job, she has to buy her own clothes and pay some on her tuition, so she's really working hard these days. She got a second job as a receptionist at a nursing home. She works the night shift after going to school all day. She told me last week she was looking for a church that met in the afternoon so she could get some rest on Sabbath. At first I laughed. That idea has about as about as much chance of being heard as I have of getting an "A" in French class! But she has a point.

**Eutychus:** Maybe she and I could start our own church. I asked my mom once if they had ever considered starting Sabbath school even a half an hour later, like maybe at 10 o'clock or something. She looked at me like I was a lazy rascal. She just doesn't get it that I need a weekend after a long hard week of school work. I need to relax. I need time with my friends. And I have a lot of stuff I need to do too. When church takes up Friday night and my whole Saturday, when am I supposed to get any rest? And why is it that everything that's happening in this town happens on Saturday!

**Chloe:** Hey, are we invited over to your place tonight whenever this gets over? Come on, Euty, give me something to look forward to!

**Eutychus:** Sorry guys. My mom's invited Paul and all the leaders of the church to discuss big problems.

**Chloe:** Yeah, like what to do with kids who lower the standards and ask hard questions! Hey, I just thought of something. (*She smiles broadly.*) You know what this church needs? A really good band!

**Ty:** Sh-h-h, be quiet. They're about to pray. (*The teens pause and bow their heads as though in prayer. Eutychus opens his eyes and peeks over at Chloe, catches her eye, and grins. A few seconds later, they resume talking in whispers.*)

**Eutychus:** Hey, any bets on how long Paul preaches? I clocked him at 1 hour, 47 minutes the last time! Well, you see that open window over there? I'm going to go sit in it. There's a lot going on in town tonight, and I'm hoping to get another look at that new girl that just moved here from Abydos (*He raises his eyebrows, whistles low under his breath, and makes a face to convey that he thinks she's a knockout.*) At least I won't have you guys elbowing me when Paul gets so deep in his theology that I go off to sleep! Besides, it's stuffy in here . . .

**Ty:** Watch that you don't fall asleep . . . and out! (*Eutychus walks away, pretending not to hear, while his friends try to control their laughter.*)

## SCENE 3

The village street below the window. Eutychus lies motionless on the ground. A cluster of town folk gather around him, looking very worried.

**Town folk 1:** It's bad. He took a terrible fall. He fell out of that window like a dead weight.

**Town folk 2:** And it looks like that's just what he is all right. Dead! And so young, too. Did someone go for the doctor?

**Town folk 3:** (*Bending down to check whether he is breathing or not.*) Well, here, let me see if he's breathing. . . . I'm not getting a pulse.

**Ty:** (*Eutychus' teenage friends rush in on the scene.*) Didn't I give him specific instructions not to fall out!

**Lois:** Just tell me. Is he going to be okay? I can't bear to look.

**Chloe:** (*Praying aloud.*) Oh God, if you're up there, please don't let Eutychus die!

**Church folk 1:** (*Church folk arriving on the scene.*) You might know it would be Eutychus! That boy is going to be the death of his parents yet!

**Church folk 2:** I know he's a bit of a rebel, but he's really a good kid at heart. He's always cheering people up and there aren't very many boys who hang around to help clean up after potluck. I tell him he's an angel! I know he didn't mean to fall out of the window. It had to be an accident. Oh dear, I will miss him so much. And his poor parents!

**Church folk 3:** Well, I don't know. Wherever there are kids, there's trouble. They're always questioning things, challenging things, wanting to change things. I find it really quite upsetting! Why can't they just trust their elders?

**Paul:** (*Paul pushes the crowd aside to get to the boy. He drops immediately over him, wrapping his arms around him and pulling him close to his breast. Paul's eyes are closed, as if in earnest prayer. After a few seconds, he opens his eyes, lifts his face toward heaven, and shouts with joy.*) Thank you, Jesus! (*Turning to the crowd.*) Don't be alarmed! He's alive! Come, let's praise God and break bread together and testify of His marvelous grace! This boy who was dead is alive! This is reason to celebrate!

## FOR SMALL GROUP DISCUSSION

Picture Eutychus perched in the window sill. Open to his view is the full panorama of both the world outside and the church inside. What do you think Eutychus sees? What makes the world outside so eye-catching, then and now? Think about the dialogue among the cast in the first two scenes of the drama. What comments ring in your ears and speak volumes about the teens' perceptions of life as a young person in the Troas congregation? What do you think there is about being raised in a Christian home and in the church that will draw Eutychus' attention inside the window? Do you think it will ultimately be enough to disciple Eutychus for Christ and to hold him in the church as a young adult? What's enticing the young people in your family and your home church inside?

---

# PART II - Facing the Numbers

Statistical research on Adventist youth and their involvement with the church presents a sobering reality. As a way to experience the statistics given below more powerfully, invite participants to "number off" taking a number from 1 to 10, repeating as many times as is necessary until everyone is numbered. When statistics are given, ask the appropriate proportion of participants to stand to represent the percentage of young people who said "yes" in response to a given item on the survey questionnaire. For example, when you report the statistic that 40-50% of young people in NAD are leaving the church by their middle 20's, ask participants with numbers 1-5 (i.e., half the participants) to stand. For the 34% who report they attend Sabbath school, you might ask participants with the numbers 8-10 to stand, representing approximately one-third of the group. This will give the group with higher numbers opportunity to participate.

From Dudley's research, "it seems reasonable to believe that at least 40 percent to 50 percent of Seventh-day Adventist teenagers in North America are essentially leaving the church by their middle 20s. This figure may well be higher. Some will return eventually (perhaps a fifth of the dropouts), but, of course, more may also leave" (Dudley, 2000, p. 35). Some additional vital statistics:

Attendance at worship. . . . . . . . . . . . . . . . . . . . 55%

Attendance at Sabbath School . . . . . . . . . . . . . . 34%

Attendance at other kinds of meetings . . . . . . . 25%

Hold church office. . . . . . . . . . . . . . . . . . . . . . . 21%

Serve on committees . . . . . . . . . . . . . . . . . . . . . 13%

Participate in share-your-faith activities . . . . . . . 21%

Personal daily prayer . . . . . . . . . . . . . . . . . . . . . 59%
(*an additional 23% report weekly or oftener*)

Personal daily Bible study . . . . . . . . . . . . . . . . . 13%
(*an additional 30% report weekly or oftener*)

Participate daily in family worship . . . . . . . . . . . 12%
(*an additional 17% report weekly or oftener*)

Say religious faith is quite/very important . . . . . . 82%

Feel accepted by members of local church . . . . . . 74%

Feel they have equal input into church operation . . 56%

Feel their mother is a positive influence in their
spiritual development . . . . . . . . . . . . . . . . . . . . 80%

Feel their father is a positive influence . . . . . . . . 62%

Feel other adults in the church are a
positive influence . . . . . . . . . . . . . . . . . . . . . . . 32%

Listen to rock music at least several times a week . . . 59%

Attend the cinema at least every month . . . . . . . 52%

Drink alcoholic beverages at least every month . . . 21%

Are sexually active with no plans for marriage . . . . 14%

A lot of credit is due those who have had the courage to face the statistics, to find out and acknowledge the real numbers representing Adventist youth and life as they live it on both sides of the back door of the church. It is not always easy to face the truth. But it is an important first step toward a positive solution to a world-church challenge.

## FOR SMALL GROUP DISCUSSION

How do you think the numbers for your local region and congregation would compare with Dr. Dudley's statistics?

# PART III - In Their Own Voices

For this part of the seminar, distribute *Handout 1 • Why Adventist Youth Leave the Church: In Their Own Voices*. This resource has been compiled from comments and letters of 1,500 teenagers and young adults who responded to Roger Dudley's 10-year longitudinal study of Adventist youth for the North American Division. These comments are a representative sampling of their actual words in answer to questions as to why they leave the church and things in the church that they find most disturbing.

In advance of the seminar, organize a small voice choir of adult volunteers to present this collage of youthful voices speaking about their church. Your voice choir will need to practice in order for the comments to flow smoothly and with feeling. You may

want to put the scripts for the readers in folders so they will distract as little as possible. Ask them to read with deep feeling, as though they had taken on the identity of the young person. When the voice choir presents their reading, consider having them cluster closely together, as in a family portrait. You may wish to elevate the readers to different heights by standing some on covered boxes, putting others in various heights of chairs and stools. Something as simple as your arrangement of people can generate curiosity and heighten the impact of the words.

## FOR SMALL GROUP DISCUSSION

What comments stirred the greatest response in you? Talk about the feelings and heart cries you hear from behind the words. Ask yourselves: Is there even one young person from our congregation, our part of the world, who might have written this comment? On what basis might they have come to these conclusions? What are the key reasons you hear the young people saying that they are leaving the church? If you were seated in the same room with these young people, what would be your response? How will you put "practical legs" on your response in your local church?

# PART IV - Why Adventist Teenagers Stay in the Church

Ask a spiritually mature young adult from your congregation to read *Handout 2 • What My Church Did Right*. If you have the courage, you may want to ask your youth group to write personal essays for you on what your church is doing right, and where they would like to see themselves be part of effecting change. Do not consider this option unless you really plan to include them and their ideas in dialogue and church planning. Sharing their comments at this point in the seminar would likely give the group plenty to think about.

## FOR SMALL GROUP DISCUSSION

How closely does this description compare with your local church? What would it take to make your church more like this? How much urgency do you feel about growing in this direction, knowing that whether or not your kids stay in the church may well depend on it? How will you translate this sense of urgency into action?

## CLOSURE

One Adventist young person who has not yet given up on effecting change in the church for her generation gives us hope: "Adventists are people; many follow the way of God fairly well; others just need time to grow up and receive teaching from the Master. At least they've come to the right place" (Dudley, 2000. p. 180).

Roger Dudley concludes: "It's up to all of us to make sure that it is the right place" (p.180).

## CLOSING EXERCISE

Give each participant a piece of paper and a few minutes to write down the names of as many children, youth and young adults as they can who are connected in any way to your congregation. Ask each person to bring their paper to the front and place it in a basket next to a large Bible that you have placed there. Take a few minutes to vision together what it will take to make your church "the right place" for the lifelong disciple-making of these precious ones entrusted to your care. Then take time to pray for them, for their friends, for their parents, for the entire community of faith as you commit yourselves anew to nurturing them and growing together with them toward unity in Christ.

*This seminar was inspired by a devotional presented by Ivan Goes and by the book *Why Teenagers Leave the Church: Personal Stories from a 10-year Study* by Roger Dudley, Review and Herald, 2000. Used by permission.

### References

Dudley, R. (2000). *Why our teenagers leave the church.* Hagerstown, MD: Review and Herald Publishing.

## HANDOUT #1
# Why Adventist Youth Leave the Church:
# In Their Own Voices

**Reader 1:** Sitting in a church pew, surrounded by people, feels more lonely than sitting in a park playing solitaire.

**Reader 2:** There is so much I want to know about God, but I never find any of it out at church.

**Reader 3:** I feel unaccepted by church members. I get more out of religious discussions with my friends than I do out of church.

**Reader 4:** I would rather spend Sabbath on my own than try to carve out a place in the ice.

**Reader 5:** I work nights, and it is very difficult to get up early enough to go to church. Why can't there be an afternoon service?

**Reader 6:** People are not accepted if they don't meet the dress codes or follow the rules.

**Reader 7:** Members are eager to judge by outward appearances and don't even bother to get to know someone inside.

**Reader 8:** There is no love. It is all talk.

**Reader 1:** They teach us one way, and in so many cases don't abide by their own teaching.

**Reader 3:** People look down their noses to discover all the bad, negative qualities about others and pretend that they alone are doing God's will.

**Reader 2:** A lot of members are "people-watching" instead of "Jesus-watching."

**Reader 4:** I was greatly discouraged with how supposed "Christians" could be so rude, unaccepting, and cruel.

**Reader 5:** The level of control that the church tries to wield over an individual's life disturbs me.

**Reader 7:** I'm disturbed by the tendency toward a judgmental response to anything new and different;

toward anything that makes people think about why they believe the way they do.

**Reader 6:** Staying spiritually alive is difficult. The church is full of gray heads—wise, needed parts of the body of Christ. But why must they be so stuffy and pharisaical, insisting the young people worship in the same silent, slow, sleepy way they do?

**Reader 8:** Jesus came and encouraged freedom and joy in our praise and worship. He shook the traditionalists to the core. I believe our youth can bring back that revival of energy and freedom in our programs.

**Reader 4:** Too long we have been stifled by the opinion that in order to be truly godly you must dress backwards to fashion and worship God *only* in slow hymns and organ music.

**Reader 2:** In desperation, I reach out to other denominations to feed me spiritually. Then I can go back and encourage and build up my own church. "You shouldn't do that," someone said. "It makes it look like we don't feed you." "You don't" was my quiet, honest answer.

**Reader 3:** The nominating committee decided to inject a mixture of older people, youth, and women into the leadership positions. The older clique was infuriated. I had supported them for years, and when they had an opportunity to support me, they basically thought I wasn't ready to be so active.

**Reader 1:** I wish so badly I could find enthusiasm. But it's very difficult to want to be involved when our ideas and opinions are considered to be too radical and not important.

**Reader 8:** Everyone tells us that we are the church of tomorrow, but I and millions of others are trying to tell you and everyone else who will listen that *there will be no church of tomorrow* if we are not recognized and accepted *as we are*, and allowed to put our youthful energy and new ideas into effect.

**Reader 6:** Much of Adventism seems to be rules, rules, rules. If it is fun, then it must be BAD! Let us not snuff out joy wherever we go. Being a Christian should not be depressing. The God I know is not like that at all!

**Reader 7:** The church focuses so much on "should's" and rules and theology, but not enough on actions, such as working in the community and accepting those who don't fit into the narrow box the church feels they should.

**Reader 4:** I need to hear about Jesus. I need to hear that He loves me. I need to hear someone remind me how He showed me His love. So I've found other places to go; places that weren't distracted by someone else's writings or other churches' teachings. They told me only about my Lord, His sacrifice and His love, and what it means to me.

HANDOUT #2

# What My Church Did Right

## By Becky Lane Scoggins

*One of Your Former Kids Just Wants to Write and Say "Thanks."*

Dudley, R. L. (2000). *Why our teenagers leave the church: Personal stories from a 10-year study.* Hagerstown, MD: Review and Herald. Used by permission.

At one time I believed that all churches were brimming with old people and young people who not only loved each other, but even liked each other. I imagined that all pastors played baseball and told campfire stories; that potlucks were significant events on everyone's social calendar.

That was more than 12 years ago. Do you remember the day I became an "official" part of you? I'll never forget it.

It was summer, of course. Because the church didn't have a baptistry, we had to wait until the Minnesota lakes were free of ice. All the church members drove over to Charlotte Johnson's home on Bass Lake. My friend Jennifer and I giggled as we struggled into the black baptismal robes, several sizes too big. We felt nervous, because we knew you were all so proud of us; and sober, because we knew it was the beginning of something important. We loved Jesus very much that day.

We saw you beaming as we tripped down the grassy bank in our robes. Everyone sang "Trust and Obey" from yellow song sheets that flapped in the breeze. Mom's camera ran out of film, and the neighbour kids abandoned their floating inner tube and climbed out on the boat dock to watch. Uncle Wilber led us through the green lily pads and quoted from Ecclesiastes 12, about remembering the Creator in the days of our youth; then he baptized us.

The elders lined up to shake our hands and solemnly welcomed us into the Blackberry church. Grandma kept saying how beautiful it was that three ducks swam by just as we were baptized. I shook my long, wet hair and didn't say anything. I knew that you loved me.

The pastor gave me a baptismal certificate that day, but what I remember even more came a few weeks later.

## THANKS FOR A PLACE TO WORK

The phone rang one evening. It was someone from the nominating committee, asking if I would be the Sabbath school secretary. Each week for the next year I picked up offering envelopes, counted the change two or three times (to make sure it was right), and recorded it in my logbook. My sixth-grade classmates served as cradle roll teachers, junior deacons, and members of the social committee. We never doubted that our church needed us.

You found out by default what surveys were just beginning to prove: youth don't want entertainment; they want something to do. So you gave us something to do, expected us to do it, and we did it. We knew you trusted us.

When you asked me to be the church communication secretary in seventh grade, you didn't laugh as I earnestly marched to the local *Herald Review* with my handwritten news releases. You asked us to read mission stories when we couldn't even pronounce the names of all the countries. You listened eagerly to our first sermons—long before we had ever heard of homiletics.

Somehow you understood that youth want more than a voice in the church's back seat—we want a hand on the steering wheel and a foot on the accelerator. Yes, we've probably caused a few crashes, but at least a church doesn't need collision insurance. We all survived, and we youth knew we were a necessary part of the team.

## THANKS FOR A PLACE TO GROW

But now you're wondering if we still need you. You've heard all the talk about youth leaving the church. You've heard that we have a long list of complaints: that we feel shut out, left out, let down, and turned off. Are you afraid you've failed?

Sure, you may have done a few things wrong, but I'm writing this letter to thank you, the Blackberry church, for *not* failing us. Thank you for doing a lot of things right.

Thank you for your time. There were many things your small church couldn't give—youth pastors, fancy Pathfinder uniforms, a satellite hookup in church. But you gave us your time. You gave your Friday evenings to plan to our Sabbath school lessons. You camped in igloos in February, watched the slides (164 of them) from my Maranatha mission trip, listened to the Christmas concerts we performed in, and prayed for us when you could have been sleeping.

Thank you for your adaptable spirit. True, you've all been sticking to your "family" pews for about eight decades now, but you've adjusted to youthful surprises with patience—even humor.

Remember the Pathfinder boating trip when Amy "caught" the pastor's shirt with a fishhook? She was embarrassed and afraid of his reaction. But he only laughed and suggested that we fry him for supper.

Then there was that picnic when Mom told me to bring the forks, but I forgot. No one fussed about the mistake (maybe because you looked so funny using potato chips for utensils).

I've seen you attempt some bold changes. I was proud when you were one of the first churches in the conference to ordain a woman elder. It meant a lot that you supported me when I decided to spend a year in public school instead of going to academy. And if my skirts were ever too short, you never said a word.

## THANKS FOR STILL TRYING

Are you wondering if you should have done anything differently while we were growing up? Are you searching for a foolproof method for reaching the younger generation? Forget it.

Are you waiting until you can really get the youth program organized? Forget that, too.

Youth ministry isn't neat, time-efficient, or organized. It's exhausting.

But I'm a Seventh-day Adventist Christian today because I discovered Jesus Christ in your church family, and I believed you needed my help to show His love to our community.

I know a youth class still meets every Sabbath morning in the same room with folding metal chairs that scrape on the green and yellow linoleum. There's probably another girl with long hair and braces who sits in my place now. I hope you give her more than a baptismal certificate and a handshake when she's baptized.

Give her a cradle roll class to teach. Give her a sermon to preach.

Let her know that you need her.

Kids hate to let people down, especially people they love. If you need them and trust them, they'll get the job done.

*Love,*

**Becky**

At the time this was written, Becky Lane was a graduate intern at the Review and Herald Publishing Association in Hagerstown, Maryland. Reprinted with permission from the *Adventist Review*, July 25, 1996.

# Everybody's *Welcome*
## Helping Your Church to be Family Friendly
**by Karen Holford and Paul Godfrey**

*Seminar resources for church leaders and church members to help encourage greater sensitivity to and attention to the needs of the wide variety of families that comprise the membership and the community around the church.*

Recently there has been an interest in making churches more child-friendly so families will feel more comfortable coming to church. While this is a worthwhile effort; we want to expand our efforts to address the needs of whole families. Becoming a *family-friendly* church goes beyond having a child-friendly worship service. It means creating a church where everybody feels welcome and comfortable, and knows that their individual needs have been considered and met wherever possible.

## ABOUT THIS SEMINAR MATERIAL

The material is designed to • Help your church explore the definition of "family-friendly." • Evaluate the "family-friendliness" of your church. • Make family-friendly changes that will impact your congregation and the community where the congregation worships. Rather than a full-blown course, it is more of an appetizer, an introductory resource to share with your church, and to reflect upon together. Some ideas may be adopted quickly, others may take longer, and some may not be appropriate for your church at all.

## THE RESOURCE MATERIAL INCLUDES THE FOLLOWING:

• **Guide for Leaders**

• **What a Family-Friendly Church Looks Like**

• **But Our Church is Really Small**

• **Survey - What Is Our Church Doing Right Now to be Family-Friendly?**

• **Starter Ideas for a Family-Friendly Church**

• **Case Studies**

• **Questionnaire for Members**

• **Community Questionnaire**

• **Creative Ways to Draw Out Views**

• **Resources for Family-Friendly Churches**

• **Some Useful Christian Websites**

• **Copier-ready Worksheet Masters**

 - "I have a dream for my church" *(This is best suited to a teen and youth group, but could also be used with older children or adults.)*

 - "Something I would like to see in my church would be a…" *(This is more suitable for younger children.) Both masters can also be enlarged to give more room for creativity and to present a whole collection of ideas to a church, on a display board, or a spare wall.*

Action by church leaders is key to changing the quality of "family-friendliness" in churches. The materials should be thoroughly studied by the Family Ministries Committee (or by the Church Board in lieu of a Family Ministries Committee). The Family Ministries committee itself should respond to the surveys and questionnaires that will later be given to the Church Board and the members. The Family Ministries Committee should then recommend an action plan to the Church Board for implementation in the church, involving surveys of the church body and the community, informative seminars and other appropriate follow-up.

**Note:** A brief or superficial discussion of this material with a few church leaders only will not likely give you the breadth of perspective that is needed, so involve a wide variety of people. You may miss the views of those who are on the fringes of your church, those who may feel that they are too busy to fill out a questionnaire, or those who may be uncomfortable with written material. A variety of approaches will be the most effective, and some of the results may be quite surprising.

# Guide for Leaders

**THINKING ABOUT THE NEEDS OF FAMILIES.** Becoming family-friendly starts with thinking about the different kinds of families in your congregation and community, then taking time to reflect on the whole of how you "do" church and the impact this has on all the various families to whom you minister. Families come in different shapes and sizes, more than just the two-parents-with-children variety. Among the assortment of families found in our churches:

- Single people who have never married

- Divorced single people, perhaps sharing the care of their children

- Couples without children

- Widows and widowers

- Lone-parent families

- Two-parent families

- Families with one or more disabled children

- Extended families

- Adoptive families

- Friends sharing housing

- Foster families

- Blended families

- Families from different cultural backgrounds

- Mixed-faith or inter-church families

- Carers and their elderly or disabled relatives

- Families where one parent may be absent for lengthy periods, e.g., working away from home or serving time in prison

- Families where someone other than parents are the carers, i.e., grandparents, aunts, etc., with one or more children

All these varied families have special needs. Families, in fact, often change shape several times across the life cycle. Each change presents differing needs and challenges to which we must be sensitive.

**WHAT A FAMILY-FRIENDLY CHURCH LOOKS LIKE.** To become familiar with some specifics of family-friendly churches, review the material in the section *What a Family-Friendly Church Looks Like*. The section *But Our Church is Really Small* suggests ways that congregations, especially those that are smaller, can implement family-friendly ideas.

**DECIDING TO BE FAMILY-FRIENDLY.** A church that wants to reach out to its community and become friendly to families faces all kinds of challenges, but these are exciting challenges. Some change will undoubtedly be called for. So a church must first decide whether it is seriously committed to becoming more family-friendly. As the process gets underway and people are asked for their views and ideas, their expectations will be raised and they will likely be looking for some positive changes. The route to increasing the level of family-friendliness will be different for each church and there may be some interesting discoveries along the way.

**GARNERING WIDE INPUT.** You will want to gather the views of as many adults and children in your church as possible on what they think a "family-friendly church" means to them. Listening to people's stories and creating an environment where open discussion can take place is itself one of the characteristics of church that has sensitivity to the relational needs of individuals and families. You will probably start by using the survey *What Is our Church Doing Right Now to be Family-Friendly?* or the *Questionnaire for Members* with the Church Board and other leadership groups in your church. As a church, you may also find it helpful to hear from those in your local community using the *Community Questionnaire*.

**USE EXISTING GROUPS/ACTIVITIES TO GATHER VIEWPOINTS.** The best way for you to gather views will depend upon your particular congregation, but you are likely to get the clearest picture by including perspectives from all areas of your church's life. So, be creative, and take the time to explore ways to gather information and ideas from those groups who might be missed. The material *Creative Ways to Draw Out Views* provides a variety of means for gathering input from different sectors of the church. *Case Studies*, with the discussion questions, offers another means of probing people's thinking about family-friendliness.

• *Congregations at different services.* Churches may find it helpful to use part of the Sabbath service to collect ideas interactively. Alternatively, *What Is our Church Doing Right Now to be Family-Friendly?* or the *Questionnaire for Members* can be distributed and collected on a subsequent week.

• *House groups.* These lend themselves easily to the informal and interactive collection of ideas.

• *Age, gender or interest groups.* See *Creative Ways to Draw Out Views* and the worksheets "Something I would like to see in my church would be a ..." and "I have a dream for my church ...."

• *A church weekend or day away.* A church retreat can be an ideal opportunity to emphasize what it means to be a church family and garner ideas.

**FORM SPECIAL GROUPS TO COLLECT IDEAS.** A wider cross-section of the church can be heard if special groups are formed. Based around existing groups, such as house-groups, the regular members of these groups can invite family, friends, and people who don't regularly attend. Personal invitations can generate a high level of involvement. These groups will be a way to build the mutual listening and relating that is at the heart of being a family-friendly church.

**DARE TO ASK THE COMMUNITY AROUND.** It is important to hear from non-church people. Some kind of "clinic," or "town hall," especially if it can be held in a neutral venue, such as the local library, may be beneficial. Questionnaires such as *Community Questionnaire* can be useful, if they have been carefully considered, but often a personal approach is better. You can ask people what they feel to be the major needs of the community, and what, if anything, they would like to see the church doing for the community. Visiting individuals, or groups on their own ground, with the purpose of exploring their needs, is much less threatening to do, and it can start to break down barriers. Of course, this open-ended questioning may generate ideas quite outside the area of family-friendliness! You might prefer to ask more specifically about the major needs of families and what the church could do. But, even then, we need to be open to hear what people *want* to say rather than what we expect them to say.

A church in London, England, asked people in their district what they would really like the church to do for their community. They consistently received the unexpected answer that the major problem was garbage in the streets! Understandably, they were reluctant to see this as a key area for Christian effort! But, when they eventually decided to see these answers as guidance, and to act on the specific request, it led to a great deal of fruitful interaction between the church and its local community. Being friendly to families in our communities may mean moving some activities out of the church and into the local community! For example, the best place for a parenting course for men may be in a sports centre rather than a church hall!

**PLANNING THE WAY AHEAD.** Managing change in a church can be challenging. But here are a few pointers.

• It is unlikely that you will be able to move ahead on several areas at once. As a leadership team, reflect on all the information you have collected, and then identify one or two priorities.

• Set out your goals in these areas with a time-scale, and plan the steps toward those goals.

• Remember that such objectives need to be achievable and measurable, so that you can know whether or not you've reached your goal.

• Evaluate. And then plan for the next steps forward.

**NOTE ON LEGAL REQUIREMENTS.** As you explore the needs and hopes of your church, keep in mind that there are some basic essentials that have the force of law in some places—such as child protection policies, disability access, hearing aids for those with hearing difficulties, and basic health and safety guidelines. It is important that you find out what these guidelines are for your community and make sure that your church aims to meet these criteria generously.

# What a Family-Friendly Church Looks Like

A church that wants to be family-friendly aims to:

• Encourage all members of the congregation to have a positive attitude towards each other, especially across generations and cultures.

• Have an awareness of current child protection policies and have clear guidelines to protect all children on any church activity. (This is not optional – it is vitally important that you have a child protection policy in place. For information, contact your pastor or conference Children's Ministry director.)

- Be aware of the spiritual, emotional, physical and social needs of its members and others in contact with the church community, and seek to meet these needs where it is appropriate.

- Provide a dynamic, multi-sensory, inspiring, and creative children's programme.

- Acknowledge that all relationships can benefit from learning and developing relationship skills, and provide opportunities for learning, such as seminars and workshops for parents, couples, teens, singles, those growing older, etc.

- Have a named person on whom people can call when they have a family crisis or a practical need of some sort. The aim of this is to relieve the immediate stress on families and individuals when emergencies arise.

- Actively involve adults and children of all ages in the church service on a regular basis.

- Share responsibilities around so that no one family or person is over-burdened with church-related tasks.

- Take care of church leaders and their families by protecting their family time.

- Have a building that is safe and accessible to everyone, i.e., access ramps, toilets, protective railings, etc.

- Provide a crèche or nursery for very small children so that their parents can focus on the worship experience without distractions.

- Finish services on time. Carers, people with certain health problems, parents, and those with non-church-attending spouses all need to know that a service will finish at a given time. (Having an atmosphere where people can leave a service at any time, without being made to feel uncomfortable, is helpful. It is also important to remember that a person can feel a sense of loss and loneliness if, because of time-schedules, bus, trolley or train schedules, etc., they have to leave the service before it is finished, and before they can chat with their friends. Church may be the only social contact available to some individuals.)

- Be aware of the needs of men and fathers as well as women and mothers, and address these in a variety of ways, i.e., men's groups, women's groups, sports groups, work-teams, networking, etc.

- Reach out to other families in the local community, using an on-going project.

- Provide a variety of non-threatening social activities to which members can comfortably invite families they know in the community. These are activities where there is no preaching and minimal or no obvious religious content, other than a child saying grace before a meal, for example.

# But Our Church is Really Small!

If, like many churches, you have a very small congregation, don't feel overwhelmed. There are still some things you may be able to do by listening to the stories of the people in your congregation. What would they like to do? What things are practical? Perhaps you have only one family attending. What would make it easier for them to attend, or to bring along their friends? Here are some ideas:

- Interview regular members and discuss how they might be involved in the service in different ways.

- Place a clearly labelled bright box near the door of the church, with some interactive Bible story books, crayons, Bible story worksheets, soft Noah's ark toys, etc., so that any visiting children can dip into the box and borrow things during the service.

- Keep a folder for each of the children at church. One church provided a bright ring binder with a pocket for pencils and crayons, etc. for each child. Each week a person designated for the task would prepare a worksheet—using a copier-ready resource or the Internet, etc.—that was on the theme of the church service. The folder had plain pages where the children could write notes and questions to the church leader. The binder was turned in at the end of the service. During the coming week the church leader wrote back a few lines to the children.

- One church let the children help in the service by collecting the offering and giving out songbooks. Sometimes the children would bring their instruments to church to play for the service.

- Another church had a "grandparent" scheme, where older members were given a "grandchild" in the congregation. Friendships formed between the generations, as they listened to each other, valued each other and gave each other gifts.

- A small church could get involved in a small community project that they could manage within their resources, such as a "coffee" morning, or a monthly soup run for the homeless in the community which could be done in a rotation with other churches.

- In one village in England there were five small churches of different denominations that formed their own Churches Together network. They realised that they could not all conduct all the different programmes they would like, so they shared the programmes between them, pooling their manpower and resources to make use of the different skills within the churches. Among them they managed to run a well-rounded programme including Carer and Toddler Groups, playgroups, aerobics groups, Holiday Bible Clubs, and midweek clubs to cover ages 7 - 21+, as well as Senior Citizens' groups, and village social events.

- Another small church wanted to conduct a Vacation Bible Club, but didn't have enough volunteer helpers. They invited students from a Bible college to run the club for them, whilst church members provided accommodation for the week and some local outings. The students also gained some valuable hands-on experience as they worked with the children.

---

Karen Holford works with her husband, Bernie, in the South England Conference, Trans-European Division, where they direct the Departments of Family Ministries and Children's Ministries. She is also currently chairing Churches Together for Families, in England.

Paul Godfrey was working as a Family Evangelist for the Scripture Union when he and Karen worked on this material for the Churches Together for Families website www.churchesandfamilies.org. Karen has adapted the material to the Adventist context for this planbook.

# What is Our Church Doing Right Now to be Family Friendly?

Take some time to think of the positive things your church is doing in your community and write them down. A church is family-friendly when it is aware of a wide range of people's needs and explores ways to meet those needs.

**1** | **We meet the spiritual needs of the people in our community by:**

**2** | **We meet the emotional and relational needs of the people in the community by:**

**3** | **We meet the physical needs of those in the community by:**

**4** | **We meet the social needs of people in our community by:**

**5** | **The positive elements in our children's programme are:**

**6** | **We host the following programmes to support relationships between people:**

**7** | **We have a named person or team of individuals for people to call on in an emergency.**

☐ YES  ☐ NO

**8** | **Our positive attitudes towards the diversity of people, including those of minority groups in our community, are evident by our . . .**

**9** The ways we actively try to involve different people of all ages in the church service are:

**10** The ways we share church responsibilities around so that no one family or person is over-burdened with church-related tasks are:

**11** The ways that we show our care for our church leaders and their families are:

**12** The improvements we have made towards creating a building that is safe and accessible to everyone are:

**13** We have a current child protection policy and we have clear guidelines to protect all children on any church activity.

☐ YES ☐ NO

**14** We provide a crèche or nursery for very small children so that their parents can focus on the worship experience without distractions:

☐ Every week ☐ Once a month ☐ Occasionally ☐ Never

**15** Our services finish promptly, at a given time, so that families can plan accordingly:

☐ Every week ☐ Once a month ☐ Occasionally ☐ Never

**16** The ways we show that we affirm the needs of men and fathers are by:

**17** The ways we are reaching out into the community and helping to meet local needs are by:

**18** If our church could change or improve three things I would like them to be:

1-

2-

3-

# Starter Ideas for a Family-Friendly Church

Share and discuss these ideas with your church group. How might they help meet some of the needs in your church and community? What additional ideas can you add? What changes will be needed to implement these ideas? What steps will need to be taken to implement them?

## MEETING SPIRITUAL NEEDS

Prayer meetings

Outreach programmes

Small study groups

Visitor/mission/welcome/seeker services

House fellowships

Prayer partners

Prayer breakfasts

Christian book-store

Broadcasting church services

Dial-a-prayer

Vacation Bible schools

Children's Bible story hour

## MEETING EMOTIONAL AND RELATIONAL NEEDS

Counselling services

Bereaved or divorced support groups

Carer and toddler groups

Befriending programmes

Lunch clubs for senior citizens

"Coffee" mornings

Seminars on different aspects of family life

Special dinner evenings for married couples, combined with interesting marriage seminars

## MEETING PEOPLE'S PHYSICAL NEEDS

Soup kitchen

Homeless shelter

Lunch clubs

Emergency food and clothing stores

Aerobics and fitness sessions

Health clinics

## MEETING PEOPLE'S SOCIAL NEEDS

Lunch clubs

Youth clubs

Carer and toddler club

Picnics

Outings

Harvest suppers

Special social events

"Over-sixties" clubs

"Coffee" mornings

Mom's drop-in center with child-care, crafts, parenting support, hairdressing, etc.

## SUPPORTING RELATIONSHIPS

Marriage preparation seminars

Parenting seminars

Marriage enrichment events

Singles' events

Child contact centers where children can meet safely on neutral ground with a parent with whom they no longer live

Teen relationship seminars

Divorce care groups

Retirement seminars

Support of families with a member in prison

## INVOLVING PEOPLE OF ALL AGES IN THE CHURCH SERVICE

Children's choir

Youth band

A mixed-age worship committee

Different aged welcomers at the door

Various groups within the church taking a special responsibility for a part of the service

A family writing a special prayer to read out together

A teen group dramatising the Scripture reading

## CARING FOR LEADERS AND THEIR FAMILIES

Protecting leaders' need for family time

Honouring their day-off

Helping provide times for relaxation, such as retreats, vacations and days out

Inviting them for meals

Supporting their ministry financially and practically, etc.

## MEETING LOCAL COMMUNITY NEEDS

Carer and toddler groups

Lone parent support groups

Over sixties club

Youth clubs

After school clubs

Lunch clubs

Sports events

Leisure classes

Parenting groups

Finding ways to improve local facilities and the environment

Playgroups, etc.

## MAKING OUR CHURCH BUILDING SAFE AND ACCESSIBLE

Ramped access

Designated car-park spaces

Washroom facilities suitable for disabled people

Child-sized washroom facilities

Stair-lifts

Induction loops/aid for hearing impaired

Protective railings

Buggy/stroller park

Diaper changing station, etc.

## MEETING NEEDS OF FAMILIES WITH YOUNG CHILDREN

A child protection policy (essential)

A crèche or nursery for very small children during church services

Services finishing promptly, so families can plan accordingly

Diaper changing facilities, supplies, and bottle warming equipment, etc.

An enjoyable children's programme

## MEETING NEEDS OF MEN AND FATHERS

Men's groups

Prayer breakfasts

Sports

Work-teams

Networking

Retirement planning seminars

Father and son sports programmes

Car maintenance classes

# Case Studies

## 1. LYN AND PAUL JENSEN

Lyn and Paul Jensen have two children – Stephen (4) and Annette (18 months). Paul commutes to the city leaving home early and often returning after the children are in bed. Lyn is a stay-at-home mom, having taken time out of her career in human relations. Lyn helps to lead the Mother & Toddler group in the week and the crèche in church on alternate Sabbaths, as well as helping out in Cradle Roll. She often finds getting to her women's Bible study group difficult because of baby-sitting arrangements. Paul conducts the gospel choir at the church and this takes up lots of his spare time. The family goes to church together, but their choir and crèche duties often prevent them from worshipping with each other. The services can also be stressful for Lyn, as she feels that the two children do not always behave as people might expect them to behave in church. Sometimes Lyn feels isolated as she bears the burden of the childcare, even though Paul does what he can in the limited time available to him.

## 2. LAURA CARTER

Laura Carter is 12, and for as long as she can remember she has come to church with her mother, Gill. Laura's father left home to live with another woman and her two children, and Laura sees him every other weekend. He is not interested in anything religious, although he has come to church at Christmas and Thanksgiving and once when Laura sang in the choir. Gill is struggling with her feelings of guilt over her failed marriage and she feels confused about her understanding of the church's teaching on divorce. Laura is feeling deserted by her father, desperately wanting to see him, and yet aware of her mom's pain. The church runs a youth group for teenagers that Laura could join when she is 13. But, right now, Laura is losing interest in the church. No one there seems to understand her struggles and dilemmas. Somehow the church seems irrelevant to her needs.

## 3. BETTY JOHN

Betty John's fiancé never returned from the war. Betty remained unmarried and had a fulfilling life as a teacher, sharing her home with her parents. Her two brothers have both married, and they now have adult children and grandchildren. Betty has taken most of the responsibility for caring for her parents as they grew older. A Christian all her life, she had been an active member of the church leadership, and had been responsible for overseeing the children's work, until her mother became so frail that Betty had to spend more time at home. Gradually she has given up her church commitments and other responsibilities in the local community. For some years, her parents have been isolated members of the church, particularly after her father's sight deteriorated. They began to have communion served to them in their own home and recently Betty has begun to join them in this. Occasionally Betty manages to get to church, but the services feel strange, and there are so many people she doesn't know. The old faces aren't there any more and the patterns of worship seem to have changed. Betty feels she no longer belongs.

## 4. HANNAH BENJAMIN

Hannah spent the first ten years of her life in Jamaica. Then she was sent to live with her aunt in Chicago, so that she could get a good education. Her family hoped that she would go to university and study for a degree. Hannah's uncle began to abuse her when she was fourteen, and a year later she ran away from Chicago to Detroit. For a few months she lived on the streets. Then she became pregnant and was provided with emergency housing. Now she has 18-month-old twins. Her family in Jamaica have rejected her, and she attends the local church mother and toddler group. She used to go to church when she was in Jamaica, but feels she's "too sinful" to attend services any more.

## 5. PETER AND KIM MOORE

Peter comes to church, but Kim was brought up in a different denomination, and she still wishes to attend her own church. One week Peter brings their three children to church; the next week, they go with Kim. Peter is finding it harder and harder to encourage the children to come with him. The eldest is fifteen and the youngest is ten. They either want to go with Kim, because her church is more lively and interesting, or stay home. Peter feels discouraged and worthless. He has admitted that Kim is very unhappy in their marriage and that she is considering separation.

## 6. MICHAEL EVANS

Michael attends church regularly and plays the piano occasionally. Recently he has started to bring Steve along too. They both live in the same house. They have offered to host a Bible study group. Some of your church members are uneasy about this.

## FOR DISCUSSION

1. What is the experience at church of the individuals and whole families described above? What perceptions do you think they have of their local church?

2. How might these families, including individual children and adults, be helped to feel welcome and comfortable at church? How might they be encouraged or enabled to worship in a more satisfying way?

3. What practical innovations might a church make to enable the families described to find church life and worship more friendly and relevant to them?

4. What kinds of support could these families use in addition to church services and current church activities?

5. How could you show these families that you care about the personal challenges they are facing?

6. Think of the families on the fringes of your church and those in your local community. What difference might it make to them if your church became more family-friendly?

## SURVEY

# Questionnaire for Members

**1** | How long have you been a part of this church?

**2** | What services and activities do you attend regularly?

**3** | Are there other services and activities that you attend occasionally?

**4** | Please give a brief description of who is "family" for you (e.g., I live alone; visit my parents occasionally; married with two children; grandparents live locally, although other relatives are scattered around the country, etc.)

**5** | Does this church help you in your family life? If so how?

**6** | Are there other ways in which you would like to see the church offering support to you as you live as a Christian in your family?

## SURVEY
# Community Questionnaire

**1** **What, in your view, are the most important needs in this community?**

**2** **Which of these needs are not being met by anyone at the moment, as far as you know?**

**3** **Are there ways in which you would like some help in your family life that is not available to you at the moment?**

**4** **To help us understand your needs, we invite you to give a brief description of who is "family" for you.**

**5** **Here is a list of some things which some churches are able to provide for their communities. Please tick how helpful you feel these would be in this community and which would be personally helpful to you.**

|  | Wouldn't help | Would help | Would help me |
|---|---|---|---|
| Carer and toddler group | ☐ | ☐ | ☐ |
| Parenting group | ☐ | ☐ | ☐ |
| Help with shopping | ☐ | ☐ | ☐ |
| Help around the house | ☐ | ☐ | ☐ |
| Pregnancy advice centre | ☐ | ☐ | ☐ |
| Contact centre for parents and children | ☐ | ☐ | ☐ |
| Family budgeting advice centre | ☐ | ☐ | ☐ |
| After school club | ☐ | ☐ | ☐ |

# Creative Ways to Draw Out Views

## ADULTS

- Place individuals in sub-groups with those who have similar circumstances (e.g., those with pre-school children, those who live alone, those caring for an elderly relative, etc.). Let each sub-group try to understand the needs of another sub-group and list ways the church could help. Share with the large group.

- Ask participants to form pairs. Discuss comparisons and contrasts between their family life as a child and today's families (including their own). Draw up a list of contrasts—favourable and unfavourable. Get opinions about the needs of modern families, as they have emerged from the conversations, and brainstorm about the different ways in which the church could offer support.

- Divide into groups and use *Case Studies* as a discussion starter for thinking about how your church can meet different needs.

## YOUNG PEOPLE

- Get plenty of pizza and fruit punch and listen to the young people!

- Give everyone a large sheet of paper and a marker pen. Ask them to draw a chart of their family (no names, just labels, e.g., brother, step-dad, auntie, dog, etc.) Collect and display them on the wall or floor for everyone to see. Chat about what you notice regarding the family charts—the similarities, differences, etc. Are there times when family life is difficult, or really good? Does church help? Could church be more helpful? You might be able to arrange the charts and add others to show how your church functions at the moment, or how it could be, e.g., a family of families.

- Sometimes young people do not want to talk about their own family but prefer to talk about families in TV programmes, e.g., as "The Simpsons" or "Neighbors," because it is less personal. Tape record a couple of video clips from current popular programmes showing family life and use them to promote discussion.

- Display the sentence: *This church is like a family.* Brainstorm things that are good about that (e.g., it feels like home), and things that are not so good (e.g., the pastor is like my dad, he never washes up the cups after church.) All sorts of issues around the young people's own families and church life may emerge.

- You could use the same sentence as above, but brainstorm all the ways in which the statement is true, and all the ways it isn't true. The sheet "I have a dream…" could be used to collect ideas and desires for change.

## CHILDREN

- Children will probably not be reflecting on their family life and we need to be careful not to make them feel bad about their families, especially as they may have no power in making decisions about how those families are. The best situation for talking about family life is a small group or one-to-one where lots of trust has been developed and where the child sets the agenda by talking about what they want to talk about. A teaching session on families can helpfully open up the subject for children who need or want to talk about their families.

- Run a "My Family" painting competition. Create a collage of the results. Older competitors could be asked to write a description to go with it. Have an attractive prize. This could be done in conjunction with a local school or newspaper and could yield interesting patterns and opinions.

- Talk a little about how the church is a family where all ages matter, and explain that the church leaders want to know how all the different parts of the family feel about things. Use the sheets "Something I would like…" and/or "I have a dream…" for them to write or draw their ideas.

- If a church event for all ages is being planned, ask the children for ideas about things to do, games to play, food to eat, etc. (rather than leaving it all to the adults to plan). Reflect afterwards on how the event was different from what might otherwise have been done, and whether that affected its success.

## ALL-AGE GROUPS

- Nearly all the above could be used with mixed age groups. Make sure that all age groups have a voice, and are heard by the others. Most adults will be much more used to making sure that they have their say than most children are, so it will probably be the children who need to be encouraged and empowered! It can be helpful to establish a convention within the groups that a small item, such as a pencil, is passed around from person to person. Only the person holding the object has the right to speak and be heard.

• Split into age groups, e.g., under 10, 11-15, 16-20 or whatever fits your group. Give each group a large sheet of paper with their age group written on the top. The papers are passed to each group in turn, who then describe the kind of church that they think would most appeal to the given age group. (Start at the bottom so that when the paper is passed to the next group it can be folded over to hide what has already been written.) When all the groups have finished this activity, return the papers to the organizer so that they can be read out and displayed.

• In some settings a similar activity could be done after dividing up the main group into subgroups of those who are married, single people, parents, children or whatever matches the experiences of those present. This needs to be done with care and sensitivity, and some people will obviously fit into more than one category. If this is the case, let them choose which group they would like to be in, or allocate them to the smaller of the groups into which they could fit.

• In mixed-age small groups try to build the tallest tower of cartons from the grocery store. Supply the groups with a good collection of cartons. Each box used in their towers must have an idea written on it describing a way in which the church could be more like a family, or a way in which the church could help families.

## Resources for Family-Friendly Churches

*The Family Friendly Church*. Ben Freudenburg with Rick Lawrence, Group, 1998. ISBN 07644 20488. (American book available from Internet suppliers)

*Family Friendly Ideas Your Church Can Do*. Ben Freudenburg et al., Group, 1998. ISBN 07644 20356. (American book available from Internet suppliers)

*Your Church Can be…Family Friendly – How You Can Launch a Successful Ministry in Your Church*. Steve Thomas, College Press, 1997. ISBN 0899 007469. (American book available from Internet suppliers)

*Families Finding Faith*. CPAS & Scripture Union. ISBN 1-85999-382.

*Men – The Challenge of Change*. James Lawrence, CPAS, 1997. ISBN 1-8976-6073-1.
This is a handbook of men's ministries tackling such issues as how to reach and keep men in our churches today. The book includes group sessions, discussion starters, Bible studies and copier-ready materials.

*Seen and Heard – Valuing Children in Your Church*. Jackie Cray, CPAS Monarch, 1995. ISBN 1-85424-270-9. This is a book of ways to integrate children more fully into church services, and make family life a subject for teaching within a church. Considers the biblical approach to children in church, and issues of protection, nurture and kinship within the church.

*Palm Tree Press Instant Art Series*. Palm Tree Press publishes various books to help with all aspects of church life, from the church magazine to the crèche. Copier-ready worksheets for preschoolers, and school-age children, simple cardboard models to illustrate Bible stories, crafts for Easter and Christmas, cartoons, clip art, posters and discussion starters. Available from Christian Bookshops, or direct from Kevin Mayhew, Buxhall, Stowmarket, Suffolk, IP14 3BW England. E-mail: sales@kevinmayhewltd.com

*CPAS*. Publishes a range of books to help churches, with a number of publications useful for those wishing to become more family-friendly. Books of sermon and programme ideas, dramas, and other practical help, including complete programmes for youth groups. Church Pastoral Aid Society, Athena Drive, Tachbrook Park, Warwick, CV34 6NG England. Website: www.cpas.org.uk

# Some Useful Christian Websites

## CHILD PROTECTION

- www.doveuk.com/pcca/index.htm - specialists in advising churches and schools about child protection issues

## CHILDREN'S MINISTRY

- www.childrensministry.net – a large resource for children's ministry ideas

- www.childrensermons.com – free resources for children's sermons, using simple props

- www.cpas.org.uk – a growing database of free resources to help with children and youth ministry in particular

- www.gospelcom.net/cbh/kfk - Bible material for children from the Children's Bible Hour

- www.scripture.org.uk – publishes material helpful for those ministering to children and young people

- www.theideabox.com – crafts and activities for children

- www.truelovewaits.org – helping teens avoid sex before marriage

- http://youthpastor.com – help for busy youth workers

## DEMOGRAPHICS

- www.upmystreet.com – local information and statistics about your community

## DISABILITY

- www.throughtheroof.org – disability outreach in the U.K. with Joni Eareckson Tada

## DRAMA

- www.drama4church.com

- www.dramashare.org – "how to" manuals and drama scripts

## FAMILY MINISTRY

- www.bethanyfamilyinstitute.com – Christian family ministry resources

- www.care-for-the-family.org.uk – help for Christian families under stress, or breaking up

- www.family.org – Focus on the Family web-site with links to many other Christian and family related sites

- http://family.nadadventist.org – General Conference of SDA, North American Division, Family Ministries departmental website

- http://familyministries.gc.adventist.org – General Conference of SDA, Family Ministries departmental website

## GRAPHICS

- www.gospelcom.net/rev-fun/ - every day this site has full colour cartoons that can be freely used in any non-profit bulletin or newsletter

- http://www.njwebworks.com/churchweb/gallery/ - Christian Graphics Gallery – graphics that have been collected from a variety of Christian sources on the Internet

## MARRIAGE

- www.2-in-2-1.co.uk - a web site full of Christian-based information and ideas to enrich, maintain and repair marriages

- www.marriageresource.org.uk – Marriage Resource and National Marriage Week

- www.marriage-preparation.co.uk – a website designed by members of Churches Together for Families in England about marriage preparation. It includes resources as well as ideas for churches to get started and making your preparation better.

## PARENTING

- www.abcparenting.com – parenting support and education

- www.activeparenting.com – a wide range of materials to help parents

- www.hannah.org – infertility and loss support

- www.parentsplace.com – support and links for parents

- www.truelovewaits.org – helping teens avoid sex before marriage

## SERMONS AND WORSHIP RESOURCES

- www.familyworship.org.uk – resources, songs and teaching materials from the Icthus Fellowship, to help whole churches enjoy worshipping together

- www.sermonillustrations.com – illustrations by topic index

- www.sermonsearch.com – searchable database of 7000 contemporary sermons

- http://youthpastor.com – help for busy youth workers

## SHOPPING FOR RESOURCES

- www.christianbookshop.com – on-line bookshop from several British Christian publishers

- www.parable.com – Christian on-line shopping

## WEB-DIRECTORY OF CHRISTIAN RESOURCES

- www.godonthenet.com – on-line directory of hundreds of useful Christian sites to help your ministry

## WOMEN

- www.hannah.org – infertility and loss support

- www.womentoday.org – helping women to share their faith in their home and community

## YOUTH MINISTRY

- www.cpas.org.uk – a growing database of free resources to help with children and youth ministry in particular

- www.cpo.uk.com – Christian publisher and media organisation producing all kinds of printed products to help churches, such as mugs for children's gifts, church bulletin covers, posters, National Marriage Week materials, and outreach ideas

- www.scripture.org.uk – publishes material helpful for those ministering to children and young people

- www.truelovewaits.org – helping teens avoid sex **before marriage**

- http://youthpastor.com – help for busy youth workers

---

# Copier-ready Worksheet Masters

## PAGE 58

"I have a dream for my church" *(This is best suited to a teen and youth group, but could also be used with older children or adults.)*

## PAGE 59

"Something I would like to see in my church would be a…" *(This is more suitable for younger children.) Both masters can also be enlarged to give more room for creativity and to present a whole collection of ideas to a church, on a display board, or a spare wall.*

*Something I would like to see in my church would be a...*

# Hearts and Homes for Him

**by Karen and Ron Flowers**

*Many will never hear what we say about God's love until they have experienced it in our midst. Hospitality in our homes can provide that experience.*

## ABOUT THIS SEMINAR

The following seminar is adapted with permission from *Christian Hospitality Made Easy* by Patrica B. Mutch, Ph.D., published by the Ministerial Association/Shepherdess International, General Conference of Seventh-day Adventists, 1987. *Christian Hospitality Made Easy* is a self-study course that uses *Open Heart, Open Home* by Karen Burton Mains as a textbook. Order from Seminars Unlimited, P.O. Box 66, Keene, TX 76059, (800) 982-3344. Includes study guide, 3 audio cassettes and textbook.

The seminar uses some didactic presentation and a number of group activities. Approximate time for the seminar: 2 – 3 hours. Be sure to make adequate copies of the handouts.

# Presentation

• *Group Starter Activity. Ask the group to reflect on the following question:* Of all that you have, what do you count most valuable? *Then give individuals a few minutes to share what they wish of their thoughts with someone sitting next to them.*

Most of you will likely value relationships at the top of the list. Human beings were made for relationships. Without them they are miserable. Ultimately, our success at relationships is rooted in our ability to love and care for others. Hospitality creates a path toward a warm network of relationships, but it will mean the giving of oneself in ways that meet the needs of others.

## A CHALLENGE TO CHRISTIANS

Ours is a world that desperately needs hospitality. People everywhere experience broken relationships, mistrust, hostility, anxiety and hopelessness. Technological advances bring benefits, but exact a cost in family togetherness and stability, trusting relationships, and enduring friendships. People are mobile, which often reduces family groups to nuclear families. Many live as singles or as single parents. The extended family is limited in its ability to supply personal support.

While people search for affection, caring, and lasting relationships, Christians find themselves so spent they can scarcely respond. Christians are no different from those around them in these respects. Yet we desperately need each other. And the world needs our love. In truth, many will never hear what we say about God's love until they have experienced it in our midst.

**GROUP ACTIVITY 1:** *Form small groups, then have these groups make a list of the challenges they see to their church family becoming a caring community of believers where the gift of hospitality is fully developed. Invite groups to share their ideas with the entire group. Use the following list to augment the responses from the groups:*

• time pressure

• energy drain

• lack of resources

• feelings of inadequacy

• tendency to protect ourselves from worldly influences by having minimal social interaction with non-church members

• awkwardness that many, particularly those raised in Adventist homes, feel outside the Adventist subculture

• fear that others will discover the reality of our lives

• the core selfishness of the human heart which does not want to make the investment in others

The purpose of this seminar is to address the challenge facing us by 1) understanding hospitality better and 2) stimulating interest in increasing our "hospitality quotient" with believers and non-members.

## HOSPITALITY AS A CONCEPT

Scripture teaches about hospitality both by providing examples and offering admonition.

**GROUP ACTIVITY 2A:** *Assign this activity to half the class, working in groups of 4. Read the following Bible passages and look for principles of hospitality. Beside the texts are principles that you may identify to augment the groups' discoveries.*

| TEXTS | PRINCIPLES |
| --- | --- |
| Exodus 23:9 | Aliens were to be treated kindly. |
| Leviticus 23:22 | Provision was to be made for the poor and for strangers. |
| Isaiah 58:6, 7, 10-12 | One's bounty was to be shared. (This passage is one of the most comprehensive biblical statements on hospitality, its responsibilities and its rewards.) |
| Matthew 5:42 | Sharing is crucial to life. |
| Luke 14:12-14 | The guest list is addressed. (Invite those in need to your feasts.) |
| 1 Peter 4:9-10 | As some became uncomfortable with all things being held in common (see Acts 4:32-35), they needed reminding about hospitality. Importance of service to one another. |
| Romans 12:13 | Sharing with those in need. |
| 1 Timothy 3:2 | Importance of church leaders being examples of hospitality. Qualifications of an elder included hospitality. |

**GROUP ACTIVITY 2B:** *Assign this activity to the other half of the class, working in groups of 4. Investigate one or more of the following scriptural examples of hospitality. For each person or situation, note what describes the quality and attributes of the gift of hospitality which is manifested.*

Abraham and Sarah (Genesis 18)

Lot in Sodom (Genesis 19)

Rebekah and Eliezer (Genesis 24)

Rahab and the spies (Joshua 2)

Abigail and Nabal (1 Samuel 25)

Elijah and the widow of Zarephath (1 Kings 17)

The Shunammite woman (2 Kings 4:8-37)

Hezekiah (2 Kings 20:9-19)

Mary, Martha, and Lazarus (Luke 10:38-42)

Christ feeding the multitude (Matthew 14:13-21)

Simon of Bethany and Mary (Matthew 26:6-13; Luke 7:36-50; John 12:1-8)

Lydia of Thyatira (Acts 16:13-15, 40)

Zacchaeus (Luke 19:1-9)

If these principles were practiced and these examples followed, hospitality would be a means for conveying Christ's love to those longing for relationships and tangible support. We might even find those who have experienced our hospitality to be more receptive to our sharing our faith. But alas, we may ask ourselves, who has the time and energy for extensive meal preparation and for keeping a spotless home suitable for company?

**Hospitality counterfeits.** Somehow a counterfeit to hospitality has arisen, a false hospitality we will call "entertainment." (This may be a different usage of the word than many are accustomed to, but here it will be used with a particular definition attached.) Entertainment mimics hospitality, but really has little to do with real biblical hospitality. Note some contrasts between the counterfeit of entertainment and real hospitality on the next page. (Also see Handout 1 *Entertainment or Hospitality*)

• Entertainment requires a spotless home, a perfectly matched and decorated table, a gourmet meal, a perfectly dressed and coiffured hostess.

- Hospitality seeks to put its priorities on the guest and meeting his or her needs.

- Entertainment leads guests to admire what the host and hostess have provided.

- Hospitality offers all that the host and hostess possess to meet the needs of the guest.

- Entertainment's motives are egocentric, to impress others with what we have and what we are able to do.

- Hospitality's motives are other-directed, focused on meeting the needs of others.

- Entertainment puts its priorities on things.

- Hospitality puts its priorities on people.

- Entertainment models arise out of the dream world of homemaker magazines.

- Hospitality models arise out of examples of persons who seek to meet the needs of others.

- Entertainment creates bondage to resources, time, perfection.

- Hospitality becomes increasingly a joy as we become channels of God's love and blessing.

**GROUP ACTIVITY 3**: *Give individuals a few minutes to complete and reflect personally on* When I Felt Welcome (Handout 2). *Invite several to share their reflections with the entire group. Discuss the irony in that often the very things we think we have to do in order to be a good host or hostess are the very things that make us uncomfortable as guests. And vice versa, the very things that would bring us concern and embarrassment are the same things that make us feel at home as a visitor.*

**GROUP ACTIVITY 4**: *In small groups spend a few minutes visioning together what your church would be like if the gift of hospitality were fully developed among the members. What kinds of things can you see happening? What kind of atmosphere can you feel? With what kinds of results? Share your dreams together in the large group.*

## DEVELOPING OUR HOSPITALITY

What can we do to bring real hospitality back into our lives as a church family and into the lives of our neighbors as we seek to meet their needs?

**COMMIT OURSELVES TO BE USED OF GOD.** Meet the needs of others through whatever aspect of hospitality He calls us to perform, recognizing our dependence upon Him for strength and the realization of our purposes (1 Peter 4:11).

**BATHE OUR EFFORTS AT HOSPITALITY IN PRAYER.** Ask God to make us discerning of the needs of others and ask Him to bless our efforts to meet those needs. Ask Him to purify our motives and to give us strength to do what He bids us to do.

**SET CLEAR PRIORITIES.** Families, neighbors and strangers constitute widening circles for our hospitality:

1. *Our families take first priority.* They should not be shunted aside for the *larger task* of hospitality. "The first work of Christians is to be united in the family. Then the work is to extend to their neighbors nigh and afar off" (*The Adventist Home*, p. 37). "As workers for God, our work is to begin with those nearest. It is to begin in our own home. There is no more important missionary field than this" (*Child Guidance*, p. 476). There are times in all families when family members are in a position to minister to others. The entire family can be included in gestures of hospitality. The next generation need not have so much to learn about this gift when it is part of their lives since childhood. But there are also seasons in the life of every family when they are not as able to minister to others. They may just need time alone to rest and recover, or they themselves may need to be ministered to.

2. *Friends, neighbors and co-workers* are next on the priority list, individuals whom we encounter on a daily basis. As part of the support network of persons to which we belong, we are privileged to be used by God to bear the burdens of those close to us.

3. *Our final priority includes the strangers* God sends our way and to whom we respond according to our ability to help. The pressing question of hospitality for all three groups is always: What are the needs of each person and how can I help to meet those needs?

**DEVELOP SUPPORTING SKILLS THAT HELP TO MAXIMIZE OUR EFFORTS.** *For this section you may wish to ask several church members to share their own experiences. Choose not only persons* *whose God-given gifts have made them naturals at hospitality, but also those who have cultivated this gift through conscious effort. The following are a summary of practical ideas and skills that you can use to stimulate additional thinking or to augment members' sharing.*

1. Tips on time management that help maximize a small amount of time for God.

2. Ways to keep the costs of hospitality affordable.

3. How to stock a "ready shelf" of long-term storage items for short notice meals. Plans for a menu/recipe exchange of quick, but nutritious meals for various occasions could be advertised so that each would come with something to share.

4. How to surmount the hurdle of feeling one must do everything, and do all things perfectly, when company comes.

5. Discovering the joy of lasting friendships born when families are able to accept themselves as they are without apology and simply take guests in as members of the family.

6. How to start conversations with strangers, both Christians and non-Christians. Practice and develop the art of asking good questions.

7. Share experiences of times when God has impressed you to reach out in hospitality and you have had the joy of sharing the good news in your home. Work together in pairs to develop a simple personal testimony suitable for sharing with another believer and with a non-Christian as the opportunity arises.

## HOSPITALITY EVANGELISM

I am firmly convinced that if Christians would open their homes and practice hospitality as defined in Scripture, we could significantly alter the fabric of society. We could play a major role in its spiritual, moral, and emotional redemption. (Mains, 1976, p. 22)

Our time here is short. We can pass through this world but once; as we pass along, let us make the most of life. The work to which we are called does not require wealth or social position or great ability. It requires a kindly, self-sacrificing spirit and a steadfast purpose. A lamp, however small, if kept steadily burning, may be the means of lighting many other lamps. Our sphere of influence may seem narrow, our ability small, our opportunities few, our acquirements limited; yet wonderful possibilities are ours through a faithful use of the opportunities of our own homes. If we will open our hearts and homes to the divine principles of life, we shall become channels for currents of life-giving power. From our homes will flow streams of healing, bringing life, and beauty, and fruitfulness where now are barrenness and dearth. (*The Adventist Home*, p. 33)

Hospitality can provide a means of building up the body of Christ, of winsomely drawing our children and youth to Jesus and His teachings and encouraging growth and commitment among members of all ages. Hospitality can also provide an avenue for reaching into the community around us. The home provides an ideal setting for drawing others close so that we may share the good news that is bursting in our hearts.

**GROUP ACTIVITY 5:** *Divide the group in half. Ask one group to generate ideas for using hospitality to build the body of Christ. Ask the other to create ideas for using hospitality to reach into circles beyond the church family. The following are suggestions with which to start the groups' thinking or to use as part of your summary.*

## HOSPITALITY TO BUILD THE BODY OF CHRIST.

1. *Social activities.* Make a list of social activities you think represent the best of true hospitality to pass on to your church's social committee.

2. *Linkages between new members and believers.* Becoming a Seventh-day Adventist requires many lifestyle changes. New believers need new and close ties with church members who can help them make these changes and provide a network of friends and family with whom to fellowship. These linkages will not just happen. They must be planned. For instance, a plan might be developed to rotate invitations to new believers to Sabbath dinner in the homes of different church members at least once a month for a year after their baptism. New members could be paired with members of longer standing in exercise classes, weight-control programs, bread baking workshops, church cleaning/gardening responsibilities, etc.

3. *Prayer fellowships.* Prayer may be for general or specific needs. You may want to form intercessory prayer groups, prayer partners, or small groups.

## HOSPITALITY TO REACH INTO THE COMMUNITY.

1. *Sabbath visitor hospitality.* Dinner with visitors—whether at the church or in homes—provides opportunity for visitors to reflect on what they have experienced and ask questions. Church members can discover the reasons for their visit to the church, perhaps even learn a part of the story of their lives if they are willing to share it, and how the church can meet the needs of their hearts.

2. *Youth socials.* Many churches open their doors to the youth of their communities, providing exercise rooms, gyms for basketball, drug and alcohol free parties, etc. as circumstances allow.

3. *Supper and Bible study.* A light meal followed by Bible study offers the opportunity not only for church members to gather for fellowship but for them to invite a friend outside the circle of the church family.

4. *Bed and breakfast for travelers.* Many Seventh-day Adventists are becoming involved in the "Bed and Breakfast" business. While business does not allow for overt evangelistic gestures, the literature left in the common areas, a kindly welcome, a Bible and devotional book left in a room, a prayer printed on a small card and placed at the breakfast setting, etc. all are means of witnessing.

Additional hospitality opportunities may be present on special occasions both within the *church family* or in the *community*:

1. *Funeral meals.* Death in a family provides the opportunity for caring Christians not only to provide food, but to offer to prepare and serve it, to sit and listen as the family talks of their loved one, and to clean up afterwards.

2. *Food for the hungry.* This may involve feeding the homeless, becoming involved in senior citizen food programs, or otherwise providing food for individuals and families in ways that are not demeaning but which meet their needs with dignity and caring concern.

3. *Family needs during hospitalization.* Even the simple tasks of maintaining a household create enormous stress on a family when one of their members is hospitalized. Meeting needs for meal preparation, child care, laundry, errands, etc., at this time will never be forgotten.

4. *Students.* Many churches have universities and boarding schools in close proximity. Students away from home revel in a home cooked meal and an evening or afternoon in the home of a church family, especially when they are taken in, even put to work, as part of the family circle.

5. *Radical hospitality.* Foster care, taking in refugees, runaways, homeless persons are examples of radical hospitality. This kind of hospitality is not for everyone, and should be attempted only when the whole family feels a commitment to it and when God is surely leading. It is a ministry of hospitality increasingly needed in our world.

## CONCLUSION

Hospitality need not be a gift which only a few possess. "Each of us," writes Karen Burton Mains, "can participate in some way in evangelism through hospitality—the use of the home as a tool of ministry. The genius of the home is that it is universal to each Christian. We all abide somewhere—in a room or a dormitory or an apartment or a bungalow. In this inhospitable world a Christian home is a miracle to be shared" (Mains, 1976, p. 137).

The hospitality of a Christian home exerts a mighty influence. David and Vera Mace, a Quaker pastor and his wife who have opened their family circle to countless individuals reflect on this influence:

The Christian home is, in fact, by far the most powerful evangelizing agency in the world. Its evangelism, however, is not aggressive; it is persuasive. It proclaims its message not by words, but by deeds. It does not tell others what they should be; it shows them what they could be. By their gracious influence, Christian homes win more converts than all the preachers put together. Give us enough of them, and the world would soon be a Christian world; for the world's life rises to the higher levels only as its homes do so. (Mace, 1985, p. 113)

## References and Additional Resources

LeFever, M. D. (1980). *Creative hospitality.* Wheaton, IL: Tyndale House.

Mace, D., & V. (1985). *In the presence of God.* Philadelphia, PA: The Westminster Press.

Mains, K. B. (1976). *Open heart, open home.* Elgin, IL: David C. Cook Publishing Co.

McGinnis, A. L. (1979). *The friendship factor.* Minneapolis, MN: Augsburg Publishing House.

Ortlund, A. (1979). *Discipling one another.* Waco, TX: Word Books.

Pippert, R. M. (1999). *Out of the saltshaker and into the world: Evangelism as a way of life*, *2nd edition.* Downers Grove, IL: InterVarsity Press.

Stott, J. (1971). *Basic Christianity.* Downers Grove, IL: InterVarsity Press.

White, E. G. (1952). *The Adventist home.* Hagerstown, MD: Review and Herald Publishing Association

White, E. G. (1954). *Child guidance.* Hagerstown, MD: Review and Herald Publishing Association

## HANDOUT #1
# Entertainment or Hospitality

| ENTERTAINMENT | OR | HOSPITALITY |
|---|---|---|
| Requires a spotless home, a perfectly matched and decorated table, a gourmet meal, a perfectly dressed and coiffured hostess. | | Seeks to put its priorities on the guest and meeting his or her needs. |
| Leads guests to admire what the host and hostess have provided. | | Offers all that the host and hostess possess to meet the needs of the guest. |
| Motives are egocentric, to impress others with what we have and what we are able to do. | | Motives are other-directed, focused on meeting the needs of others. |
| Puts its priorities on things. | | Puts its priorities on people. |
| Models arise out of the dream world of homemaker magazines. | | Models arise out of examples of persons who seek to meet the needs of others. |
| Creates bondage to resources, time, perfection. | | Becomes increasingly a joy as we become channels of God's love and blessing. |

HANDOUT #2
# When I Felt Welcome

This exercise will aid you in reflecting on the occasions when you were a guest and felt particularly welcome or unwelcome. Such reflection will help identify common elements which can be incorporated into your own hospitality efforts.

**1 Describe an occasion when you were a guest in a place where you felt particularly welcome and at home.**

In this experience, what factors contributed to your feelings of being welcome and at home?

a.

b.

c.

d.

e.

**2 Describe an occasion when you were a guest and felt quite uncomfortable or even were anxious to leave the situation.**

List below several factors which contributed to your feeling uncomfortable and unwelcome in the situation described above.

a.

b.

c.

d.

What advice would you have liked to give that host or hostess?

# Children's Stories

# One *Dad* for the Kingdom

## by Virginia Taylor and Karen Flowers

Mack and Charles were home from school today because it was a holiday. While Mother was busy cleaning up after breakfast, Mack and Charles were still at the table talking excitedly about tomorrow. It was to be a very special Sabbath. They had both been working very hard to learn the books of the Bible in order and all of the memory verses for the quarter. Tomorrow they were going to be part of a very special program. The children were going to sing several of their favorite songs during the big people's Sabbath School and then Mack and Charles were going to recite the Bible verses they had learned in front of the whole church. Each of them was going to have his very own microphone and everything.

The boys didn't need any more practice. They could say the books of the Bible and their memory verses in their sleep! But there was one more thing that was very important to them that still remained to be done. Mack's and Charles' daddy didn't go with them to church each week. He was happy for them to go, but he said he just wasn't a churchgoer himself. Every night when they said their prayers the boys asked God to bless their daddy and to help him learn to love Jesus so he would want to go to church with them. But every time they invited him, he'd say, "Well, maybe one of these days, but today I'm pretty busy. You go along to church with your mother and by the time you get home I'll have my work all done and we can play. How's that?"

All week the boys had been talking about what to say this time to get their dad to come to church tomorrow. Lots of other dads would be there to hear their kids sing and say the books of the Bible by heart. But when it came to Mack's and Charles' special moment with their own microphones and everything, only their mom would be there to see them . . . unless . . . unless they could think of a way to invite their dad so he wouldn't say, "Well, maybe one of these days, but today I'm pretty busy . . . ." And that's why the boys were still planning their strategy at the breakfast table on Friday morning. Mother heard them talking, but since she had had no better success in getting her husband to join her for church, she decided to let the boys follow through with their plans.

That night when they were ready for bed, Mack and Charles sat down on either side of their dad on the arms of his big chair. Dad put his arms around them and gave them a squeeze, and then pulled them down into his lap in a giggling heap as he tickled their sides and tummies. "Now what do you guys want?" he said laughing. "There's no way both of you would surround me like this if you weren't up to something."

"Well," Mack began, "tomorrow we're having this special program at church . . ." And then Charles started talking so fast Dad could hardly keep up with what he was saying. "Yes, tomorrow we're having this special program, and we're going to have our own microphones and everything, and we're going to sing and say the books of the Bible, and then Mack and I are going to say all our memory verses . . . all by ourselves in front of the whole church with our own microphones and everything!"

"All the Moms and Dads will be there to see their kids, and we want you to be there too, Pops! Please, oh please don't say you're busy tomorrow! We want you to come with us to church. We'll make you proud, really we will. P-L-E-A-S-E, Daddy, P-L-E-A-S-E!

Well. This had surely taken Dad by surprise. He started with his usual line, "Maybe one of these days . . . ." but when he saw the great disappointment in his boys' eyes, he started again. "Well, how about we let tomorrow be one of those days. I wouldn't want to miss hearing you guys say your memory verses with your own microphones and everything! So I guess we better be off to bed. We surely don't want to be late to church!"

Mack and Charles were so excited they could hardly sleep. They were excited about the special program. They were excited about their own special part with their very own microphones and everything. But most of all they were excited that tomorrow they would have a Dad and a Mom with them at church.

The special program was splendid indeed. All the children sang with all their hearts. Everyone called out the books of the Bible loudly—from Genesis to Revelation. And Mack and Charles grinned from ear to ear behind their very own microphones as they recited thirteen memory verses, every one! And do you know what? Mack and Charles were not the only ones grinning! Their dad sat right there by their mom and grinned from ear to ear too!

After church, there was a big potluck. Mack's and Charles' dad met quite a few more of the other dads than he had known before. He found out that quite a few of them went running together every Sunday morning in the park. Their dad liked to jog too, and before it was over, he was planning to meet up with the other dads the next day for a run. After that, the church had a parenting class, and you guessed it! Their dad was right there with all the other dads, wanting to learn how to be an even better dad to his two boys. And all the while, every Friday night when the boys climbed up on the arms of Dad's chair, he'd pull them down in a big tickle and then say, "Now, what might you want?"

And every time they'd say, "P-L-E-A-S-E, Daddy, P-L-E-A-S-E come to church with us tomorrow."

And every time he'd say, "Well, maybe one of these days . . . oh well, how about we make tomorrow another one of those days. . . . Now off to bed you go while I check if I have a clean shirt!"

One night after the parenting class, the pastor asked Mack's and Charles' mom to stop by his office. She had agreed to take some Bible lessons to a person in the community who had called the church asking for them. As the pastor and Mom were finishing their conversation, Dad poked his head into the pastor's office. "Hey, when do I get my Bible lessons?" he asked.

The pastor was so happy! Mom was so happy! "You can have them right now!" they both replied. And so it was that the pastor started studying the Bible with Dad and Mom and Mack and Charles, and before long, Dad was baptized and became a deacon in the church. Then when Mack and Charles crawled up beside their dad on Friday night and began their "P-L-E-A-S-E, P-L-E-A-S-E. . . ," they already knew the answer. Of course Dad would be going to church with them. Just think of it! It was his two boys Mack and Charles who invited him first!

Now you think about it. Is there anyone in your family you could invite to meet Jesus?

end

# Jailor and *Entire Family* Baptized in Philippi

**by Karen Flowers**

**Note to the storyteller:** This telling of the Bible story of the conversion of the Philippian jailor and his entire family is illustrated by using balloons filled with helium gas, tied with strings or ribbons approximately 1 ½ meters long. Older children will enjoy controlling the balloons while the story is being told to the younger children.

Create a barrier (i.e. a large table or two turned on their sides) behind which the balloon "puppeteers" can hide. Practice ahead of time is essential so each one knows when to let his or her balloon(s) rise above the table as marked in the script. Remind the puppeteers to hold the strings tightly so the balloons will not escape to the ceiling before the climax of the story. One child can control the entire bunch of balloons representing the crowd, another can manage the owners of the slave girl, another the prisoners, and another the jailor's family. This story is especially appropriate for a family camp or retreat setting. If used indoors and it is necessary for the balloons to come down immediately, think in advance about how you will retrieve the balloons from a high ceiling. If left alone, the helium will disperse and the balloons will fall to the ground within a week.

**If a wide variety of colors of balloons is available, the following color choices are suggested:**

| | |
|---|---|
| **PAUL** | dark blue |
| **SILAS** | dark green |
| **FORTUNETELLER** | purple |
| **SATAN'S SPIRIT** | black |
| **JESUS CHRIST** | gold (on a longer string than the rest) |
| **OWNERS OF SLAVE GIRL** | yellow |
| **CROWD** | 4-6 balloons, a mixture of pink and brown |
| **PRISONERS** | 4-6 balloons, a mixture of orange and light green |
| **JAILOR** | red |
| **JAILOR'S FAMILY** | 4-6 balloons, a mixture of assorted colors |

| STORY | ACTION |
|---|---|
| The Bible tells the story of two missionaries— one named Paul (pause), and one named Silas. | *(Paul balloon goes up on string.)* *(Silas balloon goes up on string.)* |
| One day when they were shopping in the market, they saw a girl telling fortunes. | *(Fortuneteller balloon goes up on string.)* |
| The fortuneteller was someone the people believed could predict what was going to happen to them in the future. She was really only a girl, and she really didn't know what was going to happen tomorrow, or the next week, or the next year. | *(Crowd balloons go up on strings.)* |

| | |
|---|---|
| But one of Satan's spirits lived inside of her and told her what to say. | *(Satan's spirit balloon goes up on string.)* |
| Every day when Paul and Silas came to the marketplace to talk with people about Jesus, she followed them around mocking them and shouting (in a mocking voice), "These men are servants of the Most High God, who are telling you the way to be saved." | *(Tug on Paul and Silas balloons as each name is mentioned.)*<br><br>*(Tug slowly up and down on Fortuneteller and Satan's spirit balloons, as though they were stalking Paul and Silas.)* |
| After many days of this, Paul got upset. He turned around and said to Satan's spirit, "In the name of Jesus Christ, I command you to come out of her!" | *(Jesus balloon goes up on string above all the others.)* |
| Instantly Satan's spirit came out of her! | *(Pull Satan's spirit balloon down quickly, and once it is below the barrier, pop it with a pin.)* |
| When the people who owned the fortuneteller saw what had happened, they were furious! They were angry because they knew that without Satan's spirit, the girl wouldn't be able to tell fortunes any more. And that was bad news for them, because without fortunes, there would be no money in their pockets! | *(Jesus balloon is lowered. Owner's balloons go up on strings.)* |
| They grabbed Paul and Silas and dragged them off to face the authorities. The crowd joined in, and it wasn't long before Paul and Silas found themselves all beaten up, and tied up, and in jail! (pause) | *(Tug up and down on Paul and Silas and Owner balloons as though to march them off. Then add Crowd balloons to the marching.)*<br><br>*(All balloons lowered.)* |
| About midnight, Paul and Silas were praying and singing hymns. The other prisoners were listening. | *(Paul and Silas balloons go up on strings.)*<br>*(Prisoner balloons go up on strings.)* |
| All of a sudden the earth began to shake. It was the worst earthquake they had ever experienced! | *(Shake Paul, Silas, and Prisoners balloons violently.)* |
| When the shaking stopped, Paul and Silas and the other prisoners looked around. To their amazement, they discovered the chains that bound them had dropped off and the doors to the jail were open wide! | *(Balloons very still.)* |
| Meanwhile, the man in charge of making sure none of the prisoners got loose was awakened by the earthquake too. He was so scared of what the authorities would do to him if the prisoners got away, he was ready to take his own life. Then he heard Paul's voice. "Don't harm yourself! We are all here!" | *(Jailor balloon up on string.)*<br><br><br><br>*(Tug up and down on Paul balloon.)* |
| The jailor called for lights and rushed in where Paul and Silas and the other prisoner's were. When he saw they had not run away, he knew that what they had been teaching about Jesus had to be true. "Just a minute! Don't go anywhere!" the jailor cried, "Let me get the rest of my family! I want them all to hear about Jesus too." | *(Jesus balloon up on string.)*<br><br>*(Jailor's family balloons up on strings.)* |

| | |
|---|---|
| Then he fell on his knees and asked Paul and Silas the most important question of all: "Sirs, what must I do to be saved?" | *(Partially lower first the Jailor balloon and then all visible balloons, but keep them showing just above the barrier, as though to worship Jesus.)* |
| And Paul and Silas told them the best news of all! "Believe on the Lord Jesus Christ and you will be saved!" (pause) | *(Let Jesus balloon go and rise to the ceiling.)* |
| And they did believe! The jailor, and his whole family! And everyone in the jailhouse was filled with joy! | *(All balloons up on strings and jiggling as if to celebrate good news! Puppeteers cheering aloud.)* |
| Shall we join them in a cheer to thank Jesus for saving us too? | *(Storytellers leads children in a cheer as all balloons used in the story—EXCEPT the Satan's spirit balloon—are released to join Jesus in the air.)* |

*end*

# *Thank God* We Have a Family

## by Karen Flowers

Ludi worked in a hospital. It was her job to clean the patients' rooms everyday. Ludi didn't mind cleaning, but the part she liked the best was meeting the patients. Some were too sick to talk to her, but she would always pause in her work long enough to stand by their bedsides and tell them she hoped they would be better soon. Sometimes she asked if they would like her to say a prayer for them. Sometimes, she just held their hands. Ludi hoped her kindness would be like her Mama's kisses on her cuts and scrapes when she was a little girl. They just made things so much better!

One day Ludi walked into a room where she found a lady sitting up in bed. "Hi," Ludi said. "I'm Ludi, and I'm here to clean your room. But before I do, is there anything I can do for you? It can't be much fun being in the hospital!"

The lady switched off the T.V. and looked at Ludi. "Well," she said, "there is something you could do. Do you see that stack of magazines over there? I think I'm feeling well enough today to do some reading. Would you mind bringing that pile over here to my bed?"

Ludi was happy to do that. The lady was happy to make a new friend. She was in the hospital for several days, and before her stay was over, she and Ludi had become *good* friends. The day she went home, she gave Ludi her phone number. She said she especially liked to talk with Ludi about the Bible. She had never met a regular person who knew as much about the Bible as Ludi!

Before long, Ludi was visiting her friend Ellie at home. She met her husband Mike and her two little girls, Natalie and Lorraine. One Sunday she invited Ellie's family to her house for lunch. A few weeks later, she invited them to an all-day picnic that her church was having. She knew the girls would enjoy the swimming pool, and especially the soccer game. The girls had long legs and could run very fast. They played on a soccer team at school.

All the while, Ludi and Ellie found time to talk more and more about the Bible. Ellie was curious about a lot of things. One day Ludi asked Ellie if she would like to study the Bible with her every week, using some lessons her pastor had prepared. Ellie was delighted. Mike said he'd like to join in too. In the meantime, Ellie and Mike were becoming friends with more and more people at the church. The pastor invited them to join a parenting seminar where they met other parents like themselves. Mike started lifting weights with some of the young men in the church. Ellie helped organize a big yard sale to raise money for blankets and bed sheets for a mission hospital in Africa. The girls joined Pathfinders and started coming to Sabbath school. It wasn't long before the whole family was among the "regulars" every Sabbath at church.

One Sabbath the pastor met Mike in the hall. He looked worried. "Is something wrong?" the pastor asked?

"Well, yes," Mike replied. "It's just that I've been listening to what you have been saying about your Christian school. And Ellie and I, well, we were just wishing our girls could go to your school this year. Will you please pray that we will find a way so our girls can go too?"

When it came time for the prayer during the worship service, the pastor included Mike's request in his prayer. Now there were many people in the congregation that day who heard the pastor pray that somehow Natalie and Lorraine would be able to go to the Christian school. Later that afternoon, some of these people got to talking on the phone among themselves. "We could help with the tuition," one said. "We could to," said another. And before long, with everyone helping a little, there was enough to pay the tuition.

But there was another problem. A BIG problem in Mike's mind. Their family lived in the center of the city and the school was far to the north side. How would the girls ever be able to get to the school every day? But you know what? A BIG problem for Mike was not a BIG problem at all for God. On the very next day, an apartment was found for rent right near the school. In fact there was a family from church living nearby who said they would be happy to give the girls a ride to school everyday.

The next Sabbath Mike no longer had a BIG problem, he had a BIG smile on his face. Since the pastor's prayer the week before, Mike and his family had moved to their new home and Natalie and Lorraine had started school in their new Christian school. When the pastor asked Mike and Ellie to tell all that had happened in just a week, there were a lot of other people smiling too. There were the people who had helped with the girls' tuition. There were the people who had helped Mike and his family move. There were the teachers from the Christian school. There were the children who were so happy to have their friends in school with them every day. And more than anyone, I'm sure Jesus was smiling, because Mike and Ellie and Natalie and Lorraine were His children too.

It wasn't long until there was a baptism, and Mike and Ellie went down into the water together to be baptized. As the pastor told a little bit of the story about how they met Ludi, and the pastor, and all the other people from the church, and studied the Bible together and joined in the church activities, he asked Mike if there was anything he wanted to say. And there it was, that great BIG smile again on Mike's face! He just couldn't stop smiling as he said over and over, "I'm just so thankful for my church family! Thank God we have a family!"

The Bible says God put us in families—at home and at church—so we wouldn't get lonely, and so we could love and take care of one another. Aren't you glad you have a family? I wonder who God wants us to invite into the fellowship of His family next?

# Resources for
# Family Ministries

# A *Home* is for Sharing

**by Karen and Ron Flowers**

*Our homes belong to the Lord. As stewards, we must prayerfully listen for His guidance in how all that is there—the resources of love and caring, as well as the physical accommodations—may be used in ministry for God.*

## WHAT HAVE THEY SEEN IN YOUR HOUSE?

Emissaries from Babylon once came to King Hezekiah of Judah out of interest in his miraculous recovery from a fatal illness and a supernatural sign linked with it—movement ten degrees backward of the sundial shadow. Hezekiah happily received his guests, but seems to have been silent about his healing experience and put scarce emphasis on the things in his house that would have opened the hearts of these inquiring ambassadors to the knowledge of the true God. The contrast between his gratitude for being healed in chapter 38 and his silence about it in chapter 39 is striking. Hezekiah gave the ambassadors a tour that showcased his armory and expansive treasure. When they had left, the prophet Isaiah confronted him with a penetrating question: "What have they seen in your house?" (Isa. 39:4) The question was sobering. Too late Hezekiah realized that his pride had led him to give away state secrets of national wealth and armaments. Moreover, he had missed a rare opportunity to share the truth about God with these foreign ambassadors.

**"God left him to test him."** This state visit was a most significant occasion, yet there is no record of Hezekiah seeking special guidance about it in prayer, from prophets, or from priests. Nor did God intervene. Alone, out of the public eye, with no consultation with spiritual advisors, the work of God in his life and the life of His nation was not on his agenda. The intent of the biblical historian in 2 Chron. 32:31 may have been to show how easily God's blessing can be taken for granted and how prone are the recipients of His mercy to become self-sufficient.

## STEWARDS OF THE LORD'S HOME

One renowned stewardship leader used to speak of "listening for the voice of God in our income,"

that is, listening for direction from God as to how we should use that which is His. Christians recognize that all that they have belongs to God. Over that with which He has entrusted us we are His stewards, His managers. Like our time, talents, treasure and body temple, our homes also belong to the Lord. We are stewards of our home which is really the Lord's home. In a manner similar to what we do with our financial resources, so we may lay our homes before Him, and prayerfully listen for His guidance in how all that is there—the resources of love and caring, as well as the physical accommodations—may be used in ministry for God. God wants our houses and homes to be witnessing centers. So we need to continually ask the question of ourselves today, "What have they seen in thine house?"

Some lasting lessons of faithfulness in witnessing from our home life that can be gleaned from the experience of Hezekiah:

- Every visit by individuals to the homes of Christians is an opportunity for them to be exposed to followers of Christ, their way of life and the gospel message.

- Since few visitors are likely to open conversation about spiritual things, Christians must find ways that are sensitive and appropriate to the occasion to share the good news.

- Christians are not called to show off their material prosperity or accomplishments, though they may recognize these as blessings from God.

## WHAT SHOULD WE BE SHARING?

Before the ambassadors from Babylon came, Hezekiah had just experienced a miraculous recovery from a mortal illness. That turnabout in his health was accompanied by supernatural evidence of God's blessing in a most unusual event—the sundial moved backward 10 degrees. (See Isaiah 38:4-8.) A marvelous opportunity was thus afforded the king to share the precious truth of Jehovah with which he and his nation had been entrusted.

**News about a Healer.** We are to share, and allow all our interaction with others to spring from the awareness that we have needs in common with all humankind. Christians are called to "declare the praises of Him who called you out of darkness into His wonderful light" (1 Peter 2:10). Or, to use Hezekiah's experience as a symbol, we are to declare that we were sick, yes, dying. But there is One who has healed and continues to heal us. We were spiritually lost, but there is One who looked upon our condition, had compassion upon us, and saved us.

Using our homes for ministry may range from the simple offering of a drink of water to a neighbor child playing with our children, to inviting church members or visitors to a meal, to the radical hospitality of lending a room to an abuse victim or to a homeless addict while he or she is rehabilitated. It may mean conducting neighborhood Bible studies in our home, or giving time for personal counsel and prayer with someone. Happy are those who find opportunities to open the Word of God with another and share deeply of their faith. While our sharing may not always lend itself to an in-depth disclosure of our faith, the sharing of our homes must be founded upon the bedrock of biblical teaching about Christ. While ministry may be driven by a variety of motives, ultimately the giving of the gospel alone makes service a great joy.

**Sharing the good news.** The essence of what Christians have to share is the good news of the grace of God toward sinners manifested in the life, death and resurrection of Jesus. Apart from anything we could do, God loved us unconditionally and acted in our behalf. Christ identified Himself with us (Matt. 1: 23). God looks upon the whole human race as being bonded to Christ (cf. *Steps to Christ*, p. 72); the New Testament uses the phrase "in Christ." God has made Christ the Savior of all humankind, especially of those who believe (1 Tim. 4:10). His life, His death and His resurrection are a new human history (1 Cor. 1:30; Heb. 2:9; Rom. 5:14-19). Because of Jesus, God justifies the ungodly (Rom. 4:5) and does not reckon our sins against us (2 Cor. 5:19). We were dead in our sins, but, in Him, God considers us spiritually resurrected, raised and seated in heavenly places (Eph. 2:1).

The call of God is for sinners to believe in Jesus, accept His atonement for us, and to walk worthy of the calling with which we were called (Eph. 4:1), letting God work in us to will and to do His good pleasure (Phil. 2:13). The assurance of the gospel is found in being "in Christ," a spiritual reality accomplished by God which the believer grasps by faith. God wants to do a work in the life of believers which the New Testament refers to as the indwelling of the Spirit (Rom. 8: 9), "Christ in you" (Col. 1:27), or Christ dwelling in the heart by faith (Eph. 3:17). The resulting lifestyle of the Christian is the fruit of the gospel. The second coming of Jesus is the hope of the gospel.

True Christian hospitality, the love, care and warmth displayed by a Christian home, comes from the hearts of individuals who have been touched and are being healed by the gospel. From our homes there will be the witness of a lifestyle and there may well be the sharing of many other Bible truths, all of which are important. All the good advice and good information we may share must not be a substitute for what is truly the Good News.

## OUR MISSION INSIDE OUR HOMES

**Family first.** The first use to which the resources of our Christian homes are to be put is for the salvation of our own families. God intended the family to be a natural setting for carrying out Jesus' directive, Go and make disciples (Matt. 28:19). In the circle of a caring family one's deep and abiding needs for belonging, for love, for intimacy and for social contact are all addressed. Since it is in the family that one first learns about relationships, the Christian family possesses a remarkable potential for teaching about loving God and relating lovingly to others (John 13: 35). By God's grace the family may be a powerful agency for the discipling of its members for Christ. In our rush to work for others, we must not neglect members of our own homes.

The most natural first recipients of our gospel sharing endeavors are the people in our households (John 1:40-42; cf. Deut. 6:6, 7; Ruth 1:14-18). "As workers for God, our work is to begin with those nearest. It is to begin in our own home. There is no more important missionary field than this" (*Child Guidance*, p. 476). "Our work for Christ is to begin with the family in the home. . . . By many this home field has been shamefully neglected, and it is time that divine resources and remedies were presented, that this state of evil may be corrected" (*Testimonies for the*

*Church, vol. 6*, pp. 429, 430). "You may be evangelists in the home, ministers of grace to your children" (*Child Guidance*, p. 479).

John's Gospel captures the exuberance of Andrew when He met the Savior. "The first thing Andrew did was to find his brother Simon . . . ." Andrew reacted to learning that Jesus was the Messiah in a way that is common when one has really good news. The news cannot be contained; it simply must be communicated to those who are near and dear to us. Andrew went beyond mere reporting, he arranged for Simon (whom Jesus named "Peter") to be introduced to Jesus. *An enthusiastic report about Jesus* and *an introduction to Him as a person*—what a simple formula for sharing the gospel with relatives in our homes! After the introduction, Andrew stepped back. From there on, Jesus and Peter had a relationship that was unique to them.

**Helping children to a place of faith.** Children in the home can often be overlooked as fitting recipients of gospel sharing efforts. Parents mistakenly assume that children will simply absorb family spirituality. This must not be taken for granted; while children and young people learn from the modeling they observe, it is also true that these younger members of the Lord's family need individual attention and opportunity to be personally introduced to Him. Deuteronomy 6 is insistent on this point: attention is to be given to the most effective kind of religious education. Regular spiritual habits of personal and family worship are to be encouraged in the home. Time and earnest efforts must be put forth on behalf of children and youth that the next generation may also become people of faith.

Ruth saw Naomi at the lowest of moments when she tried to push her daughter-in-law away and when, angry and depressed, she lashed out against God in recounting her losses (Ruth 1:15, 20, 21). No more eloquent testimony than Ruth's can be given to show that youth and young adults can meet and make a commitment to a perfect God, even when introduced to Him by an imperfect parent or relative.

**The blessing of a Christian partner (1 Cor. 7: 12-15; 1 Peter 3:1, 2).** Sadly, acceptance of the gospel message can lead to disruption in families. The New Testament wrestles with the dilemma that is faced by some converts to Christ—the choice to follow Christ could jeopardize their marriage, the institution Christ Himself created. The New Testament provides counsel for marriages divided by religion.

In 1 Corinthians, Paul responds to converts' concerns that staying married to an unbelieving spouse might be offensive to God or bring defilement upon themselves and their children. Not so, says Paul. The sacred state of marriage and its intimacies are to continue after a partner's conversion. The presence of one Christian partner "sanctifies" the other partner and the couple's children—not in the sense of changing their standing before God for that involves their personal response to Christ—but in the sense of being a source of blessing and bringing unbelievers into contact with the realm of grace. Heartrending as it is, the unbelieving partner may decide to abandon the marriage. Though consequences will be serious, the merciful word of God to the unbeliever is "let him do so" and to the believer, he or she "is not bound in such circumstances" (1 Cor. 7:15).

The preference of the Word of God is that, despite the challenges of a spiritually divided home, a way might be found for the peace of Christ to reign there. The hope is to keep the marriage intact, to give evidence of the triumph of the gospel in the midst of difficulty, to promote the comfort of the partner with whom the believer is one flesh, though they be unbelieving. Loving kindness, unwavering fidelity, humble service and winsome witness on the part of the believer create the greatest likelihood of winning the non-Christian spouse. The submission of Christian marriage partners to each other is mutual and out of reverence for Christ (cf. Eph. 5:21). When a spouse relates with Christian submission to an unbelieving partner, the first allegiance is always to Christ. Faithfulness to the claims of God on one's life does not require a spouse to suffer abuse at the hands of a violent partner.

## FAMILIES REACHING FAMILIES

The mission of the home extends beyond its own members. The Christian home is to be an object lesson, illustrating the excellence of the true principles of life. Such an illustration will be a power for good in the world. Far more powerful than any sermon that can be preached is the influence of a true home upon human hearts and lives. . . . Our sphere of influence may seem narrow, our ability small, our opportunities few, our acquirements limited; yet wonderful possibilities are ours through a faithful use of the opportunities of our own homes. If we will open our hearts and homes to the divine principles of life we shall become channels for currents of life-giving power. From our homes will flow streams of healing, bringing life and beauty and fruitfulness where now are barrenness and dearth. (*The Ministry of Healing*, pp. 352, 355)

The Christian home is, in fact, by far the most powerful evangelizing agency in the world. Its evangelism however is not aggressive; it is persuasive. It proclaims its message not by words, but by deeds. It does not tell others what they should be; it shows them what they could be. By their gracious influence, Christian homes win more converts than all the preachers put together. Give us enough of them, and the world would soon be a Christian world; for the world's life rises to the higher levels only as its homes do so. (Mace, 1985, p. 113)

People in homes around us need what we as Adventist Christians are privileged to have in our families. The world is starving for love. Many simply have no good example of marriage or family relationships to follow. For want of models of how real love can be born in the heart and can permeate family living, homes are suffering. Some divorce, some separate, others simply hang on as best they can, often warring under their roofs with each other or enduring pain and frustration. Those of us who are finding the way to successful Christian living at home have something to share so that others may see and know.

**Family life is for sharing.** The New Testament emphasis on *imitation* acknowledges the important role of modeling in the learning process (Eph. 5:1; 1 Cor. 4: 16; 1 Thess. 1:6; Heb. 6:12; 13:7; 3 John 1:11). People tend to become like whom or what they watch. This principle applies to relationships generally and especially to the home, where imitation is common: children imitate their parents and siblings; married partners often imitate one another. This concept provides an important clue to how couples and families can bear Christian witness to other couples and families.

**The power of social influence.** We witness from our homes when we provide opportunities for others to observe us, to share in some way in our home experience. In our homes they may see how the Spirit of Jesus makes a difference. "Social influence," wrote Ellen White, "is a wonderful power. We can use it if we will as a means of helping those about us" (*The Ministry of Healing*, p. 354). "A Christian home should be, in fact, a center of contagious friendliness, with open doors toward all human need" (Mace, 1985, p. 98).

As married couples invite other couples for meals, fellowship, Bible study, or when they attend a marital growth program together, the visitors see a model. The display of mutuality, affirmation, communication, conflict-resolution and accommodation of differences testifies of their life together in Christ. Parent classes and support groups where Christians and non-Christians mingle do the same thing. Family to family modeling takes place when Christian families invite other families for meals, recreation together, or for family worship. All human examples are flawed; however, the witness of the Christian home is not about modeling absolute perfection. The New Testament notion of imitation is a call for individuals to follow believers who follow Christ. The idea is that individuals will grasp the faith as they see it demonstrated in the lives of others who are human and fallible as they are.

**Hospitality evangelism.** The importance of hospitality is evident throughout Scripture: Abraham and Sarah (Gen. 18:1-8); Rebekah and her family (Gen. 24: 15-20; 31-33); Zacchaeus (Luke 19:1-9); cf. Isa. 58: 6, 7, 10-12; Rom. 12:13; 1 Peter 4:9. Hospitality meets another's basic needs for rest, food and fellowship. It is a tangible expression of self-giving love. Jesus attached theological significance to hospitality, when He taught that feeding the hungry and giving drink to the thirsty were acts of service done to Him (cf. Matt. 25:34-40). Using one's home for ministry may range from the simple offering of a drink of water to a child or inviting neighbors to a meal to the radical hospitality of lending a room to an abuse victim while he or she is rehabilitated. It may involve simple friendliness, or it may afford opportunity to offer prayer with someone or to conduct Bible studies. True hospitality comes from the hearts of individuals who have been touched by God's love and long to give tangible expression to that love in words and action.

Peter addressed an apparent reticence on the part of some to offer hospitality (1 Peter 4:9). Contemporary families are sometimes reticent also, complaining that they lack the facilities, the time and/or the energy to offer hospitality. Others feel awkward, unskilled and unsure about reaching beyond what is familiar in order to associate with unbelievers. Some wish to avoid the complications to their lives that may ensue from involvement with others. Many contemporary families confuse *hospitality* and *entertaining*. The following chart indicates the potential for ministry in hospitality compared to entertaining:

| | ENTERTAINING | HOSPITALITY |
|---|---|---|
| **PRIORITIES** | Things | People |
| **MOTIVES** | Self-centered:<br>To impress<br>To exhibit home and accomplishments | Other-centered:<br>To give to others<br>To enjoy mutual fellowship |
| **REQUIREMENTS** | Beautiful home<br>Fine decorating<br>Gourmet cooking | People looking for fellowship<br>Simple food |
| **FOCUS** | Make an impression | Minister to people's needs |
| **OUTCOMES** | Hosts lauded<br>House and furnishings admired | Guests uplifted and encouraged<br>Friendships made |

Pastor Samuel Monnier, retired General Conference Lay Activities leader, relates the following experience of family life and hospitality:

"In our home after family worship on Sunday mornings we would have a family council and at that time would often select someone to invite to our home for a meal. My wife Yvonne and I would cast our votes for the children's choice. Then we would pray that the chosen individuals would accept our invitation. When they did, we would pray daily that each one of our family might have a positive attitude and that our visitors would be touched by the Holy Spirit. Just before their arrival we would pray again for them.

"Around our table I announced that we were Christians and enjoyed asking for God's blessing. Yvonne then designated one of our children to pray. Such prayers by our children always impressed the hearts of visitors. We deliberately did not speak about God, church or religion in our table conversation, though I would explain that we had made some personal decisions not to use alcohol or meat. Before our guests left our home I usually shared my testimony in about two minutes—how I became a Christian and the meaning of faith in my life. I would share a Bible promise and offer a prayer. In that prayer I recalled aspects of our conversation, expressing to our heavenly Father our care and concern for the various things that had been mentioned by ourselves and our guests.

"Often our guests reciprocated by inviting us to their homes. We would respond and do our best to build the relationship, staying clear of topics related to church or God. I would have a small Bible with me and, before leaving their home, I would ask, 'May I read a Bible promise; may I pray?' In this simple, practical way our family witnessed. When individuals were ready for more, we found ways of involving them in events at church, a concert, a film, later an evangelistic series. In all these events we would be with them. In this way we made many friends and saw many begin on the road to church membership."

## CONCLUSION

Go to your neighbors one by one, and come close to them till their hearts are warmed by your unselfish interest and love. Sympathize with them, pray with them, watch for opportunities to do them good, and as you can, gather a few together and open the Word of God to their darkened minds. (*Welfare Ministry*, p. 64)

Bonds of friendship develop from acts of kindness and thoughtfulness that we show, from gifts we give, meals we share, time we spend with others in conversation on a level that deals with our and their inner feelings. Our homes provide us with countless opportunities for forming such friendships and sharing our Adventist Christianity with others. May God help us to hurtle barriers that often separate us from the families around us.

## References and Bibliography

Mace, D. & V. (1985). *In the presence of God: Readings for Christian marriage.* Philadelphia: The Westminster Press.

Mains, K. B. (1976). *Open heart, open home.* Elgin, IL: David C. Cook.

Mutch, P. B. (1987). *Christian hospitality made easy.* Silver Spring, MD: Ministerial Association/Shepherdess International, General Conference of Seventh-day Adventists.

White, E. G. (1854). *Child guidance.* Hagerstown, MD: Review and Herald Publishing Association.

White, E. G. (1979). *Faith and works.* Hagerstown, MD: Review & Herald Publishing Association.

White, E. G. (1915). *Gospel workers.* Hagerstown, MD: Review & Herald Publishing Association.

White, E. G. (1948). *Testimonies for the church, vol. 1.* Nampa, ID: Pacific Press Publishing Association.

White, E. G. (1948). *Testimonies for the church, vol. 6.* Nampa, Id: Pacific Press Publishing Association.

White, E. G. (1952). *The Adventist home.* Hagerstown, MD: Review and Herald Publishing Association.

White, E. G. (1942). *The ministry of healing.* Nampa, ID: Pacific Press Publishing Association.

White, E. G. (1955). *Sons and daughters of God.* Hagerstown, MD: Review & Herald Publishing Association.

White, E. G. (1892). *Steps to Christ.* Nampa, ID: Pacific Press Publishing Association.

White, E. G. (1952). *Welfare ministry.* Hagerstown, MD: Review and Herald Publishing Association.

# Choosing the Portrait Lens

**by Karen and Ron Flowers**

*As we sharpen the focus of our evangelistic objective, we believe it is time to intentionally readjust our thinking from individual snapshot to family portrait.*

It was common in Bible times for evangelists to proclaim the gospel in household settings and for whole family groups to respond together. The Jewish nobleman who sought Jesus to heal his son, returned home to find him well. As a result, his whole household believed (John 4:46-53). Cornelius, who with "all his family were devout and God-fearing," invited his relatives and close friends to hear the preaching of Peter. The Holy Spirit came on all who heard the message and they were baptized (Acts 10:2, 24, 44-48). Lydia responded to Paul's Sabbath message by the river in Philippi and either then, or soon after, she and her household were baptized (Acts 16:11-15). Other examples include the entire household of the synagogue ruler Crispus (Acts 18:8); of Aristobulus (Rom. 16:10); of Narcissus, whose household was said to be "in the Lord" (Rom. 16:11); of Onesiphorus (2 Tim. 4:19); of Stephanas, who were baptized by Paul (1 Cor. 1:16) and referred to as the first converts in Achaia (1 Cor 16:15). Traditionally, the household of Stephanas has been thought to be the jailer's household of Acts 16.

## THE IMPACT OF INDIVIDUALISM ON EVANGELISM AND THE FAMILY

The rise of individualism in recent centuries has had an adverse affect on attitudes toward the family and has been a factor in the subtle shift of the evangelism objective from reaching families to reaching individuals. Bellah (1996) described the beginnings of individualism as the offspring of John Locke. Locke was an educator of enormous influence in seventeenth-century England and in America. He forcefully proclaimed individual rights and viewed the individual as the foundational unit of society. In fact, he believed the individual is prior to society, and social groups such as families come into existence only through the voluntary contracts of individuals trying to maximize their own self-interest.

A strong spirit of individualism is often regarded as a desirable quality in an Adventist—certainly in the West, and increasingly around the world. It is considered advantageous because it is often necessary for an Adventist to swim against social and theological currents. But as we sharpen the focus of our evangelistic objective, we believe it is time to intentionally readjust our thinking from individual snapshot to family portrait. Bellah's point that wherever the modern philosophy of individualism is found, some appreciation for the family as a group has been lost deserves to be carefully considered. Individualism does change our thinking about families, and it inevitably changes our actions toward them and within them.

To be sure, Scripture recognizes each person as an individual. Individuals are valuable, possessing a free will (Jer. 1:5; Eze. 18:20; Matt. 10:30, 31; Acts 2:39). Jesus and the apostles gave personal attention to individuals (cf. Mark 3:14-19; 10:46-52; John 3:1; 4:7; 1, 2 Timothy; Titus; Philemon). Salvation must be individually received (Rom. 10:13, 17; Rev. 22:12). God, it has been said, has no grandchildren. Yet Scripture also affirms the groups in which individuals live in society, especially the family. The Creator established the first family and reaffirmed His original plan (Gen. 2:18-25; Matt. 19:4-6). Connectedness is essential to human well-being (Eccl. 4:11-13; Ps. 68:6; 1 Cor. 12). We are called to minister to one another (John 15:17, Rom. 15:14; Gal. 5:13; Eph. 4:32). There is evidence of an emphasis on reaching whole households in the evangelistic endeavors of the early church (see references given previously).

The challenge facing the church today is to hold in balance the biblical emphasis on both the individual and the family group. Emphasis on the individual can help to swing the pendulum back from the extremes of enmeshment, co-dependency, and loss of individual personhood in families. But the family group must also be upheld and supported as an incomparable center for nurture, support, socialization, disciple-making, and the transmission of values across generations.

**Risks when one is baptized alone.** When individuals, who must also be thought of as "pieces of families," make the decision to join the church and are baptized, there is always a change in the family dynamics. This change often has a negative impact on relationships.

- Family members may be set in opposition to one another.

- Over time, communication often diminishes, thus reducing opportunities for discipling other family members.

- The new believer often feels torn by family concerns. They may experience mixed feelings of guilt on the one hand over maintaining family connections, as though non-Adventist family members are part of the "world" on which they are supposed to have turned their backs. On the other hand, they may experience similar mixed feelings for separating themselves from family members, as though they have abandoned them in some way by becoming an Adventist.

- Changes in values and lifestyle, as well as active participation in the program of the church, may dramatically cut back on time and activities the family share. Prior networks of social support and friendship may also drop away.

- Negative attitudes toward the church may form among family members, and as a result, difficult barriers may be raised to discipling them for Christ and drawing them into the community of faith.

**Looking again at Matt. 10:35-37.** Families resist change. This fact, considered by family professionals to be fundamental to understanding families and how they function, has profound implications for our evangelistic endeavors. It helps us to anticipate the reality that working for whole families will be more challenging. It may also require more intentionality and a longer view than working to bring individuals to Christ. Sometimes Matt. 10:35-37 has been used as evidence that true believers must pull away from their families, as though families per se were their natural enemies. Closer consideration of these verses suggests otherwise:

The Jews believed that one of the features of the Day of the Lord, the day when God would break into history, would be the division of families. The Rabbis said: "In the period when the Son of David shall come, a daughter will rise up against her mother, a daughter-in-law against her mother-in-law." "The son despises his father, the daughter rebels against the mother, the daughter-in-law against her mother-in-law, and the man's enemies are they of his own household." *It is as if Jesus said, "The end you have always been waiting for has come; and the intervention of God in history is splitting home and groups and families into two."* (Barclay, 1975. p. 393, emphasis supplied)

In other words, it is not that families per se are enemies of the gospel. Rather, the text highlights the radical nature of the Messiah's call to discipleship. It is a call that demands a response, and because some will respond and some will not, there will be division in every social group, even in people's very homes. Jesus' words should not be interpreted as permission to neglect our responsibility to reach out to whole families. Rather, they speak of the hard reality that sometimes, despite our best efforts, some will reject the call of Jesus to follow Him.

Our ultimate allegiance is to the family of heaven. Certainly the strong bonds that bring families together must not be allowed to hinder anyone from making a full and complete commitment to God. The reality of a sinful world means that following the spiritual call of Jesus may require stepping apart from others who make a different decision regarding Him, especially those who would be spiritually abusive or destructive of Christian faith. However, every effort should be made to help individuals retain, to the fullest extent possible, their connections with their families.

**Continuing to think "family" when there are individual decisions.** It is time to recommit ourselves to developing evangelistic approaches with the specific objective of evangelizing whole families—together. We must find the best ways of sharing the Good News with entire households. We must think long-range for the well-being of both individuals and families. We must ask the question: "How will a decision to baptize one individual now affect the likelihood that we will be able to disciple a partner, children, an extended family in the future? When we have done all we can toward strengthening family ties and making Jesus winsome in a family circle and an individual decides the time has come to step out from their family in their commitment to Christ, we must be even more intentional about surrounding this family with networks of friendship and support. Ultimately, the only hope we have of leading other family members to Christ is by strengthening relationships—within the family, and between them and other Christian families who will love and care for them as an extension of the ministry of Christ in the world.

As family evangelists, we may face some ethical dilemmas when it appears that elements of Adventist lifestyle conflict with real life experience in a new member's family. In such times, let us not minimize the difficulty of effecting lifestyle change when it affects not only the individual but also the wider family circle. Let us not be quick to pass judgment upon new members or to offer simplistic solutions to those who are seeking to resolve such issues in ways that will not threaten or diminish marital or family bonds.

## THE CENTRALITY OF THE FAMILY TO FULFILLING THE GOSPEL COMMISSION

Jesus said, "Go and make disciples" (Matt. 28:19). A disciple is someone who is discovering God's truth and the principles of His Kingdom and is growing in their ability to make these values a personal way of life (John 8:31). The family is central to the disciple-making process because it is the primary place where values are conveyed. There is no influence greater than that of family in the development of a person's value system and the skills to live by these values amidst many pressures to live otherwise.

Jesus also marked disciples as people whose remarkable love for others makes a profound impression on everyone who comes in contact with them (John 13:35). Again, it is in the family that individuals learn first, for better or for worse, about relationships and about love. It is in the family that the capacity for a warm, close relationship with God and with others is developed. Families can either set the stage for family members to understand and experience the warmth and acceptance of God's love, or they can make such understanding and experience a virtual impossibility, but for a miracle of grace. Families also have the primary opportunity and responsibility to be agents of the Holy Spirit in the cultivation of self-giving love in their members, the kind of love that makes for winsome witness within the family and in the neighborhood. Thus it can be seen that

the Christian family is crucial to the fulfilling of the gospel commission.

Several authors stress this centrality:

> A person's image of God is often patterned after his image of his own parents, especially his father. If his parents were happy, loving, accepting and forgiving, he finds it easier to experience a positive and satisfying relationship with God. But if his parent were cold and indifferent, he may feel that God is far away and disinterested in him personally. If his parents were angry, hostile, and rejecting, he often feels that God can never accept him. If his parents are hard to please, he usually has the nagging notion that God is not very happy with him either. (Strauss, 1975, pp. 23, 24)

> Early family experience determines our adult character structure, the inner picture we harbor of ourselves, how we see others and feel about them, our concept of right and wrong, our capacity to establish the close, warm, sustained relationships necessary to have a family of our own, our attitude toward authority and toward the Ultimate Authority in our lives, and the way we attempt to make sense out of our existence. No human interaction has a greater impact on our lives than our family experience. (Nicholi, 1979, p. 11)

> If disciples are those who relate with their teacher in the context of a primary relationship, then the *capacity* to form primary relationships is necessary to the process of disciple making. Secondly, if primary relationships consist of relationship skills that are generalized from one primary group to another, then the family is key in its significance because it is the place where those skills are learned well or learned poorly. And last of all, if the family is the social organization in which these skills are learned first, and thus most essentially, then the family becomes central to the process of disciple making. It is a place where disciplelike relational skills are learned, and it is a primary group in which disciple making takes place. (Guernsey, 1982, p. 11)

**Harnessing the power of family support.** The relational principles that govern family interaction constitute a force to be reckoned with, and we must understand them if we are going to maximize our success in mission. As Ellen White emphasized, "He who seeks to transform humanity must himself understand humanity" (*Education*, p. 78). Without an understanding of families and how they function, our evangelistic impact will be unnecessarily limited.

A family is not just a collection of people living at one address. A family is a living, dynamic system with complex connections and patterns of relating to one another. It is these relational principles that we need to understand as we think about doing family evangelism. For example, in practical terms this means we must:

• *Look for ways to reinforce the strong bonds of attachment and loyalty to one another that are typically formed in families.* We are relational beings by God's design. When we reinforce family bonds in every way possible, we are not only increasing the likelihood of success in our disciple-making mission. We are also participating with God in the restoration of God's creation plan for human beings to be loved and cared for in families. To do this, we will have to place a high value on strengthening these bonds of love and loyalty, and make it a primary objective of evangelism. It may require patience to work to bring the entire family system to understanding and commitment, especially when one or two advance more rapidly than do the rest. But to work against family cohesiveness is to put at risk one of only two institutions to come from the Creator's hand in Eden.

• *Since family members typically look to each other first for support and companionship, we can help them develop the best relationships they can experience together.* Family members, aware as they are of one another's strengths and struggles, are uniquely able to provide spiritual nurture and support for one another in living the Christian life. Family can be one of the most difficult arenas in which to put one's religion into practice. When we help people to live out their Christianity at home, we have gone far toward helping them to live by Christian principles in every aspect of their lives. The church harnesses the family's potential for disciple-making when it helps its members to "in every way encourage each other in fighting the battles of life" (*The Ministry of Healing*, p. 360).

• *Parents typically want the best for their children. Parental affection has been the catalyst for drawing many a mother and father to join their children in the*

*faith. Family evangelism also empowers them for effective disciple-making through their parent-child relationships.* This parental desire to provide the best for their children is part of the natural script imprinted on human parents by God (Is. 49:15; Matt. 7:9-11; 1 Tim. 5:8). The parental responsibility to provide for the total well-being of children includes their spiritual nurture (Eph. 6:4). Ideally, God would have everyone discipled within a nurturing family unit. Family evangelism helps parents know how to lead their children to Jesus and provide for their ongoing spiritual nurture. This takes place best in the context of positive family relationships. As parents are enabled to grow in their understanding and commitment to God (Deut. 6:4, 5; cf. 2 Tim. 1:5), and as they learn how best to model and teach Christian principles in ways that children find alluring (Deut. 6:6-9), the likelihood that their children will commitment themselves to Christ and the church is greatly enhanced. Parent education is one of the best ways to cooperate with God in leading children to Jesus.

How much more effective would be our efforts to share the gospel if families could become winsome discipling centers! How much more effective our evangelism might be if ways could be found to elevate the significance of the family, to understand the relational principles at work in the family system, and to cooperate with these principles and build on them, rather than attempting to ignore or work against them. Families—extending to several generations— constitute an arena of evangelistic endeavor that is largely undeveloped. We believe, however, that this is a primary mission field to which God is calling the church at this time.

## TOWARD RECONCILIATION IN FAMILIES

In the work of sharing the gospel and helping people to receive the Good News, we focus most often on reconciliation with God and forming a relationship with Him. Often, however, people cannot fully complete that task—sometimes they cannot even undertake it—until they have been reconciled with the people who are closest to them. Jesus acknowledged this reality when He said, "First go and be reconciled to your brother" (Matt. 5:24). Families know the devastating impact of sin close up. Its devastation can be felt in the breakdown of marriage; the stress of parent-child relationships; the discord across generations and extended family lines; in the painful life experience of victims of abuse and violence, HIV/AIDS infection, addictions of every description, and much more. If we are to be faithful to the call of Christ to extend His ministry in the world—a ministry to the broken-hearted, the blind, the oppressed—the gospel must be first be applied as a healing balm for the real hurts and wounds in family experience.

This kind of evangelism will require new approaches, new skills, and much patience with a process that is perhaps more complicated than we have been willing to consider. But this kind of evangelism has the potential to do unprecedented good in the world as barriers that divide and separate are broken down by the gospel, and more and more families are brought together with Jesus becoming their Peace. It also stands to reason that the falling away that many times occurs in circumstances in which one person has been garnered out of a family might be greatly reduced. When families are together in the Lord and one becomes discouraged, the entire family can be summoned to support and encourage the struggling one, winsomely drawing them back into the family circle, and God's family circle.

## CONCLUSION

Two Old Testament stories come to mind by way of conclusion. They are found in 2 Sam. 18 and 2

Kings 7:9. We don't know what you make of these two stories, but the first suggests to us that before we consider linking family with evangelism, we must address ourselves to the task of making sure families have really good news. The poignant words of the great general Joab to the youthful runner bent on carrying news of the battle back to David have wisdom for us as well: "My son, why do you want to go? You don't have any news that will bring you a reward."

Contrary to the popular myth that involvement in evangelism will solve all people's family problems, we would like to suggest that families who have not experienced the gospel in ways that have brought them closer to God and to each other are like runners with no good news to share. Setting them running is not the answer. Bringing them really Good News is.

The second story makes it unmistakably clear that once they have found Good News, it will be all compelling! Like the starving lepers confronted with lavish bounty for the taking, we will be filled with joy as we fill ourselves and our pockets to overflowing at to the banquet table of Christ's marvelous grace. Then, full to the brim, there can be only one response: "This news is too good to keep to ourselves. Let's go!"

## References and Bibliography

Barclay, W. (1975). *The gospel of Matthew, vol. 1*. Philadelphia: Westminster Press.

Bellah, R. N., Madsen, R., Sullivan, W. M., Swidler, A., & Tipton, S. M. (1996). *Habits of the heart*. Berkeley, CA: University of California Press.

Guernsey, D. (1982). *A new design for family ministry*. Elgin, IL: David C. Cook Publishing Co.

Nicholi, A. (1979, May 25). The fractured family: Following it into the future. *Christianity Today*.

Strauss, R. (1975). *How to raise confident children*. Grand Rapids, MI: Baker Books.

White, E. G. (1952). *Education*. Nampa, ID: Pacific Press Publishing Association.

White, E. G. (1942). *The ministry of healing*. Nampa, ID: Pacific Press Publishing Association.

*end*

# Bringing the *Church* Home:
## Rediscovering Family as a Catalyst for Evangelism

**by David Yeagley**

*Throughout salvation history, God has turned to the family to be an agent of change in a dying world. Now . . . we must not forget the power of the family.*

## INTRODUCTION

When I was in sixth grade my brother gave me his old chemistry set. The directions were lost, so I spent hours in the basement of our family home randomly mixing chemicals with water and waiting for some reaction. The water turned ugly shades of green, black and red, but nothing else happened—no spark, no fizz, no smoke, no bang--nothing! Our world is like the solution I mixed up—dark, ugly and stained with sin. There is a growing sense that our world is hurtling toward the brink and no one can stop it. Preachers, politicians, and educators desperately mix all the chemicals they have, but nothing happens. What the world needs is the same thing that was missing from my brother's chemistry set—a catalyst, an agent for change.

Where are we going to find such a catalyst? Not in a pharmacy or drug store or chemistry text book. Instead, God's Word can help us discover it.

## THE FAMILY AS GOD'S AGENT

Throughout history the family has played a crucial part in God's plan.

**The first family.** At the creation of the world God stepped back and said, "Ah, this is very good." But an enemy lurked in the shadows. What did God do to protect this new world? He brought together a man and a woman and formed the first family. They were to fill and care for the earth, but more importantly their one-flesh union in marriage provided a witness to God's love and power—in the face of the forces of evil (Gen. 2:16, 17). This first family grew careless as the man and woman separated from each other in the garden. With their union broken, Satan seized the opportunity and our world fell into darkness.

**Abraham and the family of Israel.** After the confusion of language at the tower of Babel, the world once again stood at the brink. With all the nations now scattered over the earth and God's children divided by language, how would the news of salvation reach the world? God needed a catalyst, an agent. From one of the largest cities in Mesopotamia He called Abram to leave everything behind and journey to a strange new land where he and his family would be God's chosen people (Gen. 12:1-3). How could this one man and his family be a blessing to the whole world? We don't discover the answer until much later in Abraham's life (Gen. 18:18, 19). With the fate of all humanity hanging in the balance, God hinged His plan on the faith of Abraham.

**The family of Christian believers.** Abraham's faithfulness to God and the subsequent story of the family of Israel led to the greatest moment in salvation history. In a little backwater town of Palestine, a young Jewish girl miraculously conceived and God became man. Jesus came; He lived; He died and He rose again. But who would tell the world? Once again, the fate of the world hung in the balance. And once again God called upon a unique family (Matt. 12:48-50). Jesus' words seem puzzling until we dig deeper. In the New Testament understanding, the church appears as a family—a "household of faith" (Gal. 6:10), "the household of God" (Eph. 2:19), a "family" (Eph. 3:14-15). The book of Acts makes it clear that this family lived up to its calling. They carried the message from house to house. Time and again, entire households were led to Christ. In a few short years the world was turned upside down.

**A final family.** Notice the broad sweep of salvation history. Throughout time, God's family is always getting larger. It begins with a husband and wife born out of the intimacy of the Godhead. It expands to a single family camped like nomads in a strange land. Scripture ends with an extended family that spans the globe and crosses all ethnic, political and gender boundaries. Now God's family is about to expand once more. After millennia of heartache and separation, God is about to call His earthly family home to join with the heavenly family. The world is once again standing at the brink. It is zero-hour. Revelation tells us that, in the face of gathering darkness, God has called together a remnant of His original family to carry a crucial end-time gospel message to the world (Rev. 14:6, 7). Though this message has been shared for decades and considerable church growth taken place, multiplied millions continue to slip ever closer to the edge of disaster. Values and morality are crumbling, homes are fragmented and broken, and countless lives are isolated and hurting.

## RECOVERING THE FAMILY AS AN EVANGELISTIC CATALYST

Throughout salvation history, God has turned to the family to be an agent of change in a dying world. Now, with our world at the edge of eternity, we must not forget the power of this catalyst. Alongside Revelation 14 is Malachi 4 with a message that must work in tandem with the message of the three angels: "I'm sending Elijah the prophet to clear the way for the Big Day of God – the decisive Judgment Day! He will convince parents to look after their children and children to look up to their parents" (Malachi 4:5-6, *The Message Bible*).

The bottom line is this: *the catalyst of the family is crucial to the accomplishment of evangelism today*. James Dobson, a sometimes controversial advocate for the family, has correctly said:

> Here is the most important implication of family disintegration. It will represent a virtual end of evangelism, as has occurred in Western Europe ... The family is absolutely critical to the propagation of the faith. If it falls apart in nations around the world, we will, perhaps in our lifetime, see another moral collapse "as it was in the days of Noah." (Dobson, July 2001 Monthly Newletter)

**Unlearning some evangelistic habits.** I began playing cello at the age of nine. Over the years, as I moved with my parents from city to city and studied under a wide variety of teachers, I picked up some bad habits. They were small and seemingly insignificant, but, by the time I reached high school, I hit a wall and was unable to progress further. In Texas I studied with Wayne Burak, first-chair cellist with the Fort Worth Symphony Orchestra and a master teacher. One by one he diagnosed my acquired habits and slowly and patiently helped me to unlearn them. It was a grueling process, but the result was music to my ears—I was playing at a level I never thought possible.

Applying the catalyst of family to our evangelistic endeavors will likewise be a challenging process. Over the years practices have sprung up that tend to work against a model that appropriately incorporates principles of family life in our ministry. Recently, some attempts have been made to append family ministry to what we have already been doing evangelistically. However, if we are to overcome the wall before us we must be willing to unlearn some things and re-learn other things about evangelism. What follows are some ideas intended to stimulate creative thought and dialogue. I hope they will lead to a renewed focus on the crucial role of the family in evangelism and the development of practical models of true, family-based evangelism.

**Moving from saving souls to saving families.** The New Testament model of ministry is one that moves from house to house. The apostles repeatedly baptized entire households. Erwin McManus in *An Unstoppable Force* (2001) writes,

> God's purpose has always been about redeeming a people. Yet we have reduced it to the conversion of individuals. And there is a radical difference between the two ... one leads to a follower of Christ and the other to a movement. (p. 95)

**The significance of relational ministry.** Contemporary western culture is skeptical of doctrine but starving for relationships. A savings bank near me has a slogan that connects with this oft-unspoken yearning: "The Right Relationship is Everything." Jesus responds to this culture by affirming, "I am the way the truth and the life" and "this is life eternal that they might know thee the true God and Jesus Christ whom Thou hast sent." This is not a repudiation of doctrine but a call to a relational ministry. Ron Martoia says, "Relationships are the apologetics of the 21st century" (Velocity Conference 2003).

**From program to process.** Building relationships takes time and each friendship grows at a different pace. Relational ministry cannot be packaged into 26-night crusade. Traditional evangelistic series may yield some increase in numbers, but they may also be counterproductive to the health of families. Churches seeking to engage in family-based evangelism must commit to a long-term process that cannot be easily measured by numbers and immediate results. Every part of the process from making friends to strengthening marriages to going on a picnic with friends should be understood as part of this evangelistic process. Further, such a process will extend beyond the baptism of individuals and families to encourage them in ongoing discipleship.

**From church-centered to home-centered ministry.** In *The Family Friendly Church* Ben Freudenburg (1998) points out that we must move "from church-centered, home-supported ministry to home-centered, church-supported ministry" (p. 94). This is a new paradigm that has radical implications. Church leaders have long asked families to get involved in what the church is about. This new model of ministry calls the church to get involved in what families are about. Leonard Sweet, at a recent leadership conference, challenged the church to reclaim the home as an arena for ministry.

**From prophecy to prophetic movement.** For years, we have illustrated our evangelistic advertising brochures with images of beasts and dragons. Many public evangelists typically begin their series in Daniel 2. That Adventism has historic roots in the prophecies of Daniel and Revelation is a fact that should not be lost. However, neither must we forget that we have also been called to proclaim the Elijah Message of Malachi 4—to turn the hearts of the fathers to their children and the hearts of the children to their fathers. In this sense, healing broken marriages and announcing end-time events are equally prophetic. We cannot be God's prophetic movement while proclaiming one and ignoring the other.

**From broadcast to narrowcast.** As God's remnant people we must be willing to go where no church has gone before—Next Door! For this, big media blitzes, mass mailings and radio and TV spot announcements are unnecessary. As evangelistic contacts go, there is nothing better than meeting your neighbor over the back fence or hosting the family in the apartment

across the hall at your apartment for dinner. Mike Slaughter (2002) observes, "Our culture today is all about personalization. Unlearning churches focus on personalized pathways of discipleship that meet individual needs, rather than one-size fits all programs for the masses" (p. 35).

**From talking heads to textured experiences.** For more than 150 years Adventist evangelism has focused on lecturing or teaching. With the dawning of a culture that values experiences, learning has entered a whole new arena. Silently listening in a pew or behind a desk often stifles meaningful learning. Today's learners want to enter into an experience. They want to see, hear, touch, feel and smell. They want to be able to actively participate in the learning process. They respond to visual images—the use of metaphor and story. They also want the learning process to be something that connects them with other people on the journey.

**From proof texts to living proof.** Most evangelistic programs involve some variation of fill-in-the-blank learning. The sermon or lesson asks a question, the evangelist or the participant reads a text and then, mentally or quite literally, fills in the blanks. People today have little interest in such methods. They want to meet someone who's been down the same road they have. They're not interested in finding all the answers; they want to find someone who will share the journey with them—someone who is real and authentic. In a world that is skeptical of the Bible, living proof is the only proof they're willing to listen to.

**From outside in to inside out.** We have spent a lot of time worrying about how to attract people to come through our church doors. What would happen if we spent our time creating an experience within the community of faith that worshipers could carry with them when they left the church? Not *outside in*, but *inside out*. According to William Abraham (1989), "The gospel spread and the church grew because the sovereign hand of God was in the midst of the community that found itself surrounded by people who were puzzled and intrigued by what they saw happening" (p. 38).

**From proposition to a Person.** Above all else, we must remember that the message is not fundamentally a set of principles and propositions; it is a Person. When God wanted this sinful world to understand who He is, He didn't send a doctrinal statement, He sent a Savior. If absolute truth is a Person, then responding to truth is all about what we do with this Person. This reality must be the bedrock of family-based, relational evangelism. Said Jesus, "Now this is eternal life: that they may know you, the only true God, and Jesus Christ, whom you have sent" (John 17:3).

**David Yeagley is a Seventh-day Adventist pastor in Lansing, Michigan.**

## References

Abraham, W. (1989). *The logic of evangelism.* Grand Rapids: Wm. B. Eerdmans Publishing Co.

Dobson, J. (2001). July Monthly Newsletter.

Freudenburg, B. (1998). *The family friendly church.* Loveland, Co: Group Publishing.

Martoia, R. (2003). *Velocity .03 conference.* Jackson, MI: Westwinds Community Church.

McManus, E. (2001). *An unstoppable force.* Loveland, Co: Group Publishing.

Slaughter, M. (2002). *Unlearning church.* Loveland, Co: Group Publishing.

Sweet, L. (2003). *Velocity .03 conference.* Jackson, MI: Westwinds Community Church.

# *Family* Evangelism

## by Millie and John Youngberg

## A NEW PARADIGM

There is only one "everlasting gospel" which must be preached to all the inhabitants of earth to prepare a people for the great and majestic day of the Lord. Yet old truths can be presented in new ways. The "felt needs" of the public call for alternative, fresh approaches. Family Evangelism is a new paradigm. Although covering the essential doctrines, its forte is relational theology. Seventh-day Adventism is a prophetic message. Let us, then, not forget the relational "heart turning" prophecy of Malachi which closed the Old Testament canon and opened New Testament prophetism in Gabriel's announcement to Zacharias (Lk.1:16,17). There is "nothing more powerful than an idea whose time has come." As we witness the soaring divorce rates, juvenile delinquency and moral corruption everywhere, the time has surely come to rebuild the family altar and to turn hearts of parents to children and children to parents, and together turn their hearts toward home. When this Elijah Message is presented, the fire of God's power will fall and the blood of the Innocent Victim will save our families for heaven.

## GOALS OF FAMILY EVANGELISM

1. To facilitate heart-turning through the Elijah Message.

2. To combine doctrinal presentations with the practicality of family life–where life is lived. The message seeks for an integration of family and doctrinal instruction.

3. To share the gospel in a family setting with emphasis on Jesus and relational theology.

4. To encourage entire families to come to the Lord and join the church.

## PHILOSOPHY

If the gospel message means anything at all, it should be a transforming power to make a difference in the family and to show people how to live and relate to others. If the message of the Bible lacks the dynamism to make people nice, to make them kind, to make them loving in human relationships, then its relevance to the larger society of the nation and the world can be questioned. This is not to espouse a human altruism. Human nature cannot transform itself. Human virtue must find its beginning point in the self-sacrificing love of God.

We all know that the first church and the first school was the family. The first marriage performed in Eden by the Creator Himself established the basis of society. Transgression and the reality of sin marred the first family. The blaming game began and the firstborn killed his brother. The Family Breaker urged upon the fallen family his agenda, but the Family Maker intervened to show the family the road back to its Eden home. We call this conflict the "great controversy." Today its focus is not in cosmic lightning bolts, but within the doors of our own homes. Satan "is intruding his presence in every department of the household . . . breaking up families . . . ." (*The Great Controversy*, p. 508).

Do we need any further justification for "Family Evangelism?" The focus in this series is the Good News and how it can be lived out in the family. There is an integration of biblical and family instruction. The working of the Holy Spirit on the whole family as it accepts the gospel becomes extremely exciting and rewarding to the participating family members.

The Elijah Message of Mal. 4:5, 6 becomes the basis for this evangelistic series—showing how to turn the hearts of parents to children, of children to parents, and together strengthening the vertical relationship with the Author of the family. This last-day prophecy is the golden thread that winds its way through the whole series.

However, the message of Elijah must never eclipse the One whom this messenger announced—Jesus, the only hope of the family. While helping new believers to find and accept Jesus Christ as their Savior and to learn more about the gospel, participating church members are edified and grow as new family skills and techniques are learned. Consequently, the quality of the family is improved.

When two individuals unite their lives in marriage they enter a new school; they begin a process that is sometimes painful but essential. The home becomes a polishing place. Some do not wish to be polished and they may be the ones who end up in divorce. Home is the place for the development of character—which is all we can take to heaven. When the entire family is committed to Christ and they follow the Bible teaching, growing is easier within the home. All things are better with God in the family.

## THE FAMILY MESSAGE IS BIBLICAL

There are many family stories in the Bible from which we can learn and there are parables and family symbolism to stimulate thought on the family. One is that of Christ as the Bridegroom and we His people, His bride. He wants us to be ready for that great wedding. That is what this series is all about.

Elder and Mrs. Gordon Martinborough, veteran family evangelists from the Inter-American Division of the Seventh-day Adventist Church, have pointed out a few other examples of family in Scripture: After Enoch became a father he walked with God (Gen. 5:22); Isa. 49:15 says that God's love surpasses that of a mother; Eze. 16:8, 15 presents a picture of God as a lover and Israel's unfaithfulness as a wife. Matthew 25 presents the parable of 10 virgins in a marriage setting; Eph. 5:31, 32 emphasizes that a man and his wife shall be one flesh. This intimacy is compared to the intimacy that Christ desires to have with us, His church; Rev. 21:2 presents the Holy City as a bride. The Bible closes with an invitation from the Spirit and the bride to "Come . . . take the water of life freely" (Rev. 22:17). Because of these and other biblical references to family, some refer to the Bible as the "Family Book."

Thus, it is clear that family evangelism is not a gimmick. It has a biblical base. It follows Christ's method of meeting people's needs close to home and then giving them the solution to their needs and problems.

A family evangelistic campaign presents the Bible doctrines that would be covered in a traditional evangelistic campaign, making family issues an introduction to and setting for each doctrine. There is an integration of faith, doctrines, family relations, and family skills. Each sermon may focus on family issues differently. Some sermons transition from today's family needs to doctrinal topics. In others, doctrinal and family topics are more thoroughly integrated in the sermon.

## VALUE OF FAMILY EVANGELISM

For years observers have noted that both church members and non-Seventh-day Adventist attendees have flocked to introductory themes dealing with family problems. Then, as the series went on to the traditional doctrinal/prophetic approach, many Adventists stayed home since they had heard these topics before. Living an enhanced family life is an interest both of Adventists and non-Adventists, so attendance tends to hold up better than in the traditional series. In family evangelism, church members feel more comfortable inviting their neighbors because of the overt family benefits.

The family materials lend themselves well to group dynamics and audience participation in a seminar setting. This tends to lighten up the meeting. Attendees are assigned activities to do at home and report on at the next meeting, if the group size permits. The carefully planned homework assignments call for a transformational response, not just informational. People like to hear how others solve family problems.

Decisions for accepting Christ and subsequent baptism are an important part of the campaign, with the hope that whole families will be baptized and join God's family, the Church. Baptizing a whole family as a unit has many advantages. It reminds us of the experience of the Philippian jailor in which the entire family unit accepted Christ and members were baptized together. Rates of retention and faithfulness among new members are much better when there is family support. On the other side of the coin, warfare within the family is minimized when family members learn the Gospel together. Many of the problems people face have their basis in family dynamics. A systems approach which deals with the whole group can maintain the family equilibrium as it moves into a new way of life.

When this family evangelism approach was used in Russia, we noticed that there were a larger percentage of men baptized at the end of a series than in other evangelistic meetings there.

## A BRIEF HISTORY OF RECENT FAMILY EVANGELISM

Family evangelism was a preferred method of evangelism and nurture in the primitive Christian Church. Congregations were house churches then, even as they are today for the majority of the more than 300,000 Seventh-day Adventists in China. In Cuba, there are also many home churches. Many of Christ's miracles respected and restored the organic unity of the family. Believers were often baptized as families.

The recent resurgence of family evangelism has been very effective in various parts of the world. Gordon Martinborough reports thousands of people have accepted Christ and have been baptized during the time that he and his wife Waveney have been active in family evangelism campaigns. Fitzroy Maitland, Rocky Gale, Carlos Martin, Victor Collins, Adly Campos and others have produced and presented family evangelism materials in recent years with good results in the United States, Canada, the Caribbean, Russia, Cuba, Dominican Republic, Mexico, and other countries. These materials and presentations have been instrumental in proclaiming the Elijah Message of Mal. 4:5, 6 in these end times.

Our own activity in family evangelism dates back about a quarter of a century. We were catalysts in encouraging others—"gatherers" and organizers of early materials. After presenting a family evangelism campaign in Moscow during the summer of 1994, we became convicted that there was a need for a series of family evangelistic sermons for the former U.S.S.R. that didn't presuppose the audience had a Christian background given the 70 years of atheistic exile during the Communist era. Also, because of the opposition from the dominant church in Russia, the meetings started by using family topics and then crossed the bridge into doctrines which were illustrated biblically by family metaphors. There was an integration of material from the discipline of family science with Bible instruction.

After we returned from Moscow, May-Ellen Colon, Co-Director of Family Ministries of the Euro-Asia Division, asked us to prepare a series of family/doctrinal sermons to meet their special needs. *Family Life at Its Best* was the result of our efforts. It was published in Russia for use by ministers and lay persons in the former Soviet block. This material was then translated and culturally revised for use among Hispanics by Dr. Luis del Pozo in Mexico. The resulting work, *La Familia en Su Máximo Potencial*, has run through two editions and has been illustrated with PowerPoint graphics. (See Ordering Information at the end of this article). We know of some 50 pastors in Mexico who have utilized this series. Results have been heart-warming. One Mexican pastor reports 125 baptisms from one series in which he carefully organized the whole church. It has been a delight to see that local churches in many countries have rallied to use this material for the saving of families through an integrated Family-Bible series. At present, with the encouragement of Ron and Karen Flowers of the Department of Family Ministries of the General Conference, an English edition is being published in 2004. This new edition shows a progression over other language editions and attempts to bridge cultural barriers to address the universal needs of families everywhere.

Early on, we discovered that this task was bigger than we were. It has become an anthology of family evangelism sermons written by experienced Seventh-day Adventist pastors, evangelists, administrators, writers, and university professors. These sermons have been edited and re-edited with great effort to add family emphasis to each sermon. The process continues as the new edition is being prepared. Among the major contributors are John & Millie Youngberg, Joe Engelkemeier, and Melchizedek Ponniah. Other authors are Gaspar and May-Ellen Colon, Ken Corkum, Dwight Nelson (from NET 98 sermons), Larry Lichtenwalter, C.D. Brooks, Halcyon Wilson, C. Mervyn Maxwell, Thurmon Petty, Larry Yeagley, David Yeagley, Samuele Bacchiocchi, Fitzroy Maitland, Richard and Ardis Stenbakken, Joyce Lorentz and Paul A. Gordon.

As general editors, we have tried to maintain the integrity of the family component in the entire series and give a unified flow while respecting the input of the various guest contributors. For the new English 2004 edition of *Family Life at Its Best* the sermons are made fresh by new writers and updated with more current information. We view this as a resource manual which seasoned evangelists and creative lay persons can use. Each one can give authenticity to the message by combining his own family life experience, personal illustrations, stories from the host nation, and culturally relevant material to meet the needs of the audience.

## VARIED USES OF FAMILY EVANGELISM MATERIALS

**Women evangelists.** In Russia, the Ukraine, the United States, and Mexico women have done outstanding work using family evangelism methodology, with the series sometimes resulting in more than 100 baptisms. There is great potential for women evangelists to use family evangelism materials. Hearing a woman preacher is a novelty for many and often a woman's perspective is pointed and creative in dealing with family life issues.

**Cottage meetings.** Some families have used this material for cottage meetings. They invite their neighbors to their home, present family life information, and pray for the needs that their guests express. In such groups, steps have been taken toward family life changes, individuals have been stirred in their thinking about biblical and family issues, and personal transformations have taken place.

**Mini-family topics.** Because many family issues which won't be addressed in the main family-doctrinal sermon, we suggest that additional time be given during each meeting for a 10-12 minute "family nugget" feature. A component of the Family Evangelism Series that can be used is *Dynamic Family Living Series: A series of Family Talks to be used in Conjunction with Evangelistic Campaigns* which contains mini-family life lectures. Originally prepared for use in the Philippine 50,000 campaign, this material can also be used for brief "family nugget" features before the main sermon in traditional evangelistic series. A Spanish version, *Dinámica de la Vida Familiar*, is also available (see Ordering Information below).

## ADAPTATION FOR SHORT CAMPAIGNS

Dwight Nelson, NET 98 speaker and senior pastor at the Pioneer Memorial Church at Andrews University, tells us that in most western countries the long evangelistic series is a relic of the past. We have observed that this is true as well in Mexico, Cuba, and the Dominican Republic. In this post-modern age with cable television, people typically won't attend long series which tend to meet five times a week for some 30 presentations. Nor does the imperative of presenting the full message in one series still exist. In Inter-America, for example, many successful pastor-evangelists expect converts to have had three exposures to the message—through a sowing series, a reaping series, and a series of Bible studies or baptismal classes before baptism. They plan their evangelistic year and organize their churches accordingly.

Family evangelistic methodology can be used successfully in this cycle, as either a sowing or a reaping series. Some evangelists start with health topics, move to family topics and then present doctrinal messages. As a resource book containing basic Bible doctrines and some prophecy topics, *Family Life at Its Best* could be preceded by a health seminar and followed by a Revelation Seminar, for example. Some presenters hold meetings every night, others 4 or 5 times a week, and still others might have several sermons presented on Sabbath or Sunday in a seminar format. In this family evangelism resource book, we are coding the 30 topics and the 3 Sabbath sermons with suggestions as to which topics would work best in a 10-meeting series, and which in a series of 18 or 21 presentations.

## OUR PRAYER

We pray that the voice of Family Evangelism may swell into a Loud Cry (Rev. 18) throughout the world, proclaiming the end-time Elijah Message of Mal. 4:5, 6—turning the hearts of whole families from Babylon to God and to each other.

---

Millie and John Youngberg are pioneers in family life education in the Seventh-day Adventist Church, having served on the faculty of Andrews University in Berrien Springs, Michigan where they founded and directed the long-running Family Life International program.

### References

White, E. G. (1888). *The great controversy between Christ and Satan.* Boise, ID: Pacific Press Publishing Association.

---

## ORDERING INFORMATION

### English language materials.

• *Family Life at Its Best* (including PowerPoint graphics)

**Available June, 2004.**

• *Dynamic Family Living Series*

Order from Gary R. Hilbert, Manager, Christian Book Center (ABC), 8980 S. US 31, Berrien Springs, MI 49103 USA. Phone: (877) 227-4800, (269) 471-7331. E-mail: michiganabc@yahoo.com

### Spanish-language materials.

• *La Familia en Su Máximo Potencial* (including PowerPoint graphics)

• *Dinámica de la Vida Familiar*

Order from Department of Family Relations, Montemorelos University, Apartado 16, Montemorelos N.L. 67500, Mexico.

# *Father* Power

**by Millie and John Youngberg**

## INTRODUCTION

In 1989, there was a terrible earthquake in Armenia that came with the force of 8.9 on the Richter scale. In one home, the husband and wife were rocking back and forth with the force of this terrible earthquake. There was the almost deafening roar like thunder as the buildings were falling around them. But once the earthquake had subsided and they had survived, they thought of their son, Armen. The father ran along the streets toward the school. As he arrived, he saw that the school had fallen in the earthquake and it was all debris and rubble. The concerned father rushed back to a corner of the building where he had left his son that morning as he entered his school room.

There was total devastation—concrete slabs, boards and debris everywhere. The father began to work immediately, pulling away concrete slabs. Some people came questioning, "What are you doing? Don't waste your time. No one could possibly have survived in this pile of debris." But the father, taken aback by their pessimism, reprimanded them saying, "Don't talk to me that way. Help me dig in the rubble."

Soon the fire department came. The fire chief also saw the situation as hopeless. The chief chastised the father saying, "No one could have lived through this devastation. Stop digging in the rubble. As a matter of fact, you are discouraging the other people, giving them some hope when there is no hope." But Armen's father continued to work and work pulling away rubble and concrete slabs. He worked 5 hours. He worked 12 hours. He worked 24 hours. He worked 36 hours without stopping. And finally after all these hours, he heard a voice. It was his son, Armen, who answered his calls. "Father, I knew you would come, you had promised that if I ever needed you, you would be there."

Fourteen out of the 33 students in that school room were still alive. The slabs had made a wedge around them and had given them a place where they could survive. The father said, "Come out, Armen." Armen answered, "No, daddy, let the others go out first because I know that you will always be there." In these first years of the 21st century there still are true fathers. And they will be there when there children need them.

## FATHERS, CHILDREN NEED A FATHER

Deep in the heart of every child is the intense desire to be accepted and affirmed by their father. He is such an important part of the child's life. Each child wants a loving father and looks up to him as an essential constant who is there for them. The father is the provider or breadwinner, the protector, leader, the priest, the helper, and friend. Usually a loving father who has a good connection with his family strives to have a positive relationship with each of the children, tries to meet their needs, is there when they need him, attempts to effectively communicate, and spends quality time with them. These are essential for a healthy, happy bonding between father and child. The reality is that as fathers get busier they are spending less and less time and get less involved with their children's daily life. Time, however, is essential if our children are to be properly taught, trained, and spiritually nurtured. The father power of influence is crucially important in every home.

A good father-child relationship leads to successful academic achievement, sex-role identity, emotional and moral development which provides a healthy place for growing up "in favor with God and man".

Fatherhood is a highly dynamic relationship that transforms children to be all that they can be under the guidance and cooperation of their earthly and heavenly Father. Fathers have great power and responsibility in their role for the child they brought into this world. There are so many fathers that take seriously their ministry to their own children while on the other hand there are absent fathers who neglect and reject their offspring. Many of these fathers have given up their parental responsibility and power and are moving from being a central figure in the lives of their children to a more peripheral position. This is not God's plan. God said of Abraham, in Gen. 18:19 "For I have known him, in order that he may command his children and his household after him, that they keep the way of the Lord, to do righteousness and justice . . .:"

Fathers have God-given responsibilities and, when carried out, fathering is a satisfying experience. Fathers who are in-or-out of the home can provide an environment of security, love, instruction, nurture, and well-being and be a powerful influence in the child's life. The absent father, in-or-out of the home, contributes to a lasting void and pain that negatively affects the future of the child.

A young man heard that his father was dying in the hospital. He rushed as quickly as possible to his bedside but only to discover that the father was already in a coma. He grabbed his hand and sobbed, "Don't die until you tell me you love me." Over and over he repeated his need for hearing his father say, "Son, I love you." Sadly the words were never spoken before his last breath of life. The son was devastated.

Earthly fathers have such a high position that they actually are a representative for the Heavenly Father while the children are small. Spending time with children is crucial for training, bonding, counseling, educating, and is a powerful element in parenting.

Dr. Armand Nicholi II of Harvard University says, "If any one factor influences the character development and emotional stability of an individual, it is the quality of the relationship he or she experiences as a child with both parents." Yes, Dr. Nicholi is right. Parents not only give biological life to their children, but they model how they should live and how they should solve problems.

A father and his young son were walking through the woods. In some places the terrain was open and the little boy ran ahead or found his own way around obstacles. But after a while they came to a place where there was considerable undergrowth of brush and blackberry bushes. The boy had missed the path and soon found himself entangled. "Daddy, my legs are getting scratched!" His dad lifted him up and carried him back to the path. Then he instructed, "Son, take my hand and step where I step." Within a few minutes they had crossed the thorny place and arrived where they were going. In life, happy is the child who, when his "legs are getting scratched," can find guidance and support from a wise father. Such a father does not just tell the child what to do, but models in his own life the better way and can say, "Here son, step where I step." A strong, warm father model in childhood can save children from many of the thorns along life's path. That is true "father power".

## FATHER CRISIS: THE FATHER ROLE UNDER ATTACK

Throughout human history the father has played an important role in the family setting. This is true of almost all the cultures of the world. The father has been largely responsible for the rise and fall of the family. In more recent years, the role of the father in the family has been attacked on almost every front. L. Masters observes that we see the "embattled father struggling to maintain his self-image in the face of an aggressive wife-mother and a powerful adolescent peer group." Should the unfortunate man turn to television for some relief, his ego will be additionally assaulted "by programs in which women and children consistently outwit father," who is increasingly being presented in the media as incompetent and bungling (Masters, 1971, pp. 21-30). *(Note to the evangelist: please make sure that the above observation is relevant to your culture. If not, then by all means use more contextual and relevant studies.)*

On an Oprah television show teens shared that they did not feel loved, appreciated or even connected to their fathers. They often felt ignored and when there was communication, it was usually a critical session with much fault finding and they were not understood. Their deep desire was to have a close meaningful relationship with this significant person—their father—and be noticed and accepted by him. They wanted to belong even though their actions did not always show their true appreciation of their father and his values.

Today, increasing millions of children are being left fatherless. Some fathers fulfill military duties in various countries and many of them never return to their homes. Other fathers put in long hours at work, and are all too often ready to go out and drink with their friends. Some come home but spend long hours in front of a TV or on the computer and virtually are mentally absent from their children. His absence is not without consequence. As dismal as is the picture of father-absence, the greater problem is father-neglect where fathers live with their families but have lost close, regular contact with their children. How thankful we should be that our heavenly Father is not absent. He never leaves or forsakes us.

Behavioral scientists are pointing out that the neglectful father is a root-cause of many social and personal problems. In fact, two leading authorities in the area, Henry Biller and Dennis Meredith, state quite unequivocally that, "Father power is different from mother power and your child needs both in order to develop properly."

Dr. Ken Canfield, President of the National Center on Fathering (2001) reported that in his research he has found that too many fathers have abandoned their children—and this abandonment is not just physical, but also emotional and spiritual. When fathers do not connect emotionally and spiritually with their children, they become vulnerable. Biologically it is the father who determines the gender of the new child, and if the father does not play an active role in the life of the child, he or she tends to sense gender ambiguity and confusion. Those children whose father is active and connected with them tend to grow into adolescents and adults who have the capacity to translate great plans into appropriate action. These fathers also affect the self-concept of their children. They believe they are important because their fathers told them they were important. They also tend to be able to make crucial decisions.

Dr. Canfield continues, saying that in the United States there is a fathering crisis among African-Americans. Sixty percent of children under the age of 18 have never known their fathers. The lack of fathering produces the following social problems: (a) a high drop-out rate from high school, (b) a tendency is live below the poverty line, (c) more people added to the welfare rolls, (d) early marriage, (e) having children outside of wedlock, (f) higher divorce rates, (g) increased crime, (h) greater consumption of drugs and alcohol.

However, if the fathers and grandfathers involve themselves in the lives of their children, the following beneficial results will tend to be seen: (a) increased intellectual ability, (b) positive modeling for their children, (c) the children receive a better generational background, (d) there is a better ethnic and cultural legacy for the children and an understanding of their place in the family structure, (e) occupational options become clearer, (f) material resources are left for their children, (g) the way these children in turn will treat their children someday will be affected, (h) the children will have more positive attitudes toward their siblings, and (i) there will be more pleasant memories after they leave home or their parents die. But actually, not only are children benefited by involved parents, the parents themselves are also benefited, since parenting is perhaps the greatest school of life.

Dr. Ken Canfield reported extensive investigations of prison populations. He found that 38% of prisoners had a father, grandfather, uncle, or cousin who had also been in prison. Eighty percent of the prisoners studied had felt impacted by the fact that they did not have a father figure in their lives.

On the brighter side, Canfield reports a study by the Medical Center of the University of California, Los Angeles. The study found that when a father physically touches his son in a healthy way, there was an elevation of the hemoglobin count in the blood. When parents touch their children in a healthy way there seems to be healing.

Certainly, there are some fatherless or father-neglected families where sons and daughters have been successfully reared to form happy, well-adjusted homes of their own. However, this task is made so much easier and more delightful when father is a strong dynamic figure in the everyday life of the children. As the primary family executive, father is expected to supply authority, discipline, and sound judgment. Like executives in other institutions, he must be able to absorb the hostility generated by the conduct of his role.

Parents in general and fathers in particular are modeling for God. The power to model correctly really comes from God. So when we refer to "Father Power," we are talking about the power of the Father God who, through His Holy Spirit, enables earthly fathers to cooperate with God in rearing their children for the kingdom of God. Recent studies have concluded that there is a significant correlation between the way a child perceives the father and God. It is important, therefore, for a father to answer the question, "What kind of father/leader am I?"

## WHAT IS A FATHER?

**A father leads and supports.** The father is a protector, a spiritual leader, a teacher, a friend; he is very special in the home. We want our children to be successful. In order for them to be successful, certain things need to be fulfilled. First of all, the child must feel that he/she is capable and realize it: "I am capable." He/she also has to feel needed and important to the family. The child needs to feel influential over his/her own future. So, as we train our children, we need to help them to realize that they are responsible for their destiny. They are architects of their own lives. They must choose well that which they do daily. Self-discipline is another quality that we must help instill in our children. There are young people who say, "I want to do what I want to when I want to and how I want to." But that leads to trouble. The child's self-concept is affected by how he/she perceives the parents think of him/her.

One favorite author, who wrote much on the privileges of parenthood, says:

Fathers, do not discourage your children. Combine affection with authority, kindness and sympathy with firm restraint. Give some of your leisure hours to your children; become acquainted with them; associate with them in the work and in their sports, and win their confidence. Cultivate friendship with them, especially with your sons. In this way you will be a strong influence for good. (*The Ministry of Healing*, pp. 391, 392)

Each one of us and each one of our children need to be self-disciplined and to have boundaries and control. Our children learn from experiences in life. A couple who raised two sons told their children: "We want you to grow up so that you will not hurt when you are older." Sometimes they would not listen and as a result in older life, they have had to hurt and to learn from many difficult experiences of life.

Another area that we are interested in is that our children learn to have friends and develop wholesome friendships. This again is where fathers can be helpful to direct their children to prepare themselves to be friends and to choose good friends. This takes talk time. Biller and Meredith point out that father presence or involvement tends to have positive effects on their daughters' relationships with boys. Girls deprived of a father or whose father has not appropriately affirmed their specialness and femininity are more likely to become "boy-crazy" as they mistakenly seek appreciation and affirmation from another male (Biller & Meredith, 1974, pp. 176, 177).

Deut. 6:7 says that fathers should teach the principles of the word of God diligently to their children. "Talk of them when you sit in your house, when you walk by the way, when you lie down, and when you rise up." In this way they can transmit their values to the generation that is coming up.

The talking part includes teaching and training so that the child will "grow up in favor with God and man" and be prepared for life. What shall we teach them? Teach them about God, what is right and wrong, how to talk positively about others and how to look for the good and not the bad. Teach them respect, honesty, generosity, service for others, and to say "I am sorry." Teach them appreciation, to be forgiving, and much more. Training them will include becoming competent in life skills that will help them on their educational journey. God has a plan for our children and will use fathers and mothers to fashion them for God's long range design for them. One

family chose Sunday morning to talk together and evaluate their family's behavior in response to Deut. 6:7 and then targeted certain areas they would emphasize during the coming week. As a father of an adult son, John tried to spend quality time alone with him, even after the young man had left home and lived in another state. Frequently, they would each drive half way between their homes in Michigan and Illinois, meet at a designated restaurant, and enjoy father-son talk time.

Yet another important area of a child's development is to be able to respond well to boundaries and consequences. Many consequences in life result from bad choices. Parents who help their children establish and maintain boundaries enable them to be responsible and give priority to the most important things. It keeps the children from sacrificing their honor and good character.

**Fathers bless their children.** Fathers have the privilege of being a blessing to their children. In one example, a father went with his older son, who was 35 years old, and spent a weekend with him camping and canoeing in a park. On Saturday, as they were out on the lake enjoying nature and its beauty, the father grew hungry and said, "Let's go back to camp and eat dinner." But the son answered, "Wait a minute, Dad. I want to ask you a favor. Would you give me the paternal blessing?" Right there in the canoe, in the middle of the lake, the father placed his hand on his son's head and prayed. This dad prayed for him and his new job. He prayed for his children and his wife. And he invoked a biblical blessing on the him, saying, "John, the Lord bless you and keep you; the Lord make His face shine upon you, and be gracious to you; the Lord life up His countenance upon you, and give you peace" (Num. 6:24-26). As they opened their eyes, each saw tears on the other's faces. That father still speaks of this as one of the great experiences of his life.

A good father affirms his son. Where there is a "father power" relationship, there is a close interconnection and rapport. God had one Son and He sent Him into this dark world to teach us human beings what love is. In the Gospel of John, on more than 120 occasions, Jesus spoke about His Father. Notice how close they were and the love of the Father for His only begotten Son. When Jesus was graduating into His active ministry and was baptized in the Jordan River, the heavens opened and the community of observers there heard a voice from on high that said: "This is My beloved Son, in whom I am well pleased" (Matt. 3:

17). To fathers who hear this we urge you to tell your children, privately and publicly, how pleased you are to have children like they are. Tell them so regularly; tell them in the special moments in their lives.

The heavenly Father blessed His Son. A short time before His crucifixion, the voice of the Father was heard from the Mount of Transfiguration, again affirming and blessing His Son, "This is My beloved Son in whom I am well pleased. Hear Him!" (Matt. 17:5). It is a beautiful thing to bless our children. Bless them in special ceremonies in the home. Bless them when you receive the holy day Sabbath. Reach out also to other children who don't have a father and bring them into your circle and place your hands on them in blessing. It will make a difference and may transform their lives.

**Fathers are reconcilers and forgivers.** There are many times when our young people grow up angry at their fathers and mothers. Fathers and mothers do their very best, but sometimes they do hurt their children and wound their spirit. There was one father who realized that he must have done this to his son who was almost 20. One day he suggested, "Son, I would like to take you to a very nice place to eat. Would you please join me this evening?" They went to a lovely restaurant. After they had finished their meal, the father said, "I tried to do my best at being a good father, but I know that there are many times that I must have hurt you in some way. I've probably wounded you, and I have said and done the wrong things. If there was any time that I hurt you and haven't made it right, will you please forgive me? I don't want anything to stand between us in our relationship." The waiters in the fancy restaurant looked on with surprise as they saw two grown men, father and son, tenderly embracing with tears falling down their cheeks. Then the two had a wonderful time discussing the son's childhood days. The slate was made clean and then the son said, "I can think of nothing, Dad. I really appreciate you."

Another father noticed that his son seemed quiet, somewhat depressed, and asked, "Is something bothering you? Have I hurt you?" The son did not respond right away, but later returned from his room with a list of offenses that he felt violated him as a young teenager. When the father looked them over, he recognized that some were legitimate while others were not. They disagreed on some of the points, but were able to dialogue on the issues until there was satisfaction for both of them. Good communication clears the air; it can remove bitterness and bring a new beginning of positive relations. When fathers enter more fully into the feelings of their children and draw out what there is in their hearts, they will be able to draw the family together and to lead them to know God better.

**Fathers discipline their children.** How should a Father discipline his children? Recent sociological research has found that there are four basic ways parents discipline their children. Which method should we use? Let's study this and weigh the possibilities. Which method does God use with us? The following is from Dr. Donna Habenicht (1994) of Andrews University, who adapted material from psychologists Baumrind and Mussen (1983, pp. 39-48).

1. The *permissive style* characterizes parents who provide high support but low control. As a result of the parents' laissez-faire attitude toward guidance, their children tend to be impulsive. Waiting for the rewards of tomorrow doesn't appeal to these children. Responsibility is not their strongest character trait, but they are usually kind toward other people.

2. In the *authoritarian style*, parents give low support but exact high control. The results tend to be negative. Young people may rebel and reject parental values. Others become overly compliant; they can't face tough decisions, and need an authority to tell them what to do.

3. The *neglectful style* represents parents who offer low support and low control. Children from neglectful homes often react in the same way that children from authoritarian homes do—they may rebel and embrace negative values. They may have deep emotional problems related to the neglect they have experienced.

4. In the *authoritative style*, parents exhibit both high support and high control. The authoritative, child-centered parenting style sets clear standards and expectations for mature behavior for children, while also considering their needs. Children are encouraged to be independent and responsible. Authoritative parents explain rules in an overall climate of warmth. They are not consumed with their own authority. They listen to their children's viewpoints and respect their feelings. Their children generally feel whatever punishment they receive is deserved. They know that their parents care about them. Children from authoritative homes usually have

strong values and stand up for them. They are often helpful and caring toward others.

Now that we have looked at the four different ways of being a parent which are found in the best sociological literature, which of these methods do you think is the best? Which is most like the way God, the great Father, deals with you and me as His children? Yes, undoubtedly number four. The authoritative style. It combines love with firmness. It sets clear standards and expectations while also considering the needs of the children. There are boundaries. What is God really like? Perhaps each of us has a story of how we have learned about the goodness of our Heavenly Father.

Donna Habenicht observes that only the authoritative parenting style truly represents the way God deals with us—lovingly and encouragingly, while at the same time eagerly wanting to help us grow. Using the authoritative style of leadership in our homes gives our children a chance to see a true picture of God. With His divine help we can introduce our children to that God through our family leadership style. Dr. Habenicht recommends this style as the most effective manner of discipline.

As an authoritative parent:

1. Have firm standards for your child's behavior that encourage increasing maturity and talk about these with your child.

2. Communicate confidence in your child's ability to grow.

3. Explain reasons for your requests and standards. Discuss these requirements with your child. Be flexible and respect your child's viewpoint, while remaining firm about the principle involved.

4. Identify your child's feelings and be caring.

5. Treat your child as a partner in "growing up."

6. Laugh, talk, and have fun with your child.

7. Take interest in your child's activities and personal interests.

8. Show your love often and unmistakably.

To these can be added Gary Chapman's (1997) list of showing love in different ways. He suggests affirmation, telling children they are loved, spending time with them, doing some fun things, giving gifts, serving children such as helping them with difficult tasks, and by touching them appropriately—like putting an arm around them, giving them a hug or a pat, and doing "high fives." All these help the child at any age to realize they are special.

## APPRECIATING FATHERS

Fathers need encouragement and affirmation. Even Jesus appreciated a "thank you" as we are reminded in the account of the ten lepers who were healed. When only one came back to say, "Thank you," Jesus asked, "Where are the other nine?" Appreciation precipitates or generates special acts in return for acts of kindness from others.

One family wrote love and appreciation notes to the father at family worship time. What was interesting to the father was that several people mentioned in their notes, "Dad, you are funny and you make us laugh". He was surprised with the statement and after this made a greater effort to say humorous thing to the children.

Tim, a teenage son, came home after a youth meeting and went straight to Dad, "I just wanted to tell you, Dad, you are loved. At the meeting we were told that we don't tell our parents this often enough."

Two adult sons, who worked in the same family business with their father, noticed that he was a little discouraged. So they decided that they would take him out alone during the lunch hour without other family members for a noon birthday lunch at an extraordinary Italian restaurant where they had a scrumptious meal and pleasant talk. The secretary cooperated by sending cards from some of the workers. Father George returned to the business shop beaming. His love cup had been filled.

One family takes their dad out to a major league baseball game as his treat from the family. There are lots of ways of saying, "Dad, you are special." Kids and moms, you might think of some unique ways of expressing appreciation to the father. A little demonstration of love goes a long way in the family relations.

**Understanding God—the Heavenly Father.**
A teacher was working with three teen girls on the topic: Who is God? The educator asked these girls who and what was God really like? As the girls shared what they knew about God, they all began to come to one conclusion, "God is like my father." Isn't that beautiful! It's true that children learn about God from what they see of their parents. On the other

hand, God is the Great Father and is the model of what an earthly father should be. One girl commented, "God is kind but yet He is firm and that is the way Dad is." "He wants me to know the difference between right and wrong" remarked a teen and "He is loving and helpful when I need him." In Ps. 103:13 it says, "As a father pities his children so the Lord pities those who fear him." Another mentioned, "My father teaches me so many things and is patient when I do things wrong." Christ said that if earthly fathers like to give good gifts to their children, how much more will our heavenly Father give good gifts to those who ask Him! (Lk. 11:13).

What is God, the Father of us all, really like? God is merciful. He knows what is best for us. He is tender with us and yet He is a God of justice and perseverance. The Bible tells us in I Corinthians 1:9 that God is faithful. In 2 Timothy 2:13 it says, "If we are faithless, He remains faithful; He cannot deny Himself." God is a God who bears our burdens. He is our Abba Father who cares for us and is full of love and compassion. He is loyal, forgiving, and longsuffering. He assures us and is trustworthy; His promises are sure. The list could go on and on.

**Appreciating the Heavenly Father through adoration.** A prayer warrior decided to try improving her prayer and devotional life by adding adoration to the Father God at the beginning of her prayers. During her devotional reading she often identified characteristics of God which she would turn into praise or a prayer request by recording them in a continuing adoration prayer on her computer. The characteristics of God the Father are endless like eternity.

"You are the King of Glory," she wrote, "the Everlasting Father with majesty and splendor all around you. You are the Sovereign God, the One and only Holy God and yet You know me and are my Friend. That is who I praise and worship today. Help me to be obedient to you and do your will. You are the Father who Guides me. In my life you opened the Red Sea and let me walk on dry ground."

"Thank you that You are the Provider Father and the Protector," she continued on another day. "You provide our needs and protect us from the enemy of life, the enemy within, the enemies around us who take away our peace, time, and productivity."

"You, Jesus are Emmanuel, God is with Us. Be with our family, healing, teaching, showing us what we know not, communicating, empowering, freeing us of captivities, and giving us grace and mercy daily.

We worship you, Emmanuel. You are the Wonderful Counselor, The Mighty God, The Everlasting Father, and the Prince of Peace. You are the Great God of heaven and earth and our home. You are the Spirit of wisdom and understanding, the Spirit of counsel and might, the Spirit of knowledge and respect. You are infinite Love, infinite Justice, and Holy."

And so her adoration prayer went on.

We know a little about God the Father from what Jesus has revealed to us. While on earth one of Jesus' disciples requested him to tell what the Father was like. Please turn to the Gospel of John 14:8, "Philip said, Lord, show us the Father and that will be enough for us." Philip was one of the disciples of Jesus Christ. He had close contact with Jesus for three-and-a-half years. In the following verses, Jesus answered Philip's question (John 14:9-11). Jesus comforted the anxious Philip saying, "Anyone who has seen me has seen the Father." The mission of Christ to this earth included revealing the nature and character of God. You see, Jesus is God Himself.

If we should take all the virtues of all the fathers of all the countries of the world since time began and multiply them by infinity, we would have only a glimpse of the virtues and the characteristics of our Heavenly Father. History records the deeds of great men and of noble fathers, some of whom gave their lives to save their children from danger or accident. But how much greater is our Heavenly Father and Jesus the Son who is the only One who has revealed the Father to us. Earthly fathers will pass away, but God is eternal.

Timothy, another contributor to the Family Book adds to this concept in 1 Tim. 1:17, "Now to the King eternal, immortal, invisible, the only God be honor and glory for ever and ever. Amen." "Eternal" means that He lives forever and ever. He was there before you were born and He will continue to live after your life comes to an end. King David, another writer of the Family Book, says in Ps. 90:2, "Before the mountains were born or you brought forth the earth and the world, from everlasting to everlasting you are God."

As fathers and mothers, under God we can procreate life. But our Heavenly Father through Jesus and the Holy Spirit is the Creator of all things, including the human family system. The Family Book begins with the story of God's creation. The narrative further explains that God performed the first human marriage between the first created man, Adam, and the first created woman, Eve (Gen. 2:21-22). The crowning act of creation, therefore, is not only the creation of human beings, but also the creation of family. God, in His desire for more companionship, created the first family. God loves the family and wishes to be part of the human family even today.

The Heavenly Family, one in unity and purpose, includes God the Father, God the Son, and God the Holy Spirit. It was Jesus the Son who left the majestic heavenly home and chose to become a member of the human family. In John 1:14 it says that He "became flesh and dwelt among us, and we beheld His glory, the glory as of the only begotten of the Father, full of grace and truth." In the original Greek language this verse literally says that "He pitched His tent among us." He pitched His tent by our tent—the great God of the universe lived with human beings. What a wonderful Savior!

The Gospel of Matthew reveals three persons of the Godhead. In Matthew 3:16-17 it says, "Jesus was baptized" (3:16), "The Spirit of God descending like a dove" (3:16), "And a voice from heaven said, 'This is my beloved Son, with him I am well pleased'" (3:17). All three persons in the Godhead are thus represented in this account of Jesus' baptism: God the Father, God the Son, and God the Holy Spirit. These three-in-one great powers work unceasingly for the well-being of the human family.

Our power is insufficient, but God is all-powerful. We know so little, but our Heavenly Father knows everything. He knows the end from the beginning (Isa. 46:9-11). There is no problem on earth too big for Him to handle and no detail of our lives too small for Him to take an immediate interest in helping us. Read Eph. 3:20, "Now to Him who is able to do exceedingly abundantly above all that we ask or think according to the power that works in us . . . ."

The earthly father is limited but with the heavenly "Father Power" all things are possible—even the impossible, for there is nothing too hard for God. Gen. 18:14 substantiates this, "Is anything too hard for the Lord?" This father power comes when on our knees we experience dialogue time with the Father of all fathers.

## WORK THROUGH ISSUES

This presentation would be incomplete without addressing the topic of "working through issues of captivity." God's mighty power can cleanse each father or family member of past problems, cultivated habits, and generational sins. Bring the issues or pain or hurts to the Father who can cleanse them. Fathering is a battle where two forces push for supremacy. The power of God is essential for us to repulse the attack of the Enemy of families. When we are on God's side we have God's power.

When Roscoe was a child, his father had abandoned the home—emotionally that is—by not being there, not providing food for the table, clothes for their bodies, or love for their hearts. When Roscoe grew up, he became a minister, but with a bad attitude. The father-son relations and bitter emotions cast a shadow on his ministry and family. One day Roscoe's dear wife inquired of him, "If your Dad should get very sick, would you care for him?" The answer came quickly, "Never," and he went back to preparing a sermon on compassion. Then he told his wife, "You don't know how our family suffered!"

It was at that time that the Lord spoke to Roscoe, "Call your father. Unless you are healed you cannot heal others." The wife encouraged him to visit his father, but the pain was too strong. After some time, he agreed to do so. The first thing that Roscoe did was to tell his father all the bad things that he had done. But he finished by saying, "Well, maybe we can be friends". The healing process began. If we are going to successfully minister in our own families, we need to look at the hurting issues of our own life and go down the difficult road of forgiveness. God's power gives the words of love when needed. Today Roscoe and his father talk by phone weekly. The Holy Spirit burned out all the anger, resentment and hostility. Roscoe is there now for his aged father.

If you have deep, painful memories, write a letter to God expressing your hurts. Tell Him what is on your heart. By writing this out, it helps get the pent-up feelings released, it aids in finding closure on the emotional wounds, and speeds the healing process. The captive is set free. Then burn the letter.

Most families at some time are dysfunctional. It is said that 95% of families are dysfunctional at some time, and the other 5% are in denial. We don't have the ability alone to heal ourselves or our dysfunctional families, but God can. Remember, nothing is too difficult for Him. The Father has power. We can't always remove the existing problem but can process it in a positive way. Even good can come out of bad.

## CONCLUSION

Are there problems that are tearing your family apart? Are there problems with your children or your spouse? Are there problems about which you cannot even talk to your friends or family? Why not take them to the all powerful God, your Father, in prayer. Indeed, "A father to the fatherless, a defender of widows, is God in his holy dwelling. God sets the lonely in families" (Ps. 68:5). The Family Book invites you to cast "all your care upon Him, for He cares for you" (1 Peter 5:7). God can be trusted and depended upon. He is the Father of all human families. He is the God of the impossible and nothing is too difficult for Him.

The Family Book illustrates this through a story that Jesus Christ Himself narrated. A wealthy father had two sons. The younger son did not want to be part of the family anymore, but wished to see attractions in other places of the world. One day he asked and received his portion of the family inheritance. Although not rightfully his until the death of his parents, at his insistence the father gave him his part of the inheritance. Wishing to be away from the father's instruction and his mother's call, he left for a far off country, far from home. Having spent all his money on friends, enticing attractions, and unwise choices, this son of a rich man stood penniless on the street—no place to live, no food to eat, and no one to love him. Finally, he managed to land a job as a pig herder. This involved taking care of the pigs in every way. Being very hungry, he even gratefully ate pig's food.

One day he remembered his father and his love. He realized that even his father's servants lived a better life than he did. He decided, "I will rise and go home to my father." On the way home he rehearsed a confession he would make to his father, "Father, I have sinned against heaven and against you. I am no longer worthy to be called your son; make me like one of your hired men" (Lk. 15:18, 19). But the father was there waiting, looking down the road, hoping that someday his son would come back home.

The Family Book continues the story, "So he got up and went to his father. But while he was still a long way off, his father saw him and filled with compassion for him; he ran to his son, threw his arms around him and kissed him" (Lk. 15:20). This run-away son did not have a chance to complete his confession. For his father interrupted to order the servants to prepare a welcome-home banquet. When all the guests were in place, the father made a speech, "This son of mine was dead and is alive again; he was lost and found" (Lk. 15:24). And never had they had a greater celebration in the father's house.

The dictionary gives two different definitions of "prodigal": 1) "wasteful," "reckless," and 2) "lavishly abundant," "profuse." We usually speak of the story of the Prodigal Son—a son who was wasteful and reckless of his inheritance. Some have suggested that the story is really about the Prodigal Father—a father who was lavishly abundant in his love. God is the Prodigal Father. He has given and given, more than we would ever have anticipated. He gave all heaven in one gift—His own Son to save lost humanity. His gift was copious and lavish; it was abundant. He could have given no more.

## CALL FOR DECISION

Now, I'm going to speak a word to the fathers here present. I'd like to have a special prayer that God will bless you in your fatherhood. It isn't always easy being father. I would like to invite all the fathers to come forward. This is a special time for you. Would you like to be a better father? Will all the fathers please come for a special prayer? Let me ask God's blessings on you. What a great privilege and responsibility is yours. Fathers, do you have a child who is having a difficult time and needs special prayer. If so, raise your hand.

## PRAYER

Lord we have not known You as we ought. Our knowledge of You, Father, is partial and imperfect, but thank You that You have revealed to us through Jesus that You, Father, love us. What great joy it will be when one day we will be able to look at your face and know You better as our Father who helped us through our difficult times on earth.

Heavenly Father, You see this group of fathers who have come forward tonight. We want your blessing put upon each. You as the Prodigal Father have put Your best robe on each one of us fathers. Forgive us when we haven't been the kind of fathers that we should have been. Put the family ring on our finger because each of us rightfully belong to Your family. Angels sing a song of celebration for us and our children as we join the family of the Heavenly Father.

Our Heavenly Father, we thank You that You are our Father. As we bow here we say we each want to be the kind of father that You have been to us. May we each be blessed and empowered by You to lead our families toward the heavenly home. Give us wisdom and strength according to our needs and help us with the difficult tasks and problems we encounter. Remember the needs of our children and our wives. Some of the children who may be young or old may be choosing the wrong ways of life. Soften their hearts and convict them and convert each. Help them to choose You as their heavenly Father. It is our desire to turn our hearts in love towards our children as Elijah instructed. We, ourselves, accept You as our Father tonight, and rededicate ourselves to be Your children. We pray in Jesus' name. Amen.

## Seminar/Homework Activities

• Honor all fathers present in the meeting. Give them a gift or a card with promises printed or written on it. Make a covenant to reaffirm each father's responsibility to lead His children to the Heavenly Father. Invite the whole family to form a circle as family units. Emphasize the concept that the love of the Heavenly Father encircles each family circle. Others may join the circle and pray for the father specifically.

• At home during family worship or during individual devotion time, do a search for who God the Father is and record these characteristics. These can be turned into an adoration prayer. For example, God is merciful, God is just, God is faithful, etc.

• Share positive qualities of your father or other fathers you've observed OR talk about what makes a good father.

• Discuss some of the following "father guidelines":

1. Love your children unconditionally.

2. Discipline constructively.

3. Spend quality time with them.

4. Teach them right from wrong.

5. Develop mutual respect.

6. Listen! Really listen! But talk also.

7. Offer encouragement and guidance.

8. Foster independence.

9. Add other guidelines you think of.

• Make a list of things that can enhance father-child relations like:

1. Plan a fun family activity within the next 2 weeks.

2. Take one child at a time to do something special with them.

3. Write an appreciation card to each child.

4. Plan a father-son weekend with a number of fathers and their sons.

5. Add something from your experience.

• Have the fathers fill in a response card with their name, address, phone number and prayer needs. Assure them that a prayer group will continue to pray for them and their families.

• Impress on fathers that the family tie remains powerful and strong as long as the family maintains a continued connection with God. God is at the head of the triangle and the husband, wife, and children are at the base of the triangle, but without God there couldn't be a realistic triangle or a strong family. This is a "unity triangle" enabling the family on earth to be united as one. What can be done by father and family to have this vital connection with God?

### References and Bibliography

Biller, H., & Meredith, D. (1974) *Father power.* New York: David McKay & Co.

Canfield, K. (2002). Secretos de la paternidad eficaz. *Mundo Familiar.* Montemorelos, N. L., Mexico: Universidad de Montemorelos. I Seminario Internacional de Vida Familiar, 8-14.

Chapman, G. (1997). *The five love languages of children.* Chicago, IL: Moody Press.

Habenicht, D. (1994, December 8). What kind of leader are you? *Adventist Review, 171,* (49), 12-14.

Habenicht, D. (1994, December 15). You can change your leadership style. *Adventist Review, 171,* (50), 8-10.

Masters, L. (1971). The passing of the dominant husband-father. *Impact of Science on Society, 21,* 21-30.

Mussen, P. H. (Ed.) (1983). *Handbook of child psychology, 4th edition, vol. IV.* New York: John Wiley & Sons.

White, E.G. (1942). *The ministry of healing.* Boise, ID: Pacific Press Publishing Association.

# WIN!- A *Wellness* Program Integrating Needs

## by John B. Youngberg

## IN A NUTSHELL

The WIN! program is built on an acronym "wellness integrating needs." The full name is "**WIN!**—A **W**ellness Program **I**ntegrating **N**eeds." As an evangelistic tool for family life educators, health care professionals, pastors, and trained lay persons, its uniqueness lies in its human needs approach that integrates the wellness of three spheres—human relationships, mind/spirit, and body. It is informational, relational, and transformational, the first curricular approach among Seventh-day Adventists, we believe, that gives a balanced treatment to these three spheres and targets synergy where the whole of the factors is greater than the sum of their parts.

Each sphere has 7 factors—21 in all. Almost all presentations will have:

- A scientific basis, a foundation of current empirical material.

- A spiritual (mind/spirit) anchor.

- A soft center—tender (affective domain).

- Use narrative pedagogy, illustrating with personal stories of positive happenings by someone who followed the lifestyle of the particular factor.

- A conclusion calling for decision/lifestyle growth/covenant.

## BRIEF BIBLICAL EVIDENCE FOR THE WHOLISTIC APPROACH

Jesus asked the sick man at the Pool of Bethesda: "Wilt thou be made *whole*" (John 5:6)? The physician, Luke, proclaimed a truly balanced picture of human development when he said, "And Jesus increased in wisdom [mental], and stature [physical], and in favor with God [spiritual] and men [relational]" (Luke 2:52).

Speaking in Matthew of the great commandment, Jesus quotes from Deuteronomy where the imperative for our wholistic response has as its base the completeness and oneness of God: "You shall love the Lord your God with all your heart, with all your soul, and with all your mind" and "your neighbor as yourself" (Matt. 22:37, 39). Paul called believers to be set apart "completely," preserving their "whole spirit, soul, and body" blameless, awaiting the coming of Christ (1 Thess. 5:23). Although biblical statements vary slightly on the names for the dimensions, what is common is that God wants us to have a balanced state of wellness—harmony among the various integral components and factors of our being.

## PERSPECTIVE OF ELLEN WHITE ON WHOLISTIC HEALTH AND WELLNESS

If one were to attempt to compress Ellen White's writing into meta-themes, the field of theology could be captured in the phrase "the great controversy perspective." For the fields of education and healing, the word would be "balance." For well over 100 years Seventh-day Adventists have been entrusted with a message of balanced wholistic wellness to share with the world. In *Education* (1903), Mrs. White stated that true education "has to do with the whole being. . . . It is the harmonious development of the physical, the mental, and the spiritual powers" (p. 13). However, for her most keenly honed expression about health ("wellness," to use a modern term), we must turn to *The Ministry of Healing* (1905). This classic statement, marching orders for much of the health education of the SDA Church, has been called the "wheel of health" and "the eight natural remedies." "Pure air, sunlight, abstemiousness, rest, exercise, proper diet, the use of water, trust in divine power—these are the true remedies" (p. 127). Throughout *The Ministry of Healing*, all of these "eight natural remedies" are covered. Seven chapters are dedicated to the family! In the thinking of Ellen White, family relationships have something to do with healing.

The "Eight Natural Remedies" model has had success. In a day when so much of modern medicine emphasized the study of disease instead of the study of wellness, our noble small army of health educators should be lauded for their wonderful work. Emphasis on these "Eight Natural Remedies" has been a good start, yet our "blueprint" calls for an even broader and expansive vision and outreach. "There is need of a broader scope, a higher aim." (*Education*, p. 13). We can move forward on past successes. We must go beyond an institutional medical base. We must get to the multitudes and meet their felt needs. We must muster the untapped human resources of the local church and move toward "felt-needs evangelism," reaching out to the community and people in their homes.

Christ's method alone will give true success in reaching the people. The Saviour mingled with men as one who desired their good. He showed His sympathy for them, ministered to their needs, and won their confidence. Then He bade them, "Follow Me" (*The Ministry of Healing*, p. 143).

Further, an active campaign in our local churches based on wellness is not just one option among many others to be chosen at whim. An eschatological reality looms ahead: "I wish to tell you that soon there will be no work done in ministerial lines but medical missionary work" (*Counsels on Health*, p. 533; *Last Day Events*, p. 80).

## BRIEF SCIENTIFIC EVIDENCE FOR EXPANDING BEYOND THE BIOLOGICAL MODEL

As informed Christians, we should be ever seeking a coherent and integrated understanding of theological and scientific constructs. Our understanding of the universe and its laws is rooted in Scripture but we believe that empirical methodologies and statistical tools can illumine our knowledge and assist us in delving into biblical concepts. Science doesn't *prove* the Bible. Divine revelation is sufficient to engender belief. Frank Gabelein coined the phrase "All truth is God's truth." We seek truth and Truth wherever found. Scientific research is an example of faith seeking understanding.

Up-to-date research can help us catch multifaceted reflections of light on theological constructs such as forgiveness, love, hope, and service and on such relational issues as communication, commitment, and social support. This article will present brief evidence that relational and spiritual factors are vital to wholistic wellness effecting measurable changes in biological outcomes.

The classic Alameda County Study (Belloc & Breslow, 1972; Breslow & Enstrom, 1980) showed

that 7 physical health habits were predictive of age-adjusted mortality rates and lent "support to the hypothesis that good health practices and not the initial health status of the survey respondents are largely responsible for the observed mortality relationships" (p. 469). A study on the same population by Berkman and Syme (1979) showed that people who lacked social and community ties were 1.9 to 3.1 times more likely to die during the nine-year follow-up period from 1965-1974. A continuing follow-up to 1982 showed that "those with close social ties and unhealthful lifestyles actually lived longer than those with poor social ties but more healthful behaviors (Ornish, 1998, p. 42).

Ornish (1998) summarizes 8 studies from 1979-1994 in various countries." Those who were socially isolated had at least two to five times the risk of premature death from all causes when compared to those who had a strong sense of connection and community." Ornish, whose research first proved that by changing lifestyle it was possible to reverse heart disease, writes: "I am not aware of any other factor in medicine that has a greater impact on our survival than the healing power of love and intimacy. Not diet, not smoking, not exercise, not stress, not genetics, not drugs, not surgery" (1998, back cover). He reports on the Harvard Study by Dr. Stanley King, et al. who randomly chose 126 healthy men from Harvard classes and followed them for 35 years with detailed medical and psychological histories. King found a tremendous impact of warmth and closeness (love) on biological health. 100% of the subjects who perceived low warmth and closeness with both parents had diagnosed diseases in midlife, as compared with only 45% of men who indicated that their relationships in childhood with both father and mother had been warm and close. Slightly over 70% of subjects had diagnosed diseases in midlife when warmth and closeness in childhood was high with mother, but low with father. The percentage rose to nearly 80% when the warmth and closeness with mother was low, but high with father.

There is on-going research at Stanford, University of Wisconsin—Madison, Hope College and other institutions sponsored by the John Templeton Foundation since 1998 on the relationship of Forgiveness and Health. Charlotte van Oyen Witvliet (2001) reported that heart rates and blood pressures were considerably lower when participants forgave rather than when they held grudges. When they held a grudge it made them sweat, a sign that their nervous systems were on high alert. However, forgiveness left them feeling calm and in control. Witvliet writes that "forgiving and unforgiving responses could have long term effects on health if they are sufficiently frequent, intense, and enduring. When physiological systems remain activated, they can influence cardiovascular health" (p. 218). Thoresen et al. (2000) found that "increased frequency of forgiving others…could function to reduce the chronicity of distress (e.g., anger, blame, and vengeful thoughts and feelings) that has prospectively been shown to alter brain, coronary, and immune functioning" (p. 259).

Even this short listing of studies shows that there are scientific reasons for including mind/spirit factors and relational (family) factors in a wholistic model for wellness. The biological factors are necessary but not sufficient.

## THE WIN! (WELLNESS INTEGRATING NEEDS) MODEL

(See Figure 1)

## ITS SPHERES AND FACTORS
*(with synonyms and terms explaining the scope of the fields)*

**A. MIND/ SPIRIT** [God-given identity, essence of who you are. "Inner strength" (Eph. 3:16 *The Message*). The Ruler of Universe wants to rule from the center of my life. Core. Inner sanctum]

1. Love (in the hub position)

2. Brainpower/Strength of mind/the Will in lifestyle change

3. Hope/ Optimism/Positive attitude/Cheerfulness/ Humor/Joy+

4. Spirituality [include 2 Cosmic Powers as a subset]

5. Trust/Prayer

6. Forgiveness

7. Joy of service/Reason for being/*Raison d'être*/ Mission/Job satisfaction/Immersion in a noble cause bigger than you are

## FIGURE 1

**B. BODY** [*Avenue, Means, Conduit, Vehicle, Temple*]

1. Nutrition

2. Exercise

3. Water

4. Sunlight (numbers 2, 3, 4, 6 point to advantages of contact with nature)

5. Self-discipline/ Temperance

6. Air

7. Rest

**C. RELATIONSHIPS** [*Influence, Family*]

1. Appreciation

2. Family time/ Priorities

3. Communication

4. Facing crisis/ Resilience

5. Social networking/ Group support

6. Close emotional ties/ Commitment

7. Resolving problems/ Removing blocks

## COMMENTARY ON THE WIN! MODEL (Figure 1)

1. The contribution of the present model as compared to other commonly used models in wellness, is the overt recognition of a cluster of Mind/Spirit factors (especially Love) in a hub position. Mind/Spirit is not a tack-on to the biological components, but is given equal, even fountainhead standing. This is congruent with our understanding of the nature of humankind. Similarly, this model recognizes the whole cluster of relationship factors centering in the family, largely absent in other wellness models. Relationships are where life is lived and have a tremendous impact on the happiness of the individual and of the family.

2. The presenter(s) should begin with the factor which is closest to the felt needs of the targeted audience and which is in accord with his/ her expertise or experience.

3. All the 21 factors do not need to be presented in one series. The audience may need a rest at some point and then pick up the thread with renewed energy. The 7 factors in Vol. 1 would make a good opening series.

4. Balance and equilibrium are the watchwords of WIN! Often, positive factors turn negative if they are over-emphasized at the expense of other factors. Many professional athletes have super-developed bodies, for example, but are pygmies in the Relationships Sphere.

## DEALING WITH PROBLEM AREAS

WIN! deals largely with positive factors which promote well-being, i.e., with *salutaris*, "promoting or conducive to some beneficial purpose; wholesome . . .health" (Random House Unabridged Dictionary). Although wellness models do not emphasize pathology, yet they must not be blind to the fact that clinical problems and pathology do exist, and may block the creation of a wellness-friendly environment. Experience shows that the same factors which prevent disease and maintain health oftentimes assist nature in restoration from disease, especially when illness has not arrived at an advanced stage.

Attention will be paid in WIN! to resolving problems and remedying unhealthy responses which impede particular wellness factors. For example, moral failure will militate against the Close Emotional Ties/Commitment Factor. This may give rise to anger, hostility, and bitterness. If the individual feels unforgiven, he/she in turn may become unforgiving of others. The Love factor is compromised when the individual no longer expresses deep love for his/her mate. A *block* frustrates the synergy of wholistic wellness which should flow throughout Divine-human, intra- and interpersonal relationships. Sexual addictions and unfaithfulness may block the benefits of the Close Emotional Ties/ Commitment Factor. If cherished, these blocks will alter the equilibrium of the tri-dimensional model, change the flow from positive to negative energy, displace the master Love dynamic with selfishness, and compromise the individual's "Inner Strength." For wholistic healing of body, mind/spirit, and relationships, the problem of moral failure must be addressed. Other blocks or walls may also present themselves, impeding other factors. For these reasons, the Resolving Problems factor has been added to the Relationships Sphere. (See Figures 1, 2).

## USES IN EVANGELISM

WIN! could be used by family life educators, ministers, laymen, and health-care professionals in public evangelism or in neighborhood groups in homes.

The topics are different from those presented in the *Family Life at Its Best* (Family Evangelism) series described elsewhere in this planbook. *Family Life at Its Best* is slanted more to the family and has more doctrinal content. WIN! tends to be more scientific and emphasizes health benefits. The two approaches are very compatible and users may end up using a creative synthesis of the two models.

WIN! is not intended to be a whole-message doctrinal approach. WIN! could be used as an entry event, a "sowing" series. It aims at transforming minds, bringing about a conversion experience, and producing lifestyle change. If this happens, it won't be hard for the public to accept prophetic and doctrinal truths as presented in a Revelation Seminar or other follow-up series.

WIN! is built around human needs. It is relational and tends to build a sense of belongingness between participants. This is nurtured by group activities and by the encouragement people to share their positive experiences. If we capitalize on bonding and forming friendships in our evangelism, members of the public will not find it difficult to join with other friends in a community of believers.

Presentations in WIN! include an abundance of recent Internet references. As there may be more material than can be used, we recommend that users be selective, include illustrations from the culture of the audience, and use a generous sprinkling of their own experiences which will give the message authenticity and distinctiveness.

**FIGURE 2**

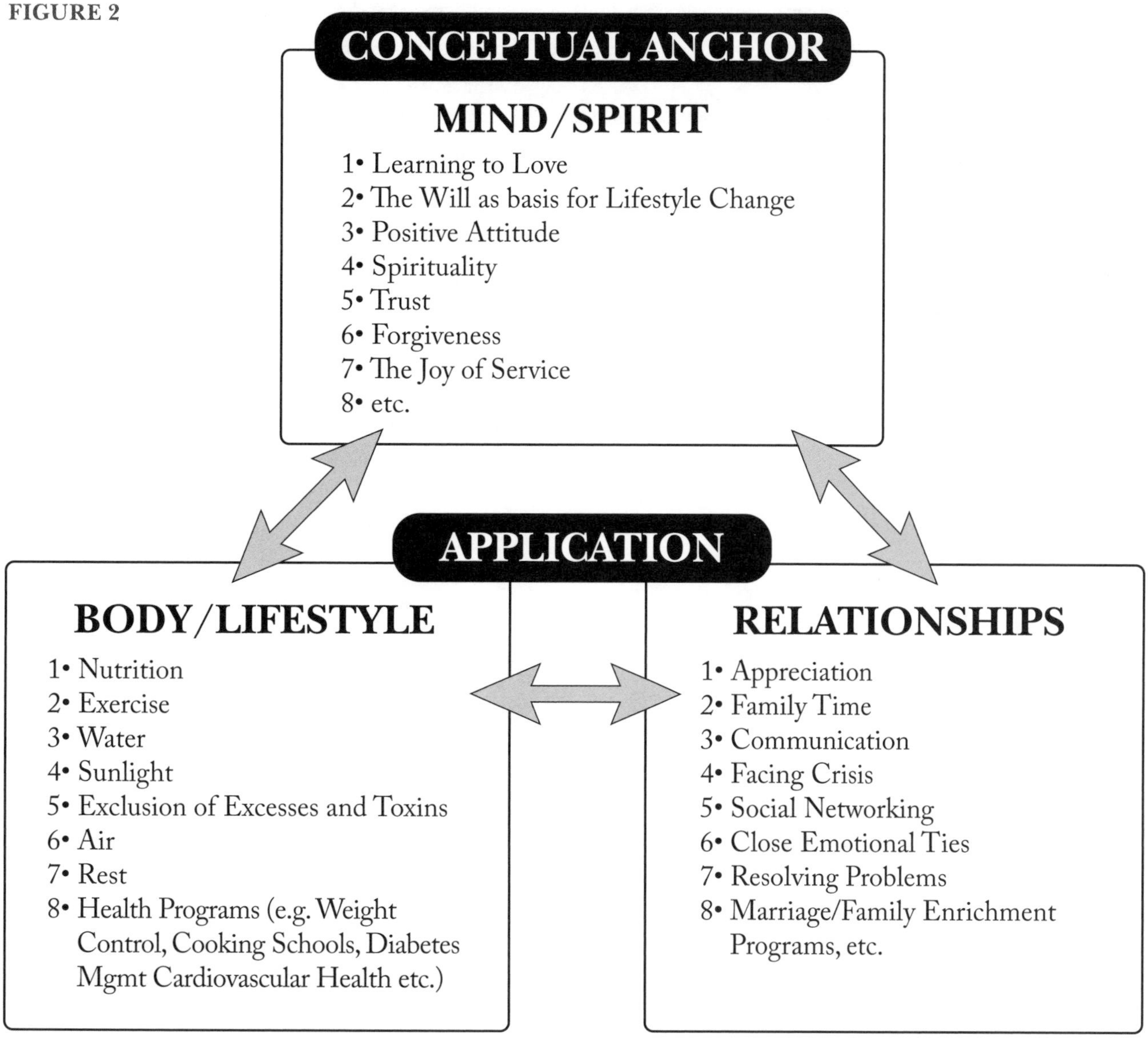

## CONCEPTUAL ANCHOR

### MIND/SPIRIT

1• Learning to Love
2• The Will as basis for Lifestyle Change
3• Positive Attitude
4• Spirituality
5• Trust
6• Forgiveness
7• The Joy of Service
8• etc.

## APPLICATION

### BODY/LIFESTYLE

1• Nutrition
2• Exercise
3• Water
4• Sunlight
5• Exclusion of Excesses and Toxins
6• Air
7• Rest
8• Health Programs (e.g. Weight Control, Cooking Schools, Diabetes Mgmt Cardiovascular Health etc.)

### RELATIONSHIPS

1• Appreciation
2• Family Time
3• Communication
4• Facing Crisis
5• Social Networking
6• Close Emotional Ties
7• Resolving Problems
8• Marriage/Family Enrichment Programs, etc.

## PUBLICATION AND AVAILABILITY

Chapters are being contributed by outstanding authorities in the respective topics. John B. Youngberg is senior editor, bringing focus, and unity of thought and presentation. John and Millie Youngberg have pilot tested 7 topics in Berrien Springs, Michigan. Results have been optimal. The audiences have been most appreciative of the new and creative approach. God willing, during Spring 2004, Volume 1, with complete presentation text and PowerPoint illustrations for these 7 topics will be published. Two other volumes will follow. Volume 1 will include a complete text on

Appreciation, Brain Power, Exercise, Forgiveness, Close Emotional Ties (Commitment), Nutrition, and Love. Notice that 3 topics are from the Mind/Spirit sphere, 2 from the Body sphere, and 2 from the Relationships sphere. Reference will be made to Inventories which can be used to evaluate and give personal insight to participants.

After April 2004, for information and availability contact: Gary R. Hilbert, Mgr., Christian Book Center (ABC), 8980 S. US 31, Berrien Springs, MI 49103. Tel. 877-227-4800 or 269-471-7331. Email: michiganabc@yahoo.com.

## Bibliography

Belloc, N. B., & Breslow, L. (1972). Relationship of physical health status and health practices. *Preventive Medicine, 1*, 409-421.

Berkman, L. F., & Syme, S. L. (1979). Social networks, host resistance, and mortality: A nine-year follow-up study of Alameda country residents. *American Journal of Epidemiology, 109* (2).

Breslow, L., & Enstrom, J. E. (1980). Persistence of health habits and their relationship to mortality. *Preventive Medicine, 9*, 469-483.

Ornish, D. (1998). Love and survival: The scientific basis for the healing power *of intimacy.* New York: HarperCollins Publishers.

Thoresen, C. E., Harris, A. H. S., & Luskin, F. (2000). Forgiveness and health: An unanswered question. In M.E. McCullough, K.I.

Pargament, & C.E. Thoresen (Eds.). *Forgiveness: Theory, research, and practicem* (254-280). New York: Guilford Press.

White, E.G. (1923). *Counsels on health.* Boise, ID: Pacific Press Publishing Association.

White, E.G. (1903). *Education.* Boise, ID: Pacific Press Publishing Association.

White, E. G. (1992). *Last day events.* Boise, ID: Pacific Press Publishing Association.

White, E.G. (1905). *The ministry of healing.* Boise, ID: Pacific Press Publishing Association.

Witvliet, C. V. O. (2001). Forgiveness and health: Review and reflections on a matter of faith, feelings, and physiology. *Journal of Psychology and Theology, 29* (3), 212-224.

# *Appreciation* — A Stimulant to Wholistic Wellness

**by John B. Youngberg**

*A sample presentation from WIN! A Wellness Program Integrating Needs*

## INTRODUCTION

Tenderly the emperor Shah Jahan spoke to his beloved wife Mumtaz, "You are such a source of strength and inspiration to me, I value your love." The ruler continued, "I do appreciate your many contributions to my life and the encouragement you give me."

It seemed to all the subjects of the kingdom that the royal couple shared a unique love for one another. Mumtaz was truly the pride of the palace and the Shah. But tragically, their life together did not last long. Mumtaz died shortly after giving birth, bringing deep sadness to Shah Jahan.

As a tangible expression of his appreciation for Mumtaz, Shah Jahan built a magnificent tomb for his wife and called it the Taj Mahal (tahj muh HAHL). It took 20,000 workmen more than ten years to construct this wonder of the world. Built with the most exquisite white marble and studded with precious stones, the Taj Mahal stands as a perpetual and perennial memorial of a husband's love and appreciation for his wife.

Although you and I may never afford to build a Taj Mahal to express appreciation to our husband, wife or child, frequent words of appreciation are buildings blocks in creating miniature "Taj Mahals" for our family members.

A northern businessman en route to Florida noticed a disabled car by the side of the road. The motorist was standing beside his car contemplating how to solve his problem. Since cell phones had not yet been invented, he was at the mercy of passing motorists. The businessman stopped and ascertained that a mechanic was needed. He took the man to the nearest town thirty miles away and arranged for towing at a garage that provided factory trained mechanic service. He drove him back to his car for security reasons and waited with the motorist for the tow truck. With the stranded motorist in his car, he followed the tow truck and crippled car back to the garage.

Numerous times on the way to the garage the man expressed his appreciation. The two men shook hands and the businessman went on his way to Florida. He gave no more thought to the incident until six months later when the Christmas season arrived. The United Parcel Service delivered a case of fresh Florida oranges and an expensive necktie. For years the businessman received oranges and a necktie at Christmas time from the recipient of his kindness who knew how to show appreciation.

These two incidents could be considered sufficient definition of appreciation, but we will receive an even broader meaning of the word by turning to the dictionary. Appreciation is recognition of the quality, the significance, or the magnitude of something or someone beneficial to you. Appreciation is an expression of gratitude. It is perceiving with aesthetic enjoyment even the little blessings. It means to cherish, prize, treasure, and value someone. Let us consider the positive effects of appreciation.

**ACTIVITY.** *Now, I want you all to stand. Think of someone you really appreciate (husband/wife, or a close friend) and share why you appreciate them. Share in groups of 2 or 3.*

## BENEFITS OF APPRECIATION TO RECIPIENTS

George Dawson, grandson of slaves, lived through the 20th century. He was born and raised in Marshall, Texas where he lived in a small cabin with his large family. Hard work kept him from schooling, but he always wanted to read. At age 98 he learned how. He and Richard Glaubman told his story in the book *Life Is So Good.*

George's father farmed him out to work for a neighbor, Mr. Little, for $1.50 a week because hard times had come, making it difficult to care for a large family. Twelve-year-old George spent four years sleeping in a dark shed and eating meals separate from the Little family. Mr. Little showed him what his work would be, emphasizing that he would be told only once. George applied himself to every task, but during his stay on the farm appreciation was not expressed.

It was not until his father came for him that he heard words of appreciation. George collected his meager belongings and put them in the burlap sack in which he had brought them four years earlier. He carried them to his father's wagon where Mr. Little was talking to his father. Mr. Little turned to George and said, "George, you've been a good worker, as good as any I've ever had." George was not used to such kind talk. All he could say was "Thank you." As he rode home in the wagon, George thought about how good the Little family treated him. That one expression of appreciation overshadowed the negatives he could have rehearsed.

An author who resides in Michigan, where winter brings cloudy days that far outweigh the number of sunny days, spent long hours at her word processor to produce her fifth book. Months after the book was released she was in the midst of the dreary days. Her spirits groaned and longed for leaves to appear on the trees. She dreamed of spring when she could shed her heavy winter coat. That's when the telephone rang.

The caller identified himself. Immediately she recognized the voice of her youth pastor when she was a child. He taught her camp craft, outdoor cooking, and hiking along with her friends who were trying to qualify for investiture in their club. He called to thank her for writing her latest book. He was deeply moved by the stories and uplifting concepts.

Later that week she told a friend, "I experienced a feeling of exhilaration for the rest of that dreary day. I completely forgot about the clouds and the leafless trees." Appreciation made a difference.

A hospice in Texas prevented professional burnout in staff members by providing a mini-retreat on a regular basis. In addition to massage, sauna, and strolls in the country, the staff engaged in an hour of affirmation. Each person expressed appreciation for some quality or helpful action on the part of every colleague. Appreciation enabled them to be emotionally present every day to dying people and their families.

A hospice chaplain, with 26 years of experience ministering to terminally ill patients, discovered that appreciation revived their sense of usefulness in spite of being bedridden. He was a master listener. When a patient reviewed his or her life, the chaplain asked him or her to teach him about their area of expertise. Before ending the visit he would say, "I really appreciate learning so much from you today. You have expanded my understanding. Thank you!"

Visit after visit the patients voluntarily taught the chaplain and received appreciation. Family members reported that their loved one was brighter and less depressed following a visit from the chaplain. This observation substantiates a study done by St. Christopher's Hospice of London. It revealed that pain levels were lower and the need for pain medication was less when the medical, social, emotional, and spiritual needs of the patients were adequately met. The chaplain was helping to meet those needs when he listened carefully and expressed appreciation.

"The consciousness of being appreciated is a wonderful stimulus and satisfaction. Sympathy and respect encourage the striving after excellence, and love itself increases as it stimulates to nobler aims" (*The Ministry of Healing*, p. 361). "Kind words, looks of sympathy, expressions of appreciation, would be to many a struggling and lonely one as the cup of cold water to a thirsty soul. A word of sympathy, an act of kindness, would lift burdens that rest heavily upon weary shoulders" (*The Ministry of Healing*, p. 23).

A stimulus, a cup of cold water—these analogies of appreciation written quite a long time ago shine a floodlight on appreciation. The word *stimulus* is defined as something that causes a response. It is an agent that elicits or accelerates a physiological or psychological activity. Synonyms of *stimulus* are words like *catalyst, impetus, impulse, incentive,* and *motivation.*

These definitions and synonyms were brought to life in the experience of an accountant who earned many thousands of dollars for the corporation where he worked for 16 years. The victim of downsizing, he took a job as a receiving clerk for a well known department store known for paying low wages. He earned a fraction of what he earned at the corporate office, but it kept bill collectors away from his door. His comments to a friend said much about appreciation.

"During my 16 years at my old job, I had 16 annual reviews. My superiors never thanked me for my accomplishments. They just told me what I did not do well. I could feel my motivation to excel declining as the years went by. I've been on the new job a year and one month. I had my first annual review. The manager's first remark was that he'd like to clone 10 of me. The manager had only words of praise and appreciation. You know what? His words of appreciation stirred something within me that made me break my back to do better work every day. I never received such words in 16 years and I savor every word my manager spoke that day." If you were to ask him whether those words of appreciation accelerated physical and psychological health, he would heartily agree. What about a cup of cold water? Can you identify with that?

Eleven men were the sole survivors of a merchant marine vessel sunk by an enemy torpedo during World War II. The ship sank in four minutes, leaving the eleven men on a life raft with enough water for a few days. For 52 days the raft bobbed up and down on the South Atlantic. In spite of severe rationing, the water supply ran out. Some of the men drank salt water from the sea and finally died. All of them pulled barnacles from the bottom of the raft and sucked the juice from them. In the morning, they licked the dew that had formed on the makeshift mast of their pitiful craft. After 52 days only 3 men were alive. The rescuers pulled the thirst-crazed survivors from the raft and gave them cold water to drink. They drank and wept at the same time.

We cannot survive without water to hydrate our bodies, neither can we be whole emotionally, physically, and spiritually without receiving and giving appreciation.

## SIGNIFICANCE OF APPRECIATION— EMPIRICAL EVIDENCE

Is there any empirical evidence to support the last statement? Very little research has been done on appreciation. Still in its fledgling state is research on the effects of gratitude, thankfulness, and appreciation on emotional, social, physical, and spiritual health. The researchers all indicate that further study is required to expand our understanding of the relationship between appreciation and full health.

Available findings are encouraging. From small beginnings we can confidently say that the principles of Scripture and observations of the helping professions are being substantiated by research.

In 1977, James J. Lynch, Professor of Psychology and Scientific Director of the Psychosomatic Clinics at the School of Medicine at the University of Maryland, wrote *The Broken Heart—The Medical Consequences of Loneliness*. While his research was not specifically about appreciation, it certainly was part of what he called *dialogue*. He indicated that without reciprocal sharing of all the joys, sorrows, hopes, and dreams, we are more apt to succumb to diseases that cause premature death. He called dialogue the elixir of life without which we cannot survive. He appealed to his readers that we either learn to live together or prematurely die alone.

In 1985, Lynch wrote *The Language of the Heart—The Body's Response to Human Dialogue*. In this work he demonstrated how the process of talking and listening to others dramatically affects the entire cardiovascular system. The human heart and circulation can be profoundly altered by human speech. We have what Lynch calls a *social membrane* that allows us to share common emotional experiences. This sharing has an effect on well-being.

In *A Cry Unheard - New Insights into the Medical Consequences of Loneliness* (2000), Lynch revised and added new material to his 1977 book at the request of medical schools. In this volume he shows how children who are underachievers in school feel isolated from the rest of the students. They do not receive affirmation and appreciation as do their peers who are scholastically successful. They find themselves unable to communicate with them and they withdraw. They experience loneliness that carries over to adulthood. This has a negative effect on total health.

Lynch states that children who receive *toxic talk - abusive language* from parents and others are forced into communicative isolation, social withdrawal, depression, and hopelessness that can last a lifetime. He believes that toxic talk can kill. It drives people into loneliness and physical disease. He even suggests that *communicative disease* will compete with *communicable disease* as a major health threat in the twenty-first century.

Memories of long-forgotten childhood struggles seem to be etched in their hearts and blood vessels, erupting as soon as they begin to talk about them. Speaking about the lack of love in childhood, the loss of love early in life, and early emotional traumas, particularly school failure, rank among the topics that elicit the greatest cardiovascular changes. (Lynch, 2000, p. 314)

Lynch suggests that rather than praising children who score highest on some achievement test, we should reward children and institutions who score high on brotherly love. Lynch's research gives us cause to believe that positive words of appreciation enhance life and produce health for those who receive them. What about the effects of appreciation on those who bestow it?

## BENEFITS OF BESTOWING APPRECIATION

In 1995 Rollin McCraty and associates analyzed heart rate variability on healthy volunteers and volunteers with a number of pathological states using the *freeze-frame* technique. Three to 24 months before the study began participants were trained to deliberately focus on sincerely appreciating someone. They also learned to deliberately focus on situations that still evoked the emotion of anger. During the study, a 5-minute baseline period was established, then half of the volunteers focused for 5 minutes on appreciation. The other half focused for 5 minutes on a situation that evoked anger.

All the volunteers had no history of cardiovascular disease and were not taking any prescription drugs known to affect cardiovascular function. Alcohol, caffeine, and nicotine were not used for 4 hours before the testing.

The researchers concluded that enhancing positive emotional states, such as appreciation, could have an important effect on cardiovascular function. The resulting positive changes in heart rate variability may be beneficial in treating people with hypertension and reducing risk of sudden death in patients who have congestive heart failure and coronary artery disease. They recommended larger studies to determine the clinical use of this type of intervention.

Researcher Michael E. McCullough stated that this experimental research indicates that discrete experiences of gratitude and appreciation may cause increases in parasympathetic myocardial control. In 2002, McCullough and associates published their research in *Journal of Personality and Social Psychology*. Their study used self-rating and observer rating to ascertain the strengths of people who have a grateful, appreciative disposition. The following traits can be attributed to recognizing and responding to the benevolence of others with gratitude and appreciation in contrast to those who are not appreciative:

1. Their feelings of gratitude are more intense, occur more frequently, span a greater number of life circumstances, and include a greater number of people.

2. They attribute their well-being to a wide range of people.

3. They appreciate the good things in life and do not take them for granted.

4. They have sensitivity toward and concern for others.

5. They are more empathic and willing to help and support others.

6. They are less materialistic.

7. They tend to be spiritually inclined and recognize non-human forces contributing to their well-being.

8. They are less envious of others.

9. They rate higher in positive emotions and life satisfaction.

Robert A. Emmons and Michael E. McCullough published their research in 2003 in *Journal of Personality and Social Psychology*. By using weekly and daily journaling of moods, coping behaviors, health practices, physical symptoms, and overall life appraisals, they found that counting blessings had emotional and interpersonal benefits compared to the control group. A few of them are listed below:

1. They experienced fewer symptoms of physical illness.

2. They spent more time exercising.

3. They felt better about life in general and were optimistic about the upcoming week.

4. They felt more connected with others.

5. They felt more loved and cared for by others.

6. They were more likely to build and strengthen a sense of spirituality.

7. They engaged in flexible and creative thinking.

8. They were better able to cope with stress and adversity.

Very few empirical studies have been done on the emotional, physical, social, and spiritual effects of appreciation, but the similarity of outcomes in the studies presented here is impressive. It appears that appreciation is a factor in total well-being. Apart from research, many people attest to the fact that being appreciative has many benefits.

A traveling lecturer often spent hours of layover time in airports. Rather than pity himself and become bored, he looked for custodial workers who were picking up discarded newspapers and emptying trash receptacles. He thanked them for keeping the airport tidy and expressed appreciation for their attention to little details. He often inquired about their family and shared pictures of his family. It provided them with a little respite from their labor. When he was asked why he did it, he said, "It allows me to switch from self-focus to others-focus. It brightens my day and gives me and the workers a chance to make a new friend."

A church pastor had to be out of town at the time when a faithful parishioner was hospitalized for surgery. Many people appreciate a pastoral visit before and after surgery, but this woman received neither. Instead of grumbling about pastoral neglect, she recounted all the times when she was encouraged by the pastor. During her recuperation she crocheted a colorful afghan for the pastor and his wife. She sincerely believed that her appreciation afghan facilitated the healing process.

In *Letters to a Young Therapist* (2003), Mary Pipher states that having a satisfying life has to do with much more than the absence of tragedy. It has to do mainly with appreciating what we have.

M. J. Ryan spends most of her book, *Attitudes of Gratitude* (1999), listing the benefits of showing appreciation and gratitude. She states that it is impossible to show appreciation and be angry at the same time. "Whenever we are appreciative, we are filled with a sense of well-being and swept up by the feeling of joy" (p. 14). She believes that counting our blessings literally bathes us inwardly with good hormones. The more we are thankful, the more light comes into our life and the more we shine out to the dark world around us.

## WHAT ARE RELIGIOUS AUTHORS SAYING?

James J. Lynch (2000) observed that we are dissolving into a tribe of *I* people without the collective *we*. Focusing on self seems to permeate many of the self-help books sold in religious book stores. It is disappointing to thumb through tables of content and indexes of book after book and not find the word *appreciation*. Michael E. McCullough (2002) is to be commended for his work in this area inasmuch as he is associate professor in the Department of Religious Studies at the University of Miami. Dr. Archibald D. Hart of Fuller Theological Seminary wrote *15 Principles for Achieving Happiness* (1988). His words are significant. "We have forgotten how to appreciate the little things of life" (p. 79). "We are constantly gifted with a stream of little things which can help restore our mental and emotional balance and provide us with a rich resource for happiness—if we learn to appreciate them" (p. 82). "A generation incapable of appreciating quiet and solitude will be a generation of people who are spiritually deaf, with no ears for

God, and spiritually mute, with no voice to sing His praises" (p. 84).

The prolific writer and church leader, Ellen G. White, wrote the classic book *The Ministry of Healing*. Three statements speak eloquently about the value of being appreciative. "If human beings would open the windows of the soul heavenward, in appreciation of the divine gifts, a flood of healing virtue would pour in" (p. 116). "Nothing tends more to promote health of body and of soul than does a spirit of gratitude and praise. It is a positive duty to resist melancholy, discontented thoughts and feelings—as much a duty as it is to pray" (p. 251). "Morning, noon, and night, let gratitude as a sweet perfume ascend to heaven" (p. 253).

A chaplain in a psychiatric hospital verified this saying. A patient, Eleanor, had been treated for depression many times in his hospital, and each time she was admitted, he visited her. Something about Eleanor aroused his curiosity. Her conversation was always negative, with complaints about the insensitive nurses, the tasteless food, the tough meat, the mean therapists, and the psychiatrists who were interested in nothing but getting rich. The chaplain knew that her observations were irrational. He also noticed that she was not responding well to her medication.

One day the chaplain announced to Eleanor that he had a cure for her depression. She perked up and wanted to know immediately what it was. The chaplain said, "Eleanor, I want you to make a list of all the things you think you *should* be thankful for. Every morning and every night read your list over several times. The second part of the cure is to express appreciation to one nurse for something each day. The third part is to write a letter to a friend back home with words of encouragement."

A few days later Eleanor enthusiastically shared her list with the chaplain. "Listen to all the things I'm thankful for." She told him what she appreciated about a nurse and talked about her letter to a friend. She began to respond to her medication better, went to chapel and sang her favorite song, "God Will Take Care of You," with enthusiasm. Her demeanor brightened. She smiled and laughed while watching TV. She was discharged from the hospital and was never admitted again.

When Ellen White spoke about a flood of healing virtue pouring in as a result of showing appreciation, she is speaking about total healing. The reason is simple. A person is not divided into parts unrelated to each other. William R. Miller and Kathleen A. Jackson wrote in *Practical Psychology for Pastors* (1995),

"Emotions have heavy physiological underpinnings" (p. 92). When one aspect of our life is unbalanced it affects every aspect of our life. When balance is maintained there is harmony and health. Appreciation opens the life to the divine gifts that otherwise could not be utilized because of self-focus.

James J. Lynch (2000) recommends that we look up and out. Too long have we been told that introspection is the way to healing. Too long have we been told that people and situations in the past are to blame for our present misery. It is high time that we are told to open the windows of the soul heavenward and outward to the needs of others. Upward and outward are the key words. Appreciation for the little things in life, for the generous gifts of God, for the blessings of relationship with others, is the way to open the windows of the soul.

A Maranatha International volunteer who has taken young Americans on many short term mission trips observed that youth who have everything handed to them experience an attitude adjustment when they come face to face with poverty. In spite of poverty, the people they come to help are happy and not self-focused. They express appreciation for the smallest favors.

Their contentment and happiness come from looking upward and outward. This was exemplified by a shoeshine boy who cleaned and polished a volunteer's shoes. When it came time to do the final buffing, the boy, for lack of a buffing cloth, took off his shirt. He buffed the shoes with his shirt, then put it on again. This is just one example of how appreciation expressed in the midst of poverty can break through the culture of self-gratification.

A cautionary word is in order when speaking about religious writers. Some authors pose as religious, when in reality they are metaphysical practitioners who believe that gratitude and appreciation are deep within the infinite soul waiting to be released by meditation and other practices. They seldom mention "God," and occasionally refer to a higher power. They promote the ideas of human potential and would totally disagree with the apostle Paul's teaching that sinful humans are incapable of good apart from the enabling of God.

In Paul's letter to the Galatians, he teaches that virtues are the fruit of the Holy Spirit within a person who has committed himself or herself to God's leading (Gal. 5:22, 23). The list that Paul gives is not exhaustive and certainly would encompass appreciation and gratitude.

A significant number of these religious authors focus on the benefits of appreciation and gratitude for *you.* The emphasis is largely self-focused. This is contrary to Christian teaching. Appreciation is a gift from God. We are not naturally appreciative. When we invite God into our life, He infuses us with His love, joy, and gratitude. When we are awed by the eternally flowing stream of God's forgiveness flooding our soul, it changes the way we look at everything in life. We are no longer self-focused, but we have the heart of a servant. We are interested in the well-being of others.

## WHAT DOES THE BIBLE SAY ABOUT APPRECIATION?

The apostle Paul speaks often about appreciation, thankfulness, and rejoicing. "But we request of you, brethren, that you appreciate those who diligently labor among you, and have charge over you in the Lord and give you instruction, and that you esteem them very highly in love because of their work. Encourage the faint hearted" (1 Thess. 5:12, 14).

Paul's work for the early Christian Church was not a soft and easy job. He was thrown in jail, beaten, and harassed at every step of the way. If anyone was a candidate for burnout it was Paul. He knew the benefits of being appreciated. No doubt he saw the ill effects of ungratefulness. He met critics who had nothing but negative words. They tried to thwart his efforts in every city in which he preached. They had sour dispositions and a way of throwing water on new ideas. Paul's counsel to encourage the faint hearted came out of his own experience. Listen to these words. "Rejoice always; pray without ceasing; in everything give thanks; for this is God's will for you in Christ Jesus" (1 Thess. 5:18). The real challenge from Paul is this: "If anything is worthy of praise, let your mind dwell on these things" (Phil. 4:8).

After examining some of the research on the effects of appreciation, this biblical advice makes a lot of sense. The mind that dwells on benefits, blessings, and praiseworthy events will be a healthy mind. Following Paul's advice will lead to good health and satisfying relationships.

The Psalms are especially full of praise and appreciation to God. When we are always aware of the little blessings, we will always have cause to express our appreciation to God. Henri J. M. Nouwen said that to pray is to live. The life is a conversation with God. As our eyes and ears take in the beauties around us, we express appreciation. As we share quiet hours with friends, we verbalize our appreciation. As our olfactory nerves detect homemade bread and freshly pressed apple sauce, we show appreciation to God and the culinary specialists who created them. As we listen to the strains of a favorite hymn or the sooth-ing melody of a piano concerto, we whisper thanks to God who gave such talent to musicians. As the day ends and our head hits the pillow our sigh is an expression of gratitude. Paul said that the Christian overflows with gratitude.

Ten lepers, outcasts from society, came within hearing distance of Jesus. They apparently heard about Jesus' healing power and decided to make their request for healing. Jesus simply told them to go show themselves to the priests. Priestly inspection and clearance opened to door to these unfortunate ones to return to their homes. As they ran they unraveled the bandages on their hands and discovered to their delight that healthy skin had replaced the crippling disease. One leper was so overwhelmed with gratitude that he reversed his steps, returned to Jesus and fell at His feet. He poured out his appreciation and his praise. Jesus asked, "Where are the nine?"

Jesus wanted more than the eradication of leprosy in their bodies. He wanted a dynamic relationship that would open the way for more and more of God's grace to enrich them. This happened to the one healed leper who came to express appreciation. The biblical account is very brief, but with a little imagination the reader can picture that thankful man following Jesus and taking in every word He spoke. Some have even pictured the man going home from the crucifixion and weeping for hours. Perhaps he was a charter member of the early apostolic church.

Jesus commended that man for his expression of appreciation. He must have known that more than a body was healed. Restored were the man's self-esteem, his dignity, his ability to earn a living, and his rela-tionships with family and friends. The entire commu-nity was richer because appreciation followed healing.

Jesus told a story about a wealthy man who entrusted his goods to three servants while he went on a journey. When he returned he discovered that only two had used his goods wisely. To the two wise servants the owner said, "Well done, good and faithful servant. Enter into the joy of your Lord." Commentators believe that Jesus was revealing his own expression of apprecia-tion that He will utter to the faithful at the time of His second advent. It is good to notice that Jesus considers the expression of appreciation important.

A careful study of the Beatitudes shows the principles of the Kingdom of Heaven. The first three beatitudes pertain to self-emptying. This comes when we realize our spiritual poverty in the light of the righteous Lord. We acknowledge and confess our waywardness and receive the peace that comes with forgiveness. In the fourth beatitude we hunger and thirst for the grace of God that strengthens us to move from self-focus to other-focus. We are filled by the power of God's Spirit. The rest of the beatitudes describe how the Christian spills into the life of others. We invest our energies into the well-being of others. It is this experience of drawing closer to God each day that empowers us to show appreciation and kindness to others.

A man named Paul tells of life growing up in Lima, Peru. "Times were hard. My father, a pilot and business executive, was starting a new airline. He had put all of his capital into the business, and I remem-ber frequently hearing, 'We just don't have the money for that now.' One day he informed us children that mother's birthday was coming. He had saved a long time to buy her a bottle of her favorite perfume.

"I'll never forget the day we gathered in the kitchen and Father presented Mother with a beauti-fully wrapped gift," he continues. "With trembling hands she unwrapped the small bottle and read the label. Delight and surprise were evident on her face. Then it happened. Somehow Mother dropped the perfume, shattering it on the floor. We all gasped in unbelief. Without a moment's hesitation, Father knelt down, put some of the spilled perfume on his finger and gently touched it to Mother's neck, then he held her in his arms and kissed away her tears.

"Four months later Father was killed in a tragic airplane crash high in the Andes. Though that was 50 years ago, the tenderness my father expressed that day and the high value he placed upon Mother will remain with me as long as I live."

## CONCLUSION

It is unwise to advocate any one of the factors in wholistic wellness as a cure-all. The ideal to be recommended is incorporating into your life all of the factors that will be addressed in this series of presen-tations.

A body builder who was named Mr. Canada six consecutive years taught a class in total fitness. He showed pictures of men and women who had bulging muscles, but they were not flexible when it came to range of motion. He demonstrated in front of the class both power lifting and flexibility. His emphasis was on balancing the social, physical, emotional, and spiritual aspects of life.

Though initially we may have thought appreciation was related only to emotional health, we have seen that it carries over into our relationships at home, our success in the work place, our physical health, our service to others, and to our relationship with God.

**The alabaster box.** A young woman entered a small shop intent on buying some perfume. She had a special purpose for it and she wanted the best she could buy. Eyeing her critically, the shopkeeper decided she wasn't wealthy, so he offered something he thought would meet her needs. The fragrance was nice, but she said, "Do you have anything better than this?"

"Yes," he said, and took something else from the shelf. "But it costs much more." He opened it, and indeed, the fragrance was very delightful.

"Is this the very best that you have–the best in the whole store?" she persisted. The shopkeeper turned and surveyed the shelf of imported perfumes, rare fragrances from Egypt, India, and faraway lands of the East. "I have one other," he replied. "But it is very expensive. It comes sealed in an alabaster box." Her heartbeat quickened as she said, "May I see it, please?"

He removed it from the shelf. Her eyes sparkled as she fingered the highly-polished alabaster which protected the rare essence of spikenard. It would take every penny she had–300 pence–a year's wages for a working man in those time. Gladly paying the fee, the young woman–whose name was Mary–quickly began to untie the knots of twine still clinging to her precious gift, whispering to herself, "Nothing is too good for my Lord."

Mary had heard Jesus say He was soon to die, and she intended to use the costly ointment to prepare His body for burial. But she couldn't wait. At a special dinner, she was moved to break open the alabaster box and pour the perfume on Jesus' head. She was thankful that Jesus had forgiven her sins and she chose to lavish her gratitude on her Savior while He was still alive.

The fragrance of her gift of appreciation filled the whole house that day. It gladdened Jesus' heart with the assurance of her love. And shortly after, as He went down into the darkness of His great trial, in which almost everyone forsook Him, Jesus carried the memory of that sweet-smelling gift of love. Until time should be no more, that broken alabaster box tells the story of love, sacrifice, and appreciation.

## HOMEWORK ACTIVITY

*What could you do to show love and appreciation to the members of your family? Put an action plan together: Who? What? When? Share your action plan with someone.*

## APPEAL

We have just considered how to unleash the Appreciation Factor in this WIN! –Wellness Integrating Needs program. It can transform your life and your family! Then untie the knots. Break the alabaster box. Let its fragrance fill the whole house–your house. With its sweet perfume it will bring healing and wellness to your hearts.

## HANDOUT 1

**The Incomplete Story... • Page 115**

## HANDOUT 2

**Appreciation Exercises • Page 116**

# HANDOUT #1
# The Incomplete Story...

**One day 10 loathsome lepers came to Jesus by the seaside. Where am I in the story?**

☐ A spectator who says "clear these unclean critters out of here!"

☐ One of the 9 who were more interested in their benefit than in saying "Thank You!"

☐ The one who turned back to express his appreciation.

☐ The One who gave a healing touch to the "untouchables."

☐ Other _____

**One day a woman with a checkered past came to Jesus and anointed his head and feet with a costly perfume in an alabaster box. Jesus said that the story of what she did would be told forever in all the world. I am also telling a story every day by my life. Am I —**

☐ Like Simon

☐ Like Judas

☐ One of the many invitees who didn't know what to think

☐ Like Mary Magdalene

☐ Like Jesus who gratefully accepted the best gift that this sinner lovingly offered

☐ Other _____

**My thoughts on how these stories relate to me**

In the past _____

_____

_____

_____

_____

Now I choose by God's grace to be a new person who _____

_____

_____

_____

_____

### "I can do all things through Christ who strengthens me."
*–Paul in Philippians 4:13.*

## HANDOUT #2
# Appreciation Exercises

1. Keep an Appreciation Diary. Record expressions of appreciation you received and your reactions. Record your expressions of appreciation to others and your reactions.

2. Concentrate on what is right and good about people and situations.

3. Set aside several days for this exercise. In the morning, list everything that went wrong or that did not meet your expectations. In the afternoon, list everything that went right or that met your expectations. At the end of the day, record your emotional tone for morning and afternoon. Compare the two.

4. Set aside a time to think deeply about something in the natural world, the qualities of a close friend or relative, and God's love and plan to redeem us. Focus on increasing your wonderment and astonishment at the big and small characteristics of each.

5. Pretend that you are forced to downsize and move into a small facility. Think about what you will keep and why you appreciate what you keep.

6. Visit periodically with an intimate friend. Share stories of people, past and present, who you appreciate. Share experiences in life that you appreciate.

7. Phone, write, or e-mail words of appreciation to one person every day. When you see a friend, express your appreciation. Make it a habit.

8. Whenever you pray, express your appreciation to God for His blessings to you.

## Bibliography

Dawson, G., & Glaubman, R. (2000). *Life is so good*. New York: Penguin Books.

Emmons, R. A., & McCullough, M. E. (2003). Counting blessings versus burdens: An experimental investigation of gratitude and subjective well-being in daily life. *Journal of Personality and Social Psychology, 84* (2), 377-389.

Emmons, R. A., McCullough, M. E., & Tsang, J. (2002). The grateful disposition: A conceptual and empirical topography. *Journal of Personality and Social Psychology, 82* (1), 112-127.

Hart, A. D. (1988). *15 principles for achieving happiness*. Dallas, TX: Word Publishing.

Intrator, S. M. (2002). *Stories of the courage to teach: Honoring the teacher's heart*. San Francisco: Jossey-Bass Publishers.

Lynch, J. J. (2000). *A cry unheard: New insights into the medical consequences of loneliness*. Baltimore: Bancroft Press.

McCraty, R., Atkinson, M., Tiller, W. A., Rein, G., & Watkins, A. D. (1995). The effects of emotions on short-term power spectrum analysis of heart rate variability. *American Journal of Cardiology, 76* (14), 1089-1093.

Miller, W. R., & Jackson, K. A. (1995). *Practical psychology for pastors, 2nd edition*. Englewood Cliffs, NJ: Prentice Hall.

Palmer, P. J. (1998). *The courage to teach: Exploring the inner landscape of a teacher's life*. San Francisco: Jossey-Bass Publishers.

Pipher, M. (2003). *Letters to a young therapist*. New York: Basic Books.

Ryan, M. J. (1999). *Attitudes of gratitude*. Berkeley, CA: Conari Press.

White, E. G. (1942). *The ministry of healing*. Nampa, ID: Pacific Press Publishing Association.

# *Family Ministries* Can Help Reap God's Harvest

by Gordon & Waveney Martinborough

*As the Church around the world reaps God's harvest in 2004, Family Ministries can help! In this presentation we shall answer five questions. · What is Family Life Evangelism? · Why should we do it? · How we can use this divine method? · Which materials are available? · What does a Family Life evangelistic presentation look like?*

## WHAT IS FAMILY LIFE EVANGELISM?

First of all, what is it? Integrated Family Life Evangelism is a divine methodology which combines vital family issues with conceptually compatible Bible doctrines in a unified Christ-centered approach.

**It's biblical.** Let us examine four reasons for doing Family Life Evangelism. The first is that it is a divine method of teaching truth. All through the Bible God uses parental love to illustrate His love. Abraham is a classical example. As the hand of that loving father trembled over the death of the son on Mount Moriah, so the tender heart of our heavenly Father shuddered over the death of His Son on Mount Calvary. The Psalmist declares, "As a father pities his children, so the Lord pities those who serve Him." (Psalm 103: 13). And the prophet adds, "Can a mother forget the baby at her breast . . . ? Though she may forget, I will not forget you!" (Isa. 49:15 NIV). And the entire world remembers the amazing parable of the loving Father hugging his prodigal son.

Throughout scripture, God also uses marital love to illustrate His fathomless love. Isn't that the message of the whole book of Hosea? Then there is the book of Ruth teaching us about the heavenly Kinsman redeeming the one He loves. And what about Song of Songs? Isn't the love of Solomon for his Shunamite wife also a parable of the love of the One "greater than Solomon" for the Church, His bride? Then there are the wedding parables of Jesus and the apocalyptic images of the Bride, the wife of the Lamb.

Ephesians chapter five deserves special attention. "Husbands, love your wives, just as Christ also loved the church" (vs. 25). "Just as the church is subject to Christ, so let the wives be to their own husbands" (vs. 24). "A man shall …be joined [sexually] to his wife, and the two shall become one flesh.' This is a great mystery, but I speak concerning Christ and the church" (vss. 31, 32). This illustrates the methodology of Family Life Evangelism. The apostle Paul combines vital family issues with conceptually compatible Bible doctrines in a unified Christ-centered approach. And he moves freely from one to the other because one is the parable of the other. In the same way, every evangelistic presentation has two parts: a family issue and a compatible Bible doctrine. So this methodology is not a human gimmick, it is a divine method! It's biblical.

**It's practical.** While the regular evangelistic campaign emphasizes preparation for heaven, Family Life Evangelism has a two-fold emphasis. It prepares people for heaven and simultaneously prepares them to live happily on earth. It deals with the "nuts and bolts" of life: love vs. infatuation, compatibility, marital roles, communication, conflict resolution, sexuality, money management, singleness, parenting, and much more. Moreover, it is focused: "Seven steps," "Five ways," "Four keys," "Six secrets." And it is not theoretical; it's practical. It does not only say "what to do," it emphasizes "how to do it."

**It's multilateral.** Today multitudes are marching in the remnant church. However, if we were to analyze the influx we would be constrained to admit that most of our converts come from the lower levels of society. Why aren't we attracting a significant number of persons from the upper levels? Why aren't we reaching people in the higher social, educational, and financial strata of society? Did not Jesus die for them also?

One reason for our reticence is that such people are difficult to reach. They are not interested in heaven because they are enjoying their own heaven here on earth! True, they are not interested in Bible doctrines, but they are interested in issues of health and family life. Family Life Evangelism has the potential for reaching such people because it satisfies the felt need of happy family life together with their unfelt need for eternal life. It uses the strategy that Jesus used.

**It's eschatological.** Seventh-day Adventists are people of eschatology with a unique view which we call the Great Controversy. We teach that in Eden God created two eternal institutions—the family and the Sabbath. We declare that the Papacy has trampled God's seventh-day Sabbath, substituting first day worship, and we believe that it has also depreciated Family Life by the celibacy of its clergy. We proclaim that we are "repairers of the breach" and "restorers of paths" (Isa. 58:12 KJV). And we are famous for restoration of the Sabbath! The big question is: Are we as famous for restoring marriage and family? When people come to our evangelistic campaigns do they expect that a significant part of our presentations will focus on family life? If we are to be faithful to the Edenic restoration, shouldn't we be restoring both institutions?

Moreover, we affirm that we are commissioned to preach the Elijah message of Malachi 4:5, 6—turning "the hearts of fathers to their children, and the hearts of children to their fathers." Doesn't that involve a family life revival?

## GOD'S MASTER PLAN

The prophet Hosea gives us God's master plan for reaping a great harvest. "Sow for yourselves righteousness; reap in mercy; break up your fallow ground ...till He comes and rains righteousness on you" (Hosea 10:12). So we need plowing, sowing, reaping and raining. How can we employ these concepts?

We plow or soften hearts by praying and caring. Church members are asked to compile a prayer list of relatives, friends, neighbors, work mates or school mates whom they would like to see accept Jesus during the campaign. Then each intercessor joins one or two other intercessors to form a "Care Cell." They choose a time and place for their weekly meeting and they name a cell leader. This Care Cell meets weekly for study, prayer for prospects on prayer lists and for Christian fellowship. In addition to praying, each intercessor looks for ways to intentionally show care for his/her prospects.

After plowing, there is sowing. And "the seed is the word of God" which is packaged in attractive new Family Life lessons. Then comes reaping, using campaign sermons or seminars.

Though not stated in our text, reaping should be followed by conserving. In too many cases, when the campaign is over, the work is done. But just as a university's graduation ceremony ends with a "commencement," so baptism should commence conservation. To put it in a graphic way—giving birth, then abandoning the baby is murder! Eight advanced lessons provide a valuable tool for the conservation of new believers.

At every stage of this divine plan, we need rain – the "early and latter rain" of God's Holy Spirit. So we need to "ask the Lord for rain" (Zech. 10:1). Following God's master plan ensures success.

## HOW TO DO FAMILY LIFE EVANGELISM

**Family Life Evangelistic Campaign.** In our approach, there are three different ways to do Family Life Evangelism. Option one is the Evangelistic Campaign. This uses short plowing, normal sowing and short reaping. Plowing lasts for one month, and employs the "Pray-Care" plan stated above. Sowing lasts two months using eight Family Life lessons called Series AA. They are short and simple with answers to the questions in small type at the end of each lesson.

Reaping lasts one month, and two tools are provided. One is the *Happy Family* Evangelism Manual, which is a comprehensive handbook of ten units containing everything one needs for an evangelistic campaign: master sheet, twenty-four sermon outlines, five Sabbath services, Series AA lessons for preparation, Series C lessons for conservation, weekly visitation guidelines, new nightly decision cards, half night prayer service, and the *Happy Family* theme song.

Accompanying the manual is the *Happy Family* CD containing 24 Power Point presentations with multiethnic graphics. All presentations are in three languages: English, Spanish and French.

**Small Group Evangelism.** While the evangelistic campaign is still the traditional route, Small Group Evangelism is fast becoming a more effective methodology. The Small Group method uses long plowing, long sowing and very short reaping.

Plowing lasts two months, using the "Pray-Care" procedures above. In addition to praying in the weekly Cell meeting, each intercessor looks for ways to intentionally show care for his/her prospects. They practice "Pray-Care" visitation, using the LAP procedure: *Look* for areas of interest, *Ask* questions to ascertain needs, and for those needs. This "Pray-Care" is spiritual "Day Care," where hearts are softened by love.

The long sowing takes three to four months, and the living dynamic of this process is the expansion of the Care Cell, which is converted into a "Family Fellowship." Each prospect is given lesson one with an invitation to the Family Fellowship. This cell, this small group meeting, becomes the center of operations.

What do we do in the weekly Family Fellowship? We study the attractive fifteen Family Life lessons called Series B. These lessons are really fifteen of the twenty four sermons that have been simplified and redesigned for home use. Like the sermon, half of each lesson is on the family and the other half on Bible doctrine. In addition to study, the Family Fellowship is for prayer. Here we pray for each other; further, we teach prospects to pray.

However although study and prayer are vital, the most important element of the Family Fellowship is fellowship! Whether it be sing-song, drink, cookies or chit-chat, we create ways to build friendship, to show care, and experience Christian love.

After this long sowing, the harvest is ripe, and we are ready for a short reaping! The reaping campaign needs just two weeks to present the sermons that were not covered by the lessons. These are decision sermons. Prospects from all the Fellowships are brought together for massive Fellowship, and the preacher, using the identified decision sermons from the manual with the matching presentations from the CD, call people to decision. A variety of baptismal services are scheduled during this reaping campaign.

When the short reaping is over, where should the new believers go? Back to the weekly Care Cells! For the next two months they study the Conservation lessons (Series C). But they do more than study together. They pray together and they fellowship together, for fellowship is the key! The greatest benefit of Small Group Evangelism is that it provides an effective conservation mechanism. The newborn is surrounded by a circle of friends who give spiritual support in a loving, caring environment.

**Professional Evangelistic Seminars.** The third way to do family life outreach is the Professional Evangelistic Seminars. This method aims at reaching persons in the upper levels of society—people who do not come to the tent or the church. This option needs very long plowing, long sowing and short reaping.

The fact is that if the gospel seed is sown on "stony ground" there will be no harvest! So we need to "break up" this "fallow ground." We do so by operating a six-month "Pray-Care" plan of praying, caring and visiting. We build strategic spiritual alliances with these professionals and businesspersons in their "marketplace" and in their "ballpark"! We visit them formally and informally, ascertaining and satisfying their felt needs, praying with them and for them. This is the plowing.

As in option two, the sowing is done in the Small Group called "Family Fellowship." Here we use Series A. These twelve lessons are specially designed for professionals. For example, "God loves businesspersons," "God loves educators," "God loves politicians." During these three months of sowing in the weekly Fellowship, we bring all the prospects of all the small groups once each month for an appropriate Group Fellowship such as a Prayer Breakfast, Gospel Concert or Stress Seminar. It would be advantageous if these monthly events are hosted at the proposed campaign venue.

The reaping is unique. We are not preaching sermons, we are conducting professional seminars! We use the twenty four *Happy Family Bible Seminar* study guides with the accompanying CD. However, professional seminars need professional dynamics: attractive venue, professional ambiance, interactive teaching methodology, appropriate materials (folder, pen and study guide for each participant) and prior registration. Moreover, since it is a professional seminar, we recommend that there be a modest registration fee. Of course, after the reaping is the conserving, as they return to their enlarged Care Cells for study, prayer and fellowship. Again, fellowship is the key to conservation.

**Summary.** Here is a summary of the three different ways to do integrated Family Life Evangelism:

| OPTIONS | PLOWING | SOWING | REAPING | CONSERVING |
|---|---|---|---|---|
| #1 - Evangelistic Campaign | Short - 1 month Pray & Care | Normal - 2 months, Series AA | Short - 1 month 24 Sermons, CD | Standard - 2 months Series C |
| #2 - Small Group Evangelism | Long - 2 months Pray & Care | Long - 3-4 months, Series B Family F/ship | Very short - 2 weeks 10 Sermons, CD | Standard - 2 months Series C |
| #3 - Professional Evangelistic Seminars | Very long - 6 months Pray, Care & Visit | Long - 3 months, Series A Family F/ship, Monthly event | Short - 1 month 24 Sermons, CD | Standard - 2 months Series C |

## MATERIALS

The materials available are:

| | |
|---|---|
| *Happy Family* Evangelism Manual | 24 Sermons/Seminars (& other units) |
| *Happy Family* multipurpose CD | 24 sermons/Seminars |
| Series AA: Preparation for Campaign | 8 lessons (in Manual) |
| Series C: Multipurpose Conservation Plan | 12 lessons (in Manual) |
| Small Group Evangelism Manual | Strategy & materials |
| Series B for Small Group Evangelism | 15 lessons |
| Upper Class Evangelism Manual* | Strategy & materials |
| Series A: Preparation for Professional Seminars* | 12 lessons (in Manual) |
| *Happy Family* Professional Seminars* | 24 study guide |

*The last 3 items are scheduled for release in June, 2004

All materials are available from the Family Ministries Department, General Conference of Seventh-day Adventists, Inter-American Division, 8100 S.W. 117th Ave., Miami, FL 33183 USA. Samples can be viewed at www.interamerica.org/familyministries.

# —————SAMPLE SERMON/SEMINAR—————

So what does a Family Life Evangelistic sermon or seminar look like? Here is an outline of Sermon/Seminar 16. This is a Decision Sermon or Seminar.

## How to Help My Child Obey– The Happy Way

### ATTENTION

- Many parents know only one way to get the child to obey—the whip!

- This seminar presents a better way—a happy way.

### I. TWO PRINCIPLES

- **Reinforcement:** Any behavior that is Rewarded is Reinforced and will be Repeated.

- **Extinction:** Any behavior that is not rewarded is starved to death and becomes Extinct.

- These two concepts give us two principles:

### A. The WW Principle

1. When a child's behavior is **W**rong, the reward is **W**ithheld.

2. God used the WW principle on his disobedient child Moses. Num.20:11, 12

3. Sometimes inadvertently we do the opposite.

4. Illustration: Jomo and the candy.

5. Questions on the story.

### B. The RR Principle

1. When a child's behavior is Right, there should be a Reward.

2. God affirmed the RR principle. 1 Cor. 3:14.

3. Sometimes unwillingly we do the very opposite.

4. Illustration: Maria and her room.

5. Questions on the story.

## II. TIMING OF REWARDS

### A. Two options

1. The Bible even tells us about the timing of rewards! Matt. 19:27, 29

2. So we can use immediate rewards and long term rewards.

### B. Recommendations

1. Reward immediately sometimes and accumulatively other times.

2. Reward small children right away, and older children either way.

3. Reward consistently at first and intermediately afterwards.

## III. TYPES OF REWARDS

### A. Verbal Reward

1. This is something that the parent says.

2. Bible example. Matt. 25:21

3. Question: What would be a verbal reward for Maria?

### B. Activity Reward

1. This is something enjoyable that the child is allowed to do.

2. A Bible example. Rev. 3:4

3. Question: What will be an activity reward for Maria?

### C. Total Reward

1. This is something of value that the parent gives.

2. A Bible example. Rev. 2:10

3. Question: What would be a token reward for Maria?

## IV. MODEL PARENT

**A. Just as we expect our children to obey us, God our Heavenly Father expects us to obey Him.**

**B. As our Model Parent God:**

1. Commands us to obey.

2. Expects us to obey.

3. Rewards us when we obey.

**C. God demonstrated this 2,600 years ago in the city of Babylon.**

## V. THE STORY

- King Nebuchadnezzar erected a huge golden image and commanded all his assembled officials to worship the idol.

- 2. Anyone who disobeyed would be thrown into the burning fiery furnace.

- The king of Babylon gave his command, "You shall fall down and worship the gold image" (Dan. 3:6).

- But the King of Heaven had given a different command: "You shall not bow down to them nor worship them." Ex.20:5, NIV

- These were two opposite commands!

- The three Hebrews had to decide whom they would obey.

- So do you and I today.

## VI. TWO CHOICES

### A. Conversion

1. God says: "Repent and be converted." Acts 3:19

2. Satan says, "No conversion is necessary. Just live like you please."

3. Question: Whom do I obey: Satan or Jesus?

### B. The Sabbath

1. God says, "Remember the Sabbath day to keep it holy." Ex. 20:8

2. Satan says you don't have to keep the Sabbath; Sunday is okay.

3. He used the emperor of Rome to legalize Sunday worship.

4. Then the Church of Rome perpetuated Sunday worship.

5. Question: Whom do I obey: God or Man?

### C. Baptism

1. God says, "Arise and be baptized." Acts 22:16

2. Satan says, "You've got plenty of time."

3. Christ says, "Now is the time!" 2 Cor. 6:2

4. Question: Whom will I obey: Satan or Jesus?

## VII. WONDERFUL SAVIOR!

• I'm glad the three Hebrews made the right choice!

• Nebuchadnezzar was "full of fury!" He intensified the furnace and threw them in.

• Suddenly the king exclaimed, "Didn't we cast three men bound into the midst of the fire?" Look! I see four men loose walking the midst of the fire…and the form of the fourth is like the Son of God!" (Dan. 3:24, 25)

• It was Jesus! Mighty Jesus! Traveling faster than light! Past galaxies, systems, stars and suns! And before the youth fell into the flames, Christ landed in the furnace! With Jesus in the fire, the flames lost their power! What a wonderful Savior!

• When I step out to follow Jesus in baptism, He will repeat that miracle for me!

• Read the precious promise. Isaiah 43:2

## VIII. REWARDS!

• As the Model Parent, God
  – Commands me to obey
  – Expects me to obey and
  – Rewards me when I obey

• He rewarded the Hebrews with deliverance--not from the fire, but in the fire!

• Then He promoted them to positions of high honor. Dan. 3:30

• When I obey Jesus and get baptized God will reward me in this life.  Deut. 28:13

• Then He will give me the much greater reward of everlasting life. Rev. 2:10

## DECISION

### A. Action

1. This Sabbath is our Big Baptism! And "I have decided to follow Jesus." (Music)

2. All who have decided to say: "No" to man and "Yes" to God, Raise your hands!

3. All who say: "No" to Rome and "Yes" to Jesus," Stand to your feet!

4. All who say: "No" to Satan and "Yes" to Jesus" Come to the altar!

### B. APPEAL: Persons

1. Parents. You expect your children to obey you because they love you. So God expects you to obey Him because you love Him. Come to the altar now!

2. Children. You want to obey your earthly mother and father. God wants you to obey Him - your Heavenly Father. Come now!

3. Men. The three Hebrews were men! Men with back bone! Be a man! Stand up for the Truth! Come to the altar now!

4. Youth. The three Hebrews were youth! God wants young men and women to give the best of your life to Him. Come now!

5. Persons of power and influence. Nebuchadnezzar was a powerful man. But he bowed to the God of heaven! God is calling leaders of government, leaders in society, business persons, professional people, and wealthy people. Come now!

6. Ex-Adventists. You went out and bowed down to the idol. Now you want to stand up for Jesus. Make a new start. Get re-baptized. Come!

### C. APPEAL: Issues

1. Worship. That day it was the golden idol or the God of heaven. Today it is Man's Sunday or God's Sabbath? Come! Choose God's Sabbath now. (1 Kings 18:21)

2. Fear. Who is your Nebuchadnezzar? At home? At school? On the job? Don't be afraid of Nebuchadnezzar. God is stronger than man. Come! (Isa. 12:2)

3. Fire. You may be thrown into the fire if you get baptized! Remember that Christ will be with you in the fire! You will not be burnt! Remember His promise. (Isa. 43:2)

4. Earthly rewards. God rewards us when we obey. He'll reward you in this life. You'll be "the head and not the tail." (Deut. 28:13) Come and Get it!

5.6. Heavenly reward. Then, when Christ returns you'll get the eternal reward. "I will give you a crown of life." (Rev. 2:10) Come to the Altar Now!

## D. Pass & Prayer

1. Distribute baptism passes

2. Prayer of commitment

---

**Pioneers in family evangelism philosophy and methods, Gordon and Waveney Martinborough direct the Department of Family Ministries in the Inter-American Division of the Seventh-day Adventist Church.**

All Scripture quotations, unless otherwise indicated, are taken from the New King James Version. Copyright © 1982 by Thomas Nelson, Inc. Used by permission. All rights reserved.

Scripture quotations designated by NIV are taken from the Holy Bible, New International Version. Copyright ©1973,1978,1984. International Bible Society. Used by permission of Zondervan Bible Publishers.

# Creating a Family-Friendly Church

**by Noelene Johnsson and Willie Oliver**

WILDEBEEST, also known as Gnu or African antelope, mate and give birth to their young during their annual migration to the Serengeti plains, in Tanzania, East Africa. Hyenas also roam the Serengeti, stalking the wildebeest calves. Aware of these predators, a mother wildebeest immediately upon giving birth begins nudging the weak newborn to its feet. It is not uncommon to see hyenas stalk the helpless young within minutes of birth. In an effort to protect her calf, the mother will counterattack. But the hyenas, working as a pack, often keep the mother distracted until a lone predator can get the calf.

Observers tell us that thousands of wildebeest graze nearby, raising their heads to watch this drama as it unfolds. If they acted together, they could easily outnumber the hyenas. But not one wildebeest makes a move to help mother or calf.

The wildebeest herd typifies a dysfunctional church—quite the opposite of a family-friendly church that makes ministry family-centered and church-supported. Family-friendly churches recognize that parents have the primary responsibility for the spiritual nurture of the child. But at the same time the church stands ready to assist and support the ministry of the home. Three ways family-friendly churches offer support are by:

1. Making church child-friendly.

2. Making church a safe place for children to accept Jesus.

3. Supporting and training parents for discipleship of the child.

## A CASE STUDY

The Kuna Seventh-day Adventist Church, near Boise, Idaho, is a family-friendly church.

"Our style of doing church is informal and can appear disorganized," confesses Aileen Sox, one of Kuna's church elders. "We'll probably always run a little late, a little long, and a whole lot casual on Sabbath morning. But for Kuna that is small stuff. With the big stuff, we get it right. We pay attention to kids."

Kuna's first Vacation Bible School in a number of years attracted 100 children and more than 50 volunteers!

Generous members subsidize part of the tuition (in some cases all of it) for a number of Kuna children to attend church school. Nobody complains about spending money for Sabbath School furniture or supplies for Vacation Bible School.

Kuna members applaud kids and involve them every week in church services. Children sometimes read the morning's Scripture passage, sing or play special music, and sing with the children's praise team. Junior deacons and deaconesses have assignments whenever their adult mentors do. Kids greet at the front door along with their parents or older siblings.

The church applauds children's achievements—honor roll, graduation, community awards—during praise or announcement time. Kid's prayer requests are taken to God's throne just as seriously as are the adults'. The children's offering may not be the biggest cash offering each Sabbath morning, but it could be the bulkiest.

Nobody can resist the children, each carrying a basket to be filled.

At Kuna they don't mind the noise generated by children during a worship service, which they hold before Sabbath school so children will endure it better. The church provides "busy" bags for each child under age 10, and has booster seats to help kids ages 1–5 see what is going on up front during the service. And Kuna gives parents wireless headsets from the sound system so they can listen to the sermon while walking their restless toddlers.

At Christmas Kuna kids each receive a book from Pacific Press or the Review and Herald; at their dedication babies receive a toddler's worship book; and at baptisms candidates receive a Bible. When a baby is born, the pastor visits the hospital with a copy of Kay Kuzma's book *Preparing for Your Baby's Dedication: A Guide for Parents*. "Kuna wants parents to know right from the beginning their church will participate in their child's spiritual life," Sox says.

Not surprising, Kuna has experienced amazing growth, from 20 families to 85—most of it n the past six years.[1]

## ANOTHER KID-FRIENDLY CHURCH.

Community Praise Church, in Alexandria, Virginia, lavishes love on their children, especially on Children's Sabbath. Last March the children and their leaders conducted the services for this special day. A children's praise team helped lead the singing, 12-year old Drey Lock preached the sermon, after which senior pastor Henry Wright "opened the doors of the church." Wright affirmed Drey's sermon, inviting those who had not joined the church to make the life-changing decision. One young father came forward.

Eight children trained by children's pastor Victoria Harrison responded affirmatively to the reading of a child-friendly version of the baptismal vows prior to their baptism. At every step of the program the congregation vigorously affirmed and applauded the efforts of the children, reinforcing the message that the children belong to and serve a truly loving church family.

Whether they realize it or not, Kuna and Community Praise benefit from being child-friendly—they attract families, they grow, and they keep their kids committed and loyal.

## CHILDHOOD'S WINDOW OF OPPORTUNITY

Bill Hybels, one of America's best-known pastors, says, "The single remaining common interest or entrance point for nonchurched people into the life of the church is children. . . . We have a wide-open door to almost every family in every community worldwide when we love and serve their kids."[2] Parents want their children involved in outstanding programs. And if the kids love being there, parents will keep bringing them back. Eventually the whole family will stay for church.

Barna Research Group, in November 1999, reported their findings that childhood is the most important time for deciding for Christ. A century ago Ellen White wrote: "It is in these early years that the affections are the most ardent, the heart most susceptible of improvement."[3]

Barna's nationwide survey showed the probability of people accepting Jesus Christ as their Savior in relation to their age. Children from 5 to 13 have a 32 percent probability of accepting Jesus; ages 14 to 18, only 4 percent; 19 and older, 6 percent. This data flies in the face of the way we do church.

If childhood is evangelism's window of opportunity, should we not be more intentional about allocating budgets and evangelism efforts where they will be most productive, rather than to an audience that is six to eight times less open?

## MAKING CHURCH SAFE FOR CHILDREN

If we would make our churches family-friendly, we must ensure that both the church facility and church family are safe for children.

Larrie Parks[4] and his wife were chatting after the church potluck one week when he suddenly missed his daughter, Shannon. Concerned to know where she was, Larrie hurried toward the church foyer calling her name. The other children playing in the hallway had not seen Shannon, adding to Larrie's concern. He hurried back along the hall, calling to Shannon as he went.

Then came the sound of a slammed door, running footsteps, and Shannon screaming for him. Larrie's relief was short-lived as Shannon breathlessly told of a man forcing her into an empty classroom. At the sound of her father's voice, the girl had found the courage to make a break and run unharmed to safety.

"I was so devastated by this experience that for a whole year my spiritual life was affected," Parks recalls. When children are molested, they do not suffer alone; the whole family grieves. Where the perpetrator is a member and denies what happened, the whole church can take sides; everyone hurts, and ministry is derailed.

Family-friendly churches plan ahead to make church a safe place for children to come to know Jesus. A few simple rules can protect both children and the church's ministry:

1. Have those who hold positions of trust in the church fill out volunteer screening forms.

2. Wait six months before giving new and previously unknown members a church office.

3. Avoid having adults working one on one with a child, but if they must, leave the classroom door open so that anyone can look in.

## SUPPORTING PARENTS, TEACHING DISCIPLESHIP

Family is the place where children learn and experience love, affection, values, and God. In the home, children learn to be connected to or disconnected from each other, not only by what parents and guardians say, but also by what the children experience.

Family experts suggest that a principal predictor of success for young people—in every aspect of their lives—is their perception of their parents' image of them; not so much what their parents think of them, but what they *think* their parents think of them.

Families who experience high rates of cohesion, connectedness, and spiritual and relational health intentionally connect with each other every day. Family worship not only connects family members at the beginning of each day, but also builds spirituality and relationships. Recently Barna Research reported that nine out of 10 parents of children under the age of 13 believe they are responsible for communicating their values and religious beliefs to their children. Yet in a typical week, most parents don't spend any time discussing religious matters or sharing religious materials with their children.[5]

Unfortunately, many families in the congregation do not understand the importance of family worship, and even if they do, they don't know how to go about it. This is where churches can help. Parenting seminars and tips from the pulpit can support parents and show them what to do.

A new opportunity is opening up for churches supporting families—children's discipleship. The Kids in Discipleship Center, at the Collegedale church in Tennessee, has developed a discipleship program in two stages. Already four churches have participated, and reports are encouraging, even electrifying.

Becky Hopper reports from the Andrews Seventh-day Adventist Church, in North Carolina, that 24 parents meeting in four groups after only seven lessons experienced revival and a new sense of unity—something that some had longed for.

"'Footprints in the Sand—Part I,' the first set of 12 lessons, helps parents, in a small group setting, become committed disciples," MacLafferty explains. "Footprints, Part II," brings together the parents and children, working as families to study through a series of 32 lessons. This series gets children into a personal relationship with Jesus, develops habits of personal and family devotions, and encourages service and witnessing. Eventually some of these families will become involved in mentoring other families in the discipleship process.

We all want our kids and grandkids to grow up to be responsible members of society at large. And we surely want them to love and serve God as they grow older. This doesn't happen by chance, or by providing random, sporadic attempts at communicating our religious and cultural values.

We need to be deliberate in how we communicate our faith to our kids. It's our responsibility to them—and to Jesus.

[1] They now have 120 kids under the age of 18!

[2] David Staal, "Take the Challenge: Lead Up," *Children's Ministry*, January/February 2003, p. 51.

[3] Ellen G. White, in *Review and Herald*, December 17, 1889.

[4] Not his real name.

[5] Barnas Research Online, May 6, 2003.

---

Noelene Johnsson is Director of Children's Ministries for the North American Division (NAD). She believes that ministry to children should be inclusive, filled with grace, and cooperative ventures between parents and church members.

Willie Oliver is NAD's Director of Family Ministries and is committed to positive change in the lives of families throughout North America.

# CONDUCTING FAMILY WORSHIP

Research and personal experience suggest that the most effective family worships are those that deliberately involve all the members of the family by giving them an opportunity to lead out in the daily exercise. Having clear goals in mind, such as what devotional material will be used, how long worship will last, where and when worship will convene, and what components will be included in the daily ritual, are important considerations.

My family has daily family worship in our (the parents') bedroom from Monday through Friday at 6:00 in the morning. We choose age-specific interactive devotional books from which we read each morning.

Our family observes a schedule for leading out in the daily devotional activities as well as the daily prayers that will be offered. After the appointed person has led out in the reading or activity, the person leading out in prayer will ask if anyone has prayer requests (spoken or unspoken) or prayer praises (answers to prayers or specific blessings experienced) that we may together bring to the Lord. After listening to the prayer requests and praises, the person scheduled to lead out in prayer prays about the specific points that have been shared.

By sharing leadership of our morning worships, our children learn to own their faith. They are also developing spiritual leadership skills and a positive self-esteem by having an audience that is attentive to what they are saying. This has also provided an excellent opportunity to practice oral reading skills and get help with unfamiliar words. By praying each day for requests and praises, our children are learning to intercede on behalf of others, and to affirm their beliefs and faith in God, especially when they get to share stories about prayers that have been answered.

Although lasting only 10-15 minutes, our daily family worships also double as scheduled time to catch up with each others' lives. During the time of prayer requests and praises, we get an opportunity to talk about things that concern us, as well as things that please us. Talking about ersonal joys and concerns fosters a spirit of connectedness, both spiritually and emotionally.

# EQUAL ACCESS TO GOD

—Willie Oliver

"Through [Jesus Christ] we [all] have access to the Father by one Spirit (Eph. 2:18, NIV).

When we gather to worship, we are all participants with access to God. Nobody should feel invisible, marginalized, or left out. So why would we design a service that is entirely over the heads of a sizeable group—the children?

Susan Scoggins tells of her precocious 2-year old granddaughter Trisney. When questioned one week about Sabbath School, Trisney confidently reported that it had been about Jairus. When asked if she had listened to the sermon in church, the child responded, "No, it was in a different language."

Many older children feel the same way. Maybe that's why they bury their heads in their *Guide* magazines when the sermon starts. The big words and abstract concepts of a sermon are too often a foreign tongue to them. The whole church enjoys the service more when the children are included.

—Noelene Johnsson

---

Reprinted from *Adventist Review*, June, 2003. Used by permission.

## Great Resources for Family-friendly Ministry

- Go to www.churchchairs4kids.com to learn more about toddler-friendly booster seats.

- Erwin, Pamela J. *The Family Powered Church*. Loveland, CO: Group Publishing, 2000.

- *Family Friendly Church Leader Guide*. Lincoln, NE: AdventSource, 2001. (*Participant Guide* also available.)

- *Family Ministries Handbook—The Complete How to Guide for Local Church Leaders*. Lincoln, NE: AdventSource, 2003.

- Flowers, Ron and Karen. *It Takes a Family—Discipling Children and Teens for Christ*. Lincoln, NE: AdventSource, 2002.

- For more information about making churches safe, go to: http://childmin.com/Resources/ VolunteerScreening.htm.

- To learn more about Kids in Discipleship, contact Don MacLafferty at kidcenter@southern.edu; Phone: (423) 396-2134.

# *Church* Planting Can Be Hazardous to Your Family Health

**Karen and Ron Flowers dialogue with Alicia Patterson, Geoff Patterson, Marti Schneider, and Doug Tilstra**

*Front-line planters offer help on keeping family relationships strong.*

**Karen:** Let me first introduce our distinguished panel of experienced church planters. *Marti Schneider* is the coordinator of the SEEDS church planting conferences and director of the General Conference Global Mission Total Employment program. She has worked for many years in pastoral evangelism with her husband Don, who now serves as the president of the North American Division. *Doug Tilstra*, with his wife Lorraine, is a pioneer in Adventist church planting. He brings this experience, as well as his doctoral research on church planting, to his current responsibility for pastoral training as a professor of religion at Southern Adventist University. *Alicia and Geoff Patterson* are a pastoral couple in team ministry in the Pacific Northwest of the United States. They are busy today parenting three young boys and planting their second congregation.

**Ron:** So talk to us first about the rewards of church planting. What gives you the most satisfaction?

**Marti:** Of course the biggest reward is the reward found in all ministry, the joy of talking about Jesus and telling people what He has done for them!

**Karen:** There was certainly a solid round of "Amen's" on that.

**Doug:** Strange as it may seem, some of the biggest rewards I have experienced have actually come as a result of the painful, more challenging aspects of church planting. There is the potential in this ministry for so much personal growth if you choose to grow through the challenges planting a church inevitably presents. I certainly made some mistakes my first time around, but I returned to church planting a much stronger individual, both personally and relationally.

**Alicia:** I can definitely pick up on that note. We have certainly learned by hard experience among church planters that your "warning label"—*Church planting can be hazardous to your family health*—is real. Karen, I remember talking to you as we were transitioning from our first church planting experience. I was concerned for our family. We had a new baby, and I knew we would have to be more intentional than ever about keeping our marriage and our connections with our children strong if we were to survive another church planting experience as a healthy family.

**Geoff:** But as you say, Doug, risk and reward go hand in hand in church planting. At the same time as Alicia and I have felt the strain on our marriage relationship and our parenting of our children in the midst of church planting, I think the biggest reward has been the team ministry aspect of our church planting experience. It's wonderful to be able to connect with your marriage partner on something you both care deeply about. It's just great to be able to talk with each other intelligently, in depth, and frequently about something you're passionate about. I love having Alicia engage with me in dialogue about our church planting project, rather than seeing her eyes glaze over when I talk to her, like she's moving into "okay-I'm-listening-but-only-because-I-love-you" mode.

**Alicia:** I am amazed at the way God has given Geoff and me just the complementary gifts we need. It's just fun to be in ministry together because he has gifts and strengths I don't have.

**Geoff:** We both enjoy watching each other's gifts and talents unfold and blossom, because there are so many needs in the church plant. It's always good to see your spouse growing and doing better and better at the things they do well.

**Ron:** It's so rewarding to do something together that neither of you could have done alone.

**Doug:** Yes. My wife and I know that satisfaction. However, as I listen to you and reflect on Lorraine's and my experience, I find myself thinking again about the reality that not every church planting couple will have the same combination of gifts and interests. Perhaps we need to open the door wider for different models of "team" ministry suited to different combinations of gifts. Just as we have become sensitive to individual differences, we can recognize and support couple differences in ministry.

**Marti:** I think this is really important. And I would also add that people and couples do sometimes change over time and in different circumstances. Doug will remember a quieter and much shyer Marti from an earlier time in our ministry. Even my husband is sometimes surprised at the woman he's married to now! I believe time and place and changing expectations have released me to be who I really am inside.

**Karen:** I think all of us who are involved in ministry know intuitively that we have entered the lives of our spouses in a unique way. And I think most of us see this as a positive. But we all need rope to do ministry in our own way. Some spouses enjoy an up-front role. Others participate in ministry in many other supportive roles, related to their giftedness.

**Doug:** One situation not unlike our own is that of military spouses. Clearly, anybody who's married to a person in the military is going to be affected by their spouse's career choice. There are certain perks, and there are also certain disadvantages. A military spouse isn't required to join the military themselves, though they may choose to. But, for sure, their lives are going to be dramatically impacted by the military connection. In a similar way, there are probably a variety of healthy responses that a spouse of a church planter can make. What I think is most important is for the husband and wife to come to at least an "eye-opening" together as to what this experience is going to be like. The spouse may choose to become deeply involved as a pastoring person, or they may choose to continue in their own career while offering differing kinds of support to the church-planting venture. But having a clear vision of what's ahead will enable couples to make their choices intelligently and with deliberate intention.

**Alicia:** In that, I think we've come a long way. Most couples considering a church-planting ministry today have a bit more general knowledge about church planting on which to base their decisions than did those pioneering this work in the early 80's. But before a couple makes the choice to take up this work, they need to move beyond general knowledge to understanding more about the real demands, opportunities, joys, heartaches, and other things that make church planting different from other pastoral situations. Only then can you realistically answer the question, "How will my spouse and I relate ourselves to it?"

**Marti:** And this is a question each of them need to ask. In other words, "What will be my role in all of this? What is God calling me to do?" Don and I are going to Nigeria soon. I am going along because Don and I want to take this trip together, not because I have been given any official assignment. But I don't want to be just a tourist, so I've been pondering the question, "What is my role?" Well, I've actually been praying about it, and I've concluded that the way I can support my husband best is to pray for him. So my role in this circumstance is prayer. I may be asked to assume some other responsibilities, and I will do my best, but I am going with the purpose in my heart to support Don in prayer. He doesn't need a nervous wife who is trying to create her own action on the sidelines. So in this situation, I feel called to minister through prayer.

**Doug:** That word *role* leads me to something else I think is very important. Roles are not rigid, defined sorts of things in my view, as much as they are something we make conscious decisions about and which change in differing times and circumstances. I think it's very important to make a distinction between *identity* and *role*. Identity has to do with who we are as persons, at the very core. Roles can change. Identity runs much deeper and shifts more slowly. I think the stronger our identity, the more comfortable we can be with changing roles. But sometimes we actually form our identity out of our role.

This was a problem for me early in ministry. My role as pastor became my identity. But when I became more in touch with my identity as a child of God, then my roles could shift much more easily because my identity was not so tied up with them.

**Karen:** I hear you saying that *identity* is more of a "being" word, while *role* is more of a "doing" word. I can point to a very specific season in my life when it broke over me that my identity was rooted in God's action in my behalf as my Creator and Redeemer. At the very core, I am His daughter—by birth and by adoption—and that is what gives my life meaning and value. What I *do*, that is, the roles to which He calls me, flow out of this core identity. They are a response to it, but they do not define who I am.

**Ron:** It seems to me that another related issue confronting ministry couples is the issue of boundaries. From listening to you I have a hunch that this issue may be high on the agenda for church planting couples. Addressing the issue of boundaries opens questions like "Where does work end and the marriage begin? In what ways is our relationship the same in both arenas, and in what ways is it different?"

**Karen:** [laughing] I well remember the day Ron said to me on the way home from the office, "Karen, I don't know what to do. I have to tell you that I'm still struggling with my anger with you for what happened at the office today, but now I'm going home with you and I don't want to be mad at you as my wife!"

**Geoff:** We know about that. What's worse is that my weaknesses at work tend to be my weaknesses in the home environment too. The same kinds of things I can do to frustrate Alicia at work, I can do to frustrate her at home. So sometimes the frustration carries over between the two places. For church-planting couples there is the potential for an "overlapping zone" between home and work where negativity is compounded, and you can start making blanket assessments and statements like, "You really are that annoying way in every aspect of your life!" It's so easy to say, at home for instance, "See, you're doing it again, just like you did at the church . . . ."

**Ron:** It just seems to me that couples in ministry have to find a way to sort out the internal dynamics of their relationship in both places. The word *boundaries* has become in one sense a shorthand for the importance of working toward establishing some distinct edges to our multiple worlds and creating a measure of separateness between them. Karen and I are finding ourselves increasingly more intentional about setting a boundary between work and home. Without it, we can literally be working together from the time we have finished praying in the morning until we go to bed at night.

**Doug:** Let me throw something in here. I haven't thought about this for a long time, but a counselor said something interesting to me once. He said that research has shown that it's a rare couple who can have both a good marriage and a strong working relationship. Usually one or the other will be sacrificed. There may be even more pressure on pastoral couples because we do have such a high ideal to stretch toward. And many of us have very high expectations of ourselves and put ourselves under a lot of pressure to achieve goals and standards which may be unrealistic.

**Alicia:** I see a real need for the church planter to invest in the spirituality of their spouse. You can't be a church planter and remain the same. As you come closer to God, your passion grows for reaching lost people, and this fuels your energy for church planting. Everything we can do to help one another continue to grow in Christ can become a powerful force in bonding us to one another and uniting us in mission. If one is struggling to find their niche in it all, a spouse might ask, "How do you feel God is leading you? How do you think God wants to use your gifts and talents in sharing the good news that is in your heart?" Helping your partner make this discovery is so much better than making demands.

**Ron:** And we all know there are seasons when we can do more, and seasons when we must draw back from responsibilities to recover balance in our lives and reestablish our own sense of priorities.

**Alicia:** I faced this when our third baby was born. Geoff and I were between church planting assignments. You know, church planting is much like birthing a child. Church plants are born out of our home. It's wonderful, but I just couldn't help thinking "Are we candidates for a church-planting ministry during this season of our lives?" I knew we could not put in as much time as we had in the past. Nor could we have so much going on in our home and be a healthy family. But then I asked myself, "Where do congregations learn about healthy families if we aren't models? People with kids the ages of ours need models of a healthy family in ministry." But despite these nagging questions, we basically decided, "No, we don't think God is calling us to a church-planting ministry right now."

And then the call came. Fortunately, the church planting project where we are now was already in process. We were not starting from scratch. All church planters will understand that going from zero to twenty in a congregation is really hard. After that, there is some momentum and more and more structure is beginning to fall into place. But at the same time, it came to me that God would not ask me to do church planting at the expense of my family. I believe God wants me to minister out of the overflow of a strong, healthy family life. I prayed, "God, I only have so much time and energy for ministry right now. Please move me to know what you want me to do. Most of all, please let me not be driven by Alicia and whatever drives Alicia. Please let me be led by your Holy Spirit, because He never drives me too hard. And whenever He calls, I feel my strength and ministry efforts being multiplied many fold." And with that prayer, I have been at peace with my decision not to accept any official ministry position at the moment. I have chosen to be involved with Geoff in this church planting effort in other supportive ways within the context of my family priorities.

**Geoff:** Of course there's the husband-wife challenge, with all the peril and opportunity associated with a ministry marriage, but you can ramp it up about five times when you add young children to the mix. I know for me personally, there's nothing more frustrating than trying to get something done at the office, while feeling the pressure to carry my share of the family responsibilities. We find ourselves needing to dialogue often about schedules and commitments, both in the family and in the church.

**Doug:** I can really identify with what you are saying, though I am at a different family life stage at this point. One of the most important conclusions to which my wife and I have come is that the most basic tool that church planters need for the task is wholeness and balance in their own lives. I like your metaphor of ministry out of a full "family cup" as opposed to one that needs to be filled.

Let me just add that your comments also highlight the importance of clear expectations. I know it seems pretty basic, but it's one of those basic things that it is pretty easy to ignore. I learned early on—in the school of hard experience I'm afraid—that each person involved in planting a church brings their own set of expectations. People come to the task with many different motives, and their expectations vary with the motives that drive their involvement. It was months before I realized how wide a gulf existed between the mission statement we wrote on paper as a leadership team and the real mission statements that were etched on each person's mind and heart.

Specific answers must be determined for questions like "Why is this church being planted?" "Who are we trying to reach?" "How long might it take?" "What has to happen before we open the door on the first Sabbath?" "What does it mean to be a member of this leadership team?" "How will decisions be made?" "What about accountability?" "Are these expectations realistic?"

**Karen:** These sound like the really important questions, Doug. I'm thinking they need to be talked through as carefully by husband and wife in church-planting ministry as by the entire leadership team. The lack of clear and realistic expectations is the perfect set up for a tidal wave of anger and conflict in marriage.

**Marti:** And I think that the person upon whom the expectations fall should have the final say on those expectations. I think they are the ones who should determine whether or not the expectations are clear and realistic. Beyond that, they are the ones who should decide whether or not they are willing to accept these expectations of themselves.

**Ron:** There's sometimes talk among family professionals about whether the marriage or the parent-child relationship is the foundational relationship in the family. Karen and I have come down for a long time on the side of the marriage as the foundational relationship in God's design. It seems to us that it is the marriage that sets the atmosphere in the family. There is ample research support for the fact that the quality of the husband-wife relationship and their family management style profoundly impacts the health and well-being of the children.

**Alicia:** I know that is true. But it can be quite a journey from knowing in your head to working through your own issues enough to relate to your partner in the way the gospel calls you to and you really want to in your heart. In our shared ministry, I am often the one who looks at the big picture. Geoff says I have ideas before their time. Now, both of us have similar academic preparation for ministry, so it's not like I know things Geoff doesn't know. It's just that my way of looking at things is different. But in the beginning, we did a lot of butting heads because I was thinking about what we needed to do long-range while Geoff was trying to deal with the nitty-gritty of what had to be done today.

**Geoff:** (laughing) Talk about a set up for a good fight!

**Alicia:** For sure. But I have done a lot of praying about this, and I have come to the conclusion that if I have a choice between a great ministry idea and my relationship with Geoff, my relationship with Geoff is definitely the most important. Of course I still have ideas, and of course I still voice them. But I'd like to think I'm getting better at making my best case for what I think and then giving the issue to God and letting Him impress us with how we should proceed.

**Karen:** Each couple has to find their own way through these impasses. I have to be chagrined when Ron begins a dialogue with me with a long preamble like "Now I haven't made any decisions, this is only an idea. Nothing's in concrete here. I really want to make this decision with you. . . ." I hate to admit that I think I know exactly why he thinks such a preamble is necessary. Too often I have shot his ideas down and been quick to declare why it's obvious they won't work, while at the same time becoming defensive about my own ideas. I hope I'm getting better at receiving his ideas and letting him talk to me about the plusses and the downsides he has already identi-fied before I share my own thoughts.

**Geoff:** The text that always comes to my mind is "Quench not the Spirit, despise not prophesying, hold on to that which is good!" Actually I have to use that text on myself quite often!

**Ron:** That's good! It has really been a growth process for Karen and me to recognize that we process ideas differently. I tend to do a lot of internal processing. When I finally talk to Karen about it, my ideas sound quite formulated and set to her. Karen, on the other hand, processes out loud. She talks to sort out what she thinks. She gets all her ideas—even some that seem quite wild—out on the table before she evalu-ates them. We have both had a steep learning curve to understand one another and to give one another the chance to operate in our own modes. It's so easy to jump to the conclusion that the other is not going to give us a chance to share our perspective and participate in ministry decision- making. I'm trying to get better at communicating to Karen that I'm really looking to enter into mutual decision-making here.

**Alicia:** Yeah, me too, and to actually mean it! (laugh-ter) I think the discussion we had about roles comes in here too. I try to respect Geoff's role as head pastor and the measure of authority that comes with that. On the other hand, when the church gives me a responsibility, I appreciate Geoff respecting that and treating me and my ideas the same way he would those of another member of the church who had been given the same responsibility. This may seem obvious, but it's hard to do! It's not good for our relationship, and it's not good for the church plant, if we don't extend the respect due one another in our respec-tive ministry roles, just because of our familiarity as husband and wife.

**Karen:** It seems like a lot of what we have been talking about could be applied to all couples in min-istry. What's harder about church planting than other kinds of ministry?

**Doug:** I have been thinking about Alicia's analogy that church planting is like birthing a child. I think it's very apt. The whole experience is new and exhilarat-ing, like being new parents. I was just looking through a paper I wrote for one of my classes about our first church-planting experience. I confessed in that paper that the church plant became my life. I felt that everything up to that point in my ministry had led up to this climactic project. I described the experience as a rollercoaster. The ride was exhilarating and thrilling. There were times when you held your hands in the air and screamed with wild abandon. There were also times when you had to hold on for dear life. What I didn't know at the beginning was that there would also be times when you just wanted to get off and vomit.

**Geoff:** I could have written that!

**Marti:** I think a huge challenge to church planting is the enormous amount of energy it takes.

**Geoff:** An established church has so much momen-tum, it's like there is already a force within it carrying it along.

**Alicia:** In a church plant there is no status quo. There are no pews. There is no sound system. There's no dear old person who turns up early before services and turns the light on. It just doesn't run unless you do it yourself or inspire someone else to do it.

**Geoff:** A church plant exists more in the mind of a church planter than it does in the minds of the congregation for a long time. So much emotional energy is invested every week in showing up and being the one who believes in this more than anybody else. So much energy has to flow out of you. So much depends on you. Alicia and I both remember well the Sabbath we met each other out in the hall at a point when someone else was leading the service. We had two toddlers at that time, and they were screaming. We were both in a state of total physical and emotional exhaustion. We were ready to give up. It wasn't until later that we learned that at the very moment we were crying in the hall, everything was just starting to come together in the minds and hearts of the people in the congregation and the vision for this church was becoming theirs as well as ours.

**Alicia:** And I think there's a special contingent of demons specifically assigned to disrupt your plans! This is a frontline ministry, and it seems like you've got a huge bulls eye target painted on your back. I think we are targeted by the devil. And I think he puts special effort into getting adulterous relationships going. He knows that in a real sense, as goes our marriage, so goes our ministry.

**Doug:** I strongly agree with that. I think we need to remind ourselves every day that this is a supernatural battle we're engaged in. We are not wrestling against flesh and blood, but truly against principalities and powers.

**Ron:** What kinds of relational safeguards have you put in place that you could pass on to other church-planting couples?

**Geoff:** One of the mentalities I try to maintain is the awareness that there aren't any sins that I am above committing. I try to keep consciously before me the devastating effects an affair would have on my life, my marriage, my children, my ministry. Infidelity has the potential to destroy everything important to me. I'm painfully aware of my own human frailties. I need affirmation. It feels good when someone agrees with me, pats me on the back, notices when I'm down. I recognize my vulnerability in such moments. I know that these human needs, when combined with unique opportunities for close relationships, can be set ups for a moral fall. I pray I will be delivered from that. And part of my strategy is to ask God to help me keep up my guard and never assume I'm safe from it.

**Ron:** Karen and I well remember reading an article some ten years into our ministry that caught us up short with the realization of our vulnerability. Ministry is a profession that offers many opportunities for men and women to work closely together and to disclose at deep levels about personal and spiritual things. I remember covenanting with Karen to talk to her and listen to her about keeping our relationship strong. And I remember turning a corner in our relationships when, at a deeper level than was possible on our wedding day, I pledged myself to her again and committed everything within me to building my relationship with her and her alone.

**Alicia:** Yeah. I find myself praying too, that my desire will be for Geoff, that God will increase my love for him, and that I will be able to express my love in many ways. Sometimes I decide to go on a fast—a fast from criticizing.

**Marti:** I'm going to put something in here from our experience. Now, of course, I don't want to give the impression that Don and I aren't perfect (laughter), but one day I found myself so aggravated with him. When he was shaving, he would let the water run down his arm. It would drip off his elbow and splash onto the sink, and he would not wipe it up. I nagged him and nagged him about it, but one day it came to me that there's nothing worth ruining a good relationship over. I decided that day to make that my motto. I learned it in my "old age," but I was able to put this small annoyance in perspective with how much I love Don. I found myself praying, "Lord, help me to love Don more." And all of a sudden, as I picked up the towel and wiped up the water, I had this sense of caressing Don. It's like God gives us each other to practice on, so we can truly relate to the people out there as Jesus would.

**Karen:** We find ourselves—in our "old age"—finally catching on to fun! Ron and I are on different body clocks. He's a morning person, and I'm a night person. When he's in play mode, I'm usually in work mode. The other day, I was deep into a project when Ron suddenly turned up wanting to go for a boat ride. I was about to make excuses, when it was like I was hit in the head with a brick. "Are you crazy, woman?" a voice said in my head. "Your husband, who works so hard, wants to go for a boat ride and you want to sit at your computer?" I find myself saying to God like, "I know you know I haven't been lazy, but there's so much to get done. Please comfort me that you'll help me with the work, because right now we need to play."

**Alicia:** I can relate to that. It's so hard for me to put down a project. We've come up with what Geoff calls "porch sitting time." It's a time for just sitting down in the cool of the day after the kids are in bed. Actually, I bought Geoff a gliding rocker for the front porch so we'd have a place to sit. We have had some wonderful nights just looking at the stars.

**Geoff:** We have also tried to institute a "date night" once a week. We think it's a great idea. We haven't been able to pull it off consistently, but when we have, it really helps us feel close to each other, even if we don't leave our home but just watch a fun video or something.

**Ron:** There's so much wisdom and experience resident in this group, I wish we could talk often. Let's think of this as a beginning dialogue, to be continued . . .

**Marti:** . . . at the 2005 Seeds Conference!

**Ron:** That would be fun. Meantime, we can't thank all of you enough for sharing so openly of yourselves for the sake of the growth of couples in ministry. We pray that your sharing will touch the lives of kindred spirits engaged in church planting and other ministry callings around the world, strengthening the love ties between them and encouraging them amidst the challenges of ministry on the front lines of evangelism.

# Contextualising *Family Life* Education

**by Valerie Fidelia**

*"It is true that moral guidance and counsel need to be given, but the way you say it and to whom you say it are as important as what you say." ( 1 Timothy 1:8 The Message Bible)*

## INTRODUCTION

This presentation is designed to give us an introduction to contextualisation and to open our eyes to the pitfalls and possibilities that contextualisation presents. There are some basics we need to take into consideration, but each contextualisation will depend on the culture we are addressing.

## DEFINITION

What do we mean by contextualisation? One definition is, "Making the teaching meaningful and understandable to all people within their cultural setting" (Oxford English Dictionary). We cannot separate contextualisation from culture; so, what is "culture"? "Culture" implies "a set of values and beliefs," "language and thinking style" or "world view." Culture is "a system of meanings and values that shape one's behaviour" (Huang & Nieves-Grafals, 1994).

> As people, we share a common human nature. Beyond that, our unique genetic makeup determines much of who we are. That is the "nature" part of us, or our birth characteristics. Our life experience, the "nurture" part, is just a complex as our genetic code. It involves our culture, gender, spiritual development, socio-economic status, personal history, generational concerns, geography, phase of life, personality type and many other factors. (Lane, 2002, pp. 33, 34)

## WHY CONTEXTUALISE?

We must find common ground with the people we want to reach; to meet the needs of the people within our community of faith and the needs of those in the wider community. There is so much in our family life education that is relevant to and necessary for the wider community. We should view all family life education teaching as an opportunity to meet the heart needs of those around us. It is a wonderful means of offering the love of Jesus to a soul-sick society. We cannot minister effectively to any group if we do not contextualise.

**Examples of simple contextualisation.** There are very simple examples of contextualisation that we practise every day without even thinking about it.

*Spelling and words.* I use UK English and the first thing I do with any American English printed communication that I intend to pass on is to "correct" the spelling, e.g. labor/labour, program/programme, etc. We change words too, such as trunk/boot, diapers/nappies, etc.

We regularly make *adaptations*, that is, changing places and names to fit the context in which we are teaching. For example, many moral-building stories for children set originally in North America or Western Europe can be adapted to other societies by a simple change of town name and child's forename. Thus it becomes relevant to the audience.

We also make *modifications*, adapting and changing what we are presenting to fit the mindset and actual expectations of the target audience. For example, in premarital counselling it is very important to discuss family finances, but the context in which we are doing the counselling will determine how we approach the issue. In many parts of the world, women are not involved with family finances. Finances are strictly in the hands of the males in the family. Cultural sensitivity therefore needs to be applied when dealing with topics.

When we are planning to hold family life education programmes it would be good to list all the cultures in our congregation—or target audience. It may surprise us to find the breadth of cultural differences we have in one small congregation. In the Nicosia, Cyprus, Seventh-day Adventist church where

I worship, for example, there are about 48 members and these represent 20 nationalities—each with a distinct culture. There are also other kinds of diversity within the group: socio-economic, linguistic, liberal and conservative approaches to parenting, etc. One size certainly does not fit all.

We may further subdivide race and ethnicity and consider social/economic/educational factors, class, income, profession etc. Gender, personality type, birth order and spiritual growth are further subsets within these various groups that comprise our audience. How well we understand the various cultural subsets in our target audience will determine how effective our teaching is. Therefore, preparation is essential in order to minister to a particular people group. One must become well acquainted with each culture to do effective ministry.

**Contexualised ministry in Scripture.** There are many biblical examples of preparation for contextualised ministry. Moses was an expert in Egyptian life, culture, religion, and protocol. Was this part of his preparation for the work of leading God's people out of Egypt? He would have been thinking as an Egyptian when he was addressing the Pharaoh. Daniel and his friends were schooled in Babylonian language, literature and history. Daniel was quite at ease in the presence of the King and Ministers of State. Paul was versed in Greek classics to the extent that, in Athens, he was able to quote a Greek philosopher (Whitehouse, 2003). People from other culture groups and other religious backgrounds deserve our serious study and respect.

## UNIVERSAL TRUTHS OR CULTURALLY DETERMINED TRUTHS

Crossing cultures is easier when one understands which differences are culturally based and which are not. No one culture is "right" and the others "wrong." Following are eight "truths." Are they universal or culturally determined?

1. **People should always try to arrive at the appointed time.** In one field where I worked, meetings would be announced for "9:00 a.m., European time." There was a gap in the cultural understanding of what 'on time' meant.

2. **It is best to tell a person if they have offended you.** In some cultures this is acceptable, but in others it would never happen.

3. **It is rude to accept an offer the first time.** In the Middle East it is impolite to accept an offer the first time. The story is told of a young Middle Eastern woman visiting London for the first time. It was bitterly cold and she was looking forward to being in a warm house with a warm drink. Arriving at her destination, the hostess offered the young woman a cup of tea. Being from the Middle East, she politely refused, expecting a second and third invitation. Her British hostess, who was used to "no means no," made no further offers. The young woman went without her drink (Roden, 1968). Cultural differences indeed.

4. **It is better to be rich than to be poor.** Some civilisations put great store on wealth and possessions, but other cultures values things like health and family before wealth.

5. **One should choose one's own spouse.** Arranged marriages are still common in some cultures although they are less popular than in the past.

6. **Polite men will allow women to walk through doorways first.** There are many cultures where this would not be acceptable practice. A man would not defer to a woman and a woman would be reluctant to go through a doorway ahead of a man.

7. **Individuals have the right to make decisions about their future, regardless of what their family wants.** Individualistic societies take this view. Collective societies would not subscribe to this.

8. **Good children will always agree with their parents.** Some cultures believe this. Others encourage their children to ask question and explore; these parents are not unhappy when their children take a different view from the parents—providing they present it with respect (Lane, 2002).

## APPROACHES TO CULTURAL DIFFERENCES

There are a number of ways societies respond to other cultures:

**Xenophobia.** Fear of other cultures may lead to racism, hate groups and crimes.

**Ethnocentricity.** Believing one's own culture is superior leads to patronising, stereotyping, bigotry and intolerance of those who are different.

**Forced assimilation.** This approach says essentially, "Your culture is not okay. My culture is the best so you must be like me."

**Segregationist.** For cultures to co-exist they must be separate. The worst example is apartheid.

**Accepting.** In this approach there is a willingness to co-exist, accommodate, and build relationships. All cultures are equal and should be respected. While acceptance is good, God calls us to do more.

**Celebrating.** This means learning from and enjoying the diversity of others. God created us cultural beings and He values diversity in all creation. "Each person, and each culture, has a unique secret. Each is capable of knowing something of God which no one else knows. In the meeting of strangers we have the opportunity to share that treasure with each other" (Adeney, 1995, p. 141).

## COMMON CULTURAL DIFFERENCES THAT IMPACT FAMILY LIFE EDUCATION

Cultural differences are real and significantly impact our cross-cultural relationships. As family life educators cultural differences may have a significant impact on our ability to instruct and influence others. Cultural sensitivity is needed, for example, in the following areas of beliefs about family life.

**Child-rearing.** We differ in our various cultures on discipline, sleep habits, feeding, and acceptable public behaviour.

**Living with in-laws as a way of life.**

**Marrying close relatives.**

**Role of the extended family.** Individualistic societies cater to the nuclear family. Collective societies embrace what the extended family has to offer.

**Physical touch.** Societies differ in showing affection through physical touch in public places or at home in front of strangers.

**Arranged marriages.** What is the role of premarital counselling? Should the in-laws be included?

**Gender groups.** In many cultures men and women congregate in gender groups. They socialise separately—women at home, men in the coffee shop. They have separate eating arrangements.

**Sharing marital secrets.** Some cultures advocate keeping marital secrets between the couple; in other cultures the wife may be closer to other women than she is to her husband. It is common to share confidences.

**Sexuality.** Can it be discussed? How to teach and help in a culturally sensitive way is an important question for family life educators to consider.

**Monogamy.**

**Abuse and incest awareness.**

**Hospitality.** Some cultures view Westerners as "stingy" because they do not offer extravagantly laden tables, which is a normal rule of hospitality in many cultures.

**Gender roles.** In some cultures a man will not discuss finances or any important family decision with his wife. She must accept what he says. In some cultures it is difficult for a woman to live alone. Prior to marriage she is reliant on her father or brothers, during marriage she relies on her husband and, should she be divorced or widowed, she may have to rely on her own family again or the males in her husband's family.

## CONCLUSION

**Need for culturally sensitive resources.** It is easy to see from the simple examples set out above how wide our cultural gap is on so many topics. A problem we face is that most good literature on family life education comes from a Western culture mind-set. It must be modified significantly for some cultures. For instance, there is an urgent need to develop culturally sensitive exercises and assignments for use in marriage enrichment courses and for premarital counselling. Some parts of the world field cope with this very well, but others with fewer finances are constantly frustrated with the lack of resources.

For those who are wishing to understand cultural differences better, I would recommend *A Beginner's Guide to Crossing Cultures and Making Friends in a Multicultural World* by Patty Lane (InterVarsity, 2002 ISBN 0-8308-2346-8). She is the director of the Office of Intercultural Initiatives for the Baptist General Convention of Texas.

Valerie Fidelia is the Family Ministries director for the Middle East Union, Trans-European Division. This paper was originally presented as an interactive seminar with participants of the TED Certificate in Family Life Education program, March 2003. Used by permission.

## References

Adeney, B. T. (1995). *Strange virtues: Ethics in a multicultural world*. Downers Grove, IL: InterVarsity Press.

Huang, L. N., & Nieves-Grafals, S. (1994). Unpublished cross-cultural counselling lecture. Washington, D.C.

Lane, P. (2002). *A beginner's guide to crossing cultures: Making friends in a multicultural world*. Downers Grove, IL: InterVarsity Press.

Roden, C. (1968). *A book of Middle Eastern cookery*. London: Penguin Books, Ltd.

Whitehouse, G. (2003). Unpublished presentation at Adventist and Muslim relationship conference, Paphos, Cyprus.

# *Mission* of Fellowship

**by Gottfried Oosterwal**

## INTRODUCTION

Recent research on church growth has shown that a church's understanding of itself and its role in mission critically affects its growth and advance. Right concepts of ourselves as God's people and of His commission lead to growth. False concepts of purpose and mission or narrow views of the biblical concept of mission impede progress. Examples from historical Adventism illustrate this.

**"Shut door" to "open door."** After the Great Disappointment of 1844, Adventists struggled with the questions, What are we here for now? What is our mission? At first they used the image of Noah's ark to define themselves and their purpose. The faithful few were safely hidden in the "ark." The Lord Himself had shut the door and now they were anxiously awaiting His return. James White defined their mission as "to encourage the brethren of Laodicea." Thus they spoke only to themselves. There was no growth. No advance. Their framework for understanding seemed biblical, yet they were all too limited in their self-understanding. For them the door of salvation was shut, and nobody could be added. After a decade or so, following the guidance given by God to our church, we suddenly changed and grew in our self-understanding as a church and mission. In the 1850's James White defined the church as "an open door to the world." The church began to grow and its mission began to advance.

**Daniels and the "little flock."** In the 1920's, when difficulties, doubts, debates, and questions about revelation and inspiration bred a decline in church growth, A. G. Daniels was asked by the General Conference to hold meetings and stimulate a new self-understanding. At the first meeting Brother Daniels held, he said in effect, "If we had the right understanding of ourselves as a people and would act accordingly, millions would join this church and make preparations for the coming of Christ." Immediately after the meeting the brethren took him aside and rebuked him for what he had said, admonishing him, "Don't teach that heresy again." "What heresy?" he asked. "*Millions* of people would join," they said. "That is a wrong understanding; we are God's remnant; we are a little flock. 'Millions' is

a characteristic of Babylon. We, however, are only a small little flock who have chosen to go the narrow path, to go through the narrow gate." He reported that the prevailing idea of the church as a "little flock" presented considerable resistance to efforts to move the membership into missionary action. This view, despite being based on a biblical metaphor, had resulted in a lopsided, limited perspective.

Today, despite considerable growth in our self-understanding and our mission, some three billion people have never even heard the name of Christ. Though more is involved in accomplishing mission than a proper self-understanding as a church, many are convinced we need to grow in this area of self-understanding so that the mission may advance. How shall we grow?

## OUR IMAGE OF THE CHURCH SHAPES OUR MISSION

The New Testament uses many word images to describe the church, such as *truth, remnant, mountain, Zion, ship, sheep, body, people of God.* No one word can fully define the many aspects of what it means to be the church of God. Each image stands in need of being complemented and corrected by the others. Further, the church as *truth, remnant,* or as *little flock* needs to adapt and change when new circumstances arise in the world, so that it may be *present truth,* and respond to new challenges.

Our church, which once identified itself as the "warning message," is now coming to understand itself as a "caring church." It is not a matter of choosing between one image and another. Each image needs the other. One supports the other, compliments the other, and corrects the other.

**Proclamation of truth.** Until now our Adventist Church has been guided by two or three typical, biblical images of the church. We have identified ourselves with the "truth" and see our mission as *proclamation of the truth.* While nothing should detract from this very biblical self-understanding of the church and its mission, which has had such an impact upon the world, there is more to mission than proclamation.

**Service.** We've also seen our mission as *service*; we've established many hospitals and clinics and schools and are increasingly engaged in technical development. We thank God for the progress, yet there is something very basic missing in our self-understanding as a church.

**Fellowship.** Mission is not only proclamation, be it in word, in publications, through the media. Nor is it only proclamation and service. A third characteristic is the hallmark of mission, the notion of *fellowship*.

A study by the Southern Baptist Convention asked their new members from the last five years why they had joined. The leading reason: "We joined because we loved the fellowship in the Baptist churches." When that study was mentioned at a meeting of the administrative committee responsible for the growth of the Adventist church, the chairman commented, "Brethren, I'm so glad that this is not the case with the Seventh-day Adventist Church." He believed that people join the church because they love and hear the truth and that church mission is a matter of proclaiming the truth with clarity. The fact is that today people love this church not in the first place because of the truth, even though it is an essential pillar, but because of the fellowship.

Recently the Southeastern California Conference asked new members of the last five years about their reasons for joining the Adventist church. The conference secretary reported, "Most of the people said, 'We were loved into the truth.'"

## FELLOWSHIP: CORE OF THE BIBLICAL IMAGES OF CHURCH

**Importance of fellowship shown by sociology.** Sociologists tell us the greatest disease of modern humanity is alienation and utter loneliness. Families are breaking down; primary groups are breaking down; urbanization makes us just lonely individuals. The greatest need of humanity today is a new sense of belonging, a new sense of fellowship.

**Biblical teaching about fellowship.** Paul speaks of the church as a "fellowship in the gospel" (Phil. 1:5). The apostle John writes, "If we walk in the light as He is the light, we have fellowship with one another" (1 John 1:7, NKJV). Other images may not use the word, but emphasize the same thing. The church is compared to a human body (1 Cor. 12), with every member needing every other and linked to every other. When one receives honor all receive

honor; when one of the members is hurting we are all hurting. That's the core of the fellowship.

This fellowship is the reflection of the relationship between the Father and the Son. "The believers devoted themselves to the apostles' doctrine and to fellowship," says Acts 2:42. "And the Lord added to their number day by day those who were being saved." We don't read here of mighty evangelistic campaigns, as powerful as they are. We don't read here of establishing schools and hospitals, as important as they are. The reason for the growth of the early church was the fellowship of the believers.

**When fellowship is missing.** Often the church can be a place of insensitivity and great hurt rather than a place of fellowship. The presence or absence of fellowship is conveyed by our attitude and our behavior, in the way we greet one another, in our conversations with one another. How do we treat strangers among us? Do we take pains to create a feeling of fellowship?

For every 100 members we bring into the Adventist church 40 leave and most of these do so within the first two years after their baptism. The Institute of World Mission conducted a study on why this is so. More than 2,000 former Adventists in North America and Europe were interviewed. Of those interviewed 70% reported, "We would have stayed in the church if there would have been a genuine fellowship among the believers."

Not long ago my family and I went to a church where we were not known. We arrived early and sat down. When the service was about to begin a sister suddenly appeared in front of us and said, "That's my seat." If I hadn't been a long standing member of the Adventist church I would have left, never to come back.

Recently a sister in one of our Adventist centers took her own life, leaving behind a note which began, "I have nobody . . . ." How is it possible to be a member of an Adventist church for 22 years and end your life with the words, "I have nobody." How is it possible to be a member of a choir for 12 years and end your life with the words, "I have nobody."

## BARRIERS TO FELLOWSHIP

Why is it so difficult for many of us to accept this concept of the church as fellowship? Ellen White tells us that, because of the conditions of the people, God is holding His hand over the church so that not many people are joining (*Testimonies, vol. 6*, p. 371; *Testimonies, vol. 9*, p. 189). Among those conditions she describes are lack of love and lack of fellowship.

She indicates that many more people could have been baptized. That means that instead of the membership we have now there could have been many millions.

**Theological barriers.** Our mission to proclaim truth has become almost sacred to us. It is a core pillar of the Adventist mission, and I pray to God that it ever will remain so, but it is only one aspect of what it means to be the church in mission. The text says, "They continued steadfastly in the apostles' doctrine and fellowship . . ." (Acts 2:42). They devoted themselves to Bible study, to the truth, *and* to fellowship. We need to see ourselves, not just as proclaimers, messengers of the truth (which we are) but also as people who are fellowshipping with their own kind, with their neighbors and even with their enemies.

My mother was an Adventist and my father often went along, but I hated to go to church as a boy, for a number of reasons. In the first place I couldn't play soccer, and all Dutch boys grow up playing soccer. I never could join the junior league and of course all my friends said, "Hey, Bobby (that was my name when I was young), when are you going to join the rest of us playing soccer?" The second reason was that we didn't have a church. We had no building, no tower, no organ, no choir, no minister with a beautiful robe. The little handful of church members in Rotterdam were meeting in the greasy basement of a bicycle repair shop. There was never a moment of quiet, all the time you heard the metal hitting metal. I hated to go there. On top of that, the building we used was located in the most run down part of that large port city. You can't imagine how that section of the city looked and smelled. And coming from a better part of town, I hated it.

At times I attended the Dutch Reformed churches of my friends. They were huge—with towers and organs, choirs, and reverent ministers with long robes. I sat in them with awe. And my friends would say, "Hey, Bobby, where do you go to church?"

I replied, "Don't worry, don't worry." I was so ashamed; I was angry.

One Saturday as we set off for church I spied some of my friends waiting for me behind the corner. School was closed that particular day and they wanted to follow me and see my church. Noticing them and guessing what they intended, I excused myself, "Momma, I better run on ahead." I started running as fast as I could. I could run very fast in those days, so I lost my friends across the railroad tracks. Every Sabbath after that I would watch to make sure my friends weren't watching. If they were, I'd say, "Bye-bye, Momma," and I'd run

to church. One Sabbath I overheard my mother say to a church sister, "Our Bobby loves to go to church. He can't wait for us; he's always running!"

But all that changed. The church became the center of my life. I found meaning here and the deepest fellowship that ever can be experienced by a human being. I know the day and I know the hour. The date was May 10, 1940, a Friday, when troops from Nazi Germany invaded the Netherlands. The Germans had used their crack paratroopers for the first time in the war, landing them in the southern part of Rotterdam where I lived, while the Dutch Marines were defending the bridges in the northern part of the city.

The battle raged from house to house—shooting, bombing. The next day was the Sabbath and as our family huddled in our basement, afraid of the bombs, mother began dressing my brother and my sister.

"What are you doing?" father asked.

"I'm dressing the children."

"I see that, but what for?"

Answered mother, "We are going to church."

My startled father stated, "Today? There's a war going on!" The paratroopers were firing a machine gun right in front of our house. Father sought to reason with her, "Not even a dog is outside. How can we go on the streets?"

My mother simply responded, "Today is the day of fellowship."

When she said "day of fellowship," something hit me right there and then as a young teenager. You see the Sabbath is not only a great memorial to God's creative activity as in Exodus 20, but Deuteronomy 5 indicates that the Sabbath was given as a memorial of redemption, a memorial to the time when one nation was molded together. Once we were slaves, with divisions among us as human beings, divisions between slaves and masters, between tribes, between people of different races and ethnic groups. But the Lord has given us the Sabbath, so that we can celebrate the fellowship of the believers.

As we entered the street, a soldier, with hand grenades in his belt and a machine gun under his arm, confronted us.

"Halt, where are you going?"

"We're going to church."

He said, "Go back, go back, there's a war going on, there is shooting all the time."

My mother said, "No, we want to go to church."

Then he suddenly thought of something and said, "No, no, no, not today. Tomorrow. Everybody is confused in the war."

"No, no," my mother said opening her Bible to Exodus 20. At that point he called in his sergeant.

The sergeant said, "You better go home."

"Oh, no, we go to church today."

And he thought for a moment and said, "Jewish people."

"No, no," my mother said, knowing the love the Nazis had for the Jewish people, "we are Seventh-day Adventists. Look the Bible says . . . ." But that was too powerful for the sergeant, and so he called the lieutenant.

The lieutenant listened for awhile and, realizing what was in the minds of my parents, said, "Go, and may God be with you."

I'll not give here the details of how we crossed the front line between the Dutch Marines and the German Paratroopers. Some of us in the family are still bearing the scars. When we got to the greasy basement of the bicycle repair shop, without an organ, without a tower, the whole congregation was there. The bombs were falling and the grenades exploding, but the church was there. It was there because the very hallmark of the church is not the building, not the tower, but the fellowship of the believers. There was hugging and kissing. They did what the Bible says to do when you get together. Greet each other warmly. Hug, give each other a kiss, a kiss of love, or a holy kiss. I still see before me the hugging and the kissing . . . . And suddenly then I felt so proud to be a Seventh-day Adventist.

We didn't have an organ or a tower, or a big building, only a greasy basement in a bicycle repair shop, but we were celebrating the very essence of what it means to be the church, we were a fellowship of believers. It was that fellowship that saw us through those five terrible years of the war when there was hunger and when people were taken captive and put into concentration camps. Some children lost their fathers but they had many other fathers because of the church. Some people lost mothers, but we had many mothers as long as we had sisters in the church. That's the core of being the church. As long as one member had some soap (and my mother had hoarded a lot of soap), then the whole church had soap. And as long as some people had bread or flour or sugar or salt, the whole church had bread and flour and sugar and salt. That is what saw us through.

Some who were teenagers then owe their lives to the fellowship of believers. When all the food was rationed to one quarter loaf of bread per family, some older Adventists came to our home and gave us their bread. Before the war was over these very people had collapsed in the street. Some of us can tell the story because we are alive and well because of their sacrifice.

The next week, so proud was I of this people that I made my stand to be joined to this people of God. But all the churches were closed because the Germans forbade any meeting of more than two people. However, the following week, May 25, the churches were open again. We met, even though our city had been bombed to pieces, the second city in the Second World War after Warsaw. Many of us had lost everything we had. Some had lost their lives. And here the church was together again in sadness, thanking God for our lives but being so sad about the lives of the brothers and sisters, for when one is hurting the whole church is hurting.

We had barely sat down and our organ, the little harmonium, had begun to play when suddenly we heard a sound in the stairway to the basement of the repair shop. It was the sound of boots. The door opened and there stood a German soldier. A hush fell over us all. Forgive us, but when you lose everything through bombing, when everything is being taken away, when your country's being occupied by an enemy, you hate that enemy and we did, we did. There was hatred in our hearts and in our minds.

The first deacon went up to him and said, "Get out, leave us alone! Isn't it enough that you bomb our city and destroy our lives? Isn't it enough that you rob us of everything? This is a little church! Get away; get out; leave us alone!"

The German soldier just stood there and said, "But, I've come here to worship. I'm a brother."

I saw the first deacon swallow very hard. Just a few days before, his home and everything he owned had been destroyed. From a wealthy businessman he had been turned into a pauper because of the bombings by the Nazis. Then, suddenly, he throws his arm around the young soldier and says to him, "If you have come here to worship God, you are my brother." And he took him to the front seat of the church and held his hand through the whole service.

Fellowship isn't just for people like ourselves, fellowship extends to the foreigner and the stranger, fellowship extends to the enemy surrounding us. That's the core of the church in mission.

**Cultural barriers.** Often when we speak about fellowship we think of fun, having a good time, eating, laughing, but not doing things that pertain to God and the church. We have relegated the concept of fellowship to the social, that is, the secular realm of life, which is of a much lower nature than the spiritual. Again, this is an unbiblical division and the sooner we get rid of it the better. We must recognize that to be in fellowship with each other is a spiritual experience of great magnitude. The Psalmist constantly speaks about the joy of fellowshipping with the believers in the temple of God. The New Testament is full of this notion of fellowship as wholistic. Fellowship is at the very core of being a Christian.

To the extent that culture focuses on the individual; the fellowship of the group tends to become only an appendix. Cultural individualism tends to shape our Adventist theology, our church services, as well as our church buildings. When we enter the church we look only at each other's neck, when we look at each other we see only each other's neck, and when we leave the church we look at each other's neck again. Instead we should be looking each other in the eye and saying, "Brother, how are you; sister, how are you?" Our theology defines the church as a group of individuals meeting with God, instead of a communal feast, the celebration of the fellowship of the believers on the very day of fellowship.

## VISITING: MAKING FELLOWSHIP A REALITY

Let's start to overcome obstacles to fellowship by visiting each other. Let's speak *to* each other instead of speaking *about* each other. Let's eat and drink together. The greatest criticism of Jesus was that He ate and drank with sinners. But that was the very core of fellowshipping with people whom He loved.

Let's feast together, let's do things together. Ellen White describes the annual feasts among ancient Israel and indicates that it would be a good thing for us as a church to have such a celebration (see *Patriarchs and Prophets*, pp. 540, 541). God knew what was good for the believers then, divided and separated into tribes as they were. All met together and slept together in little huts. Can you image what kind of forced fellowship it was? But it worked.

As a boy I was always afraid that my friends wouldn't accept me. But they did, and one reason was

that I had so many people I knew in Rotterdam. As we boys roamed throughout that big city, we would need a drink or to use the toilet. My friends would say, "Hey, Bobby, don't you have an uncle or an aunt around here somewhere?" So I would walk to a door, ring the bell, and inevitably a man or woman would open the door and say, "Aye, Bobby, I'm so glad you are here, come up." Whatever we needed the people behind these doors would provide. It didn't matter that sometimes there were 12 or 15 of us. "That's alright," they'd say, "your friends are our friends."

Who were these people? Not blood relatives, for my mother came from far away Lithuania and my father from the most northern part of Holland. I grew up without uncles and aunts. Who then were these "aunts" and "uncles" all over the city? They were members of the church, that little group of people that met in the bicycle repair shop. And how did I know where they lived? Because my father and mother, like all the members of our church, were visiting others.

It is not easy to be a genuine Adventist in life in general; you need the comfort and the strength of each other. When my father was in an accident our family experienced great poverty. Yet almost every day there was a brother or sister of the church who visited us and each time they left a dollar, a Dutch gilder, in the hands of my mother. And we didn't have to be afraid of having nothing to eat. We were a fellowship of believers, the very core of what it means to be the church.

## CONCLUSION

Let us visit each other, let us speak with each other, let us eat together, let's do things together, let's feast together, let's meet in small groups for prayer and Bible study to see how we can advance the work. But above all, let our whole life be one fellowship with each other. It is as Scripture says, "If we walk in the Light, as He is in the Light, we have fellowship with one another" (1 John 1:7, NKJV). God bless you.

Adapted with permission from a sermon by Gottfried Oosterwal presented at Pioneer Memorial Church, Andrews University, Berrien Springs, Michigan, July 18, 1992.

### References

White, E. G. (1958). *Patriarchs and prophets*. Nampa, ID: Pacific Press Publishing Association.

White, E. G. (1948). *Testimonies for the church, vol. 6*. Nampa, ID: Pacific Press Publishing Association.

White, E. G. (1948). *Testimonies for the church, vol. 9*. Nampa, ID: Pacific Press Publishing Association.

# 101 *Ideas* for Family Evangelism

**by Karen and Ron Flowers**

## PERSONAL PREPARATION

- Study carefully such Bible verses as Eph. 2:4-8, 13; 2 Cor. 5:21; Rom. 5:12-20; 8:1 which convey the good news of salvation in Christ.

- Reflect on the love of God. What human instruments have profoundly influenced you in your understanding of God's love? How is your understanding of God's love growing?

- Prayerfully develop your personal testimony of faith and assurance of salvation in Christ. Writing your testimony may help you to think it through.

- Make a personal list of Bible verses which speak to you of God's love. Study and memorize these for sharing with your personal testimony.

## SHARING FAITH IN MARRIAGE

- Share your testimony with your spouse. Listen to your spouse's testimony. How has the gospel influenced your relationship?

- Give evidence of God's grace at work in your life by your empathy with your spouse, in sharing thoughts and inner feelings together.

- Take time to communicate about the meaning of your faith with your spouse. How does your faith affect the way you handle anger, resolve conflict, deal with depression?

- Endeavor to uplift and encourage your spouse with affirmation and appropriate compliments.

- Worship and pray together regularly.

## WINNING WAYS WITH UNBELIEVING SPOUSES

- Be a source of emotional and spiritual encouragement for your non-believing spouse, striving not to be judgmental of his/her behavior, but offering compliments and affirmation regularly.

- Provide an example of your belief in God's grace by living your Adventist Christianity before your spouse honestly. Be candid about weaknesses and faults, recognizing these as areas where Christian growth is needed.

- Communicate with your spouse about the forgiveness and continual renewal you are finding in Christ. Let everything you have learned about relationships in Christ make your experience in marriage better.

- Make extra efforts to identify and emphasize the things you and your spouse have in common. Seek points of agreement.

- Enter willingly and happily into every possible aspect of your spouse's life which you can without compromising principle.

- Discover together new activities and friends to replace those that may have been left behind because of your beliefs, realizing that the strength of your love bond together is the greatest asset you have in winning your loved one for Christ.

- As you develop acquaintances at church, invite men to befriend your husband, or women your wife.

- Invite your spouse to participate in activities of church life: social activities, health seminars, family life events, retreats, camp-outs, or church building/ maintenance programs.

- Encourage the participation of your spouse by recruiting and enlisting his or her expertise in some aspect of church life.

## EVANGELISTIC PARENTING

- Prepare a list of changes you would like to make to give a more evangelistic approach to your parenting.

- Make the gospel attractive to your children by your positive relationships with them, by smiling often, by entering into your child's feelings.

- Sing songs to your children which tell of God's love.

- Pray with each of your children, rehearsing God's love and your love for your child in your prayer.

- Tell your child in simple terms about God's love as described in His Word.

- Ask forgiveness of your child for something you have done which brought pain to him or her.

- Show unconditional love and acceptance of your child. Avoid conveying the message, "I will love you if . . ."

- Plan ways for giving each of your children special opportunities to make their decisions to trust in Christ personally.

## RELATIVES

- Pray regularly that relatives will accept the gospel.

- Work together as a family to prepare a list of specific efforts your family can make to lead unsaved relatives to Christ.

- Plan ways for making contact with each relative for whom the family is praying—by phone, by letter, by personal visit to give, first of all, an expression of your love and to share encouragement.

## FRIENDS AND NEIGHBORS

- During family worship relate what special opportunities for gospel sharing have occurred for each one during the day—in your family, at work, at school, in the neighborhood.

- Discuss as a family the prospective spiritual interest of individuals in work, neighborhood, school, family circles.

- Start a prayer list on which are the names of your 10 closest neighbors.

- During family worship talk about special ways of witnessing to the individuals on the prayer list.

- Encourage your children to do little errands of love and mercy for those less fortunate than themselves.

- Cooperate with your child in some task of Christian service to which their abilities, strengths and interests are suited and from which they will gain success and joy.

- Assist your older children and young people to form missionary bands with their playmates and school-mates for some task of Christian help work.

## SPIRITUAL GIFTS

- Spend some family worship periods reading and studying the Bible texts on spiritual gifts—Rom. 12; 1 Cor. 12, 13; Eph. 4. Discuss: How do these texts help us to identify our spiritual gifts?

- Read biographies of Seventh-day Adventist pioneers or other notable Christian leaders whose spirit of service and spiritual gifts will inspire and encourage your family.

- Think together, pray about and discover what each family member's talents and abilities are. Thank God together for these gifts and abilities of each one.

- The gifts that God has given your children may differ from yours as parents. Invite other Adventist Christian relatives or church members who may have spiritual gifts and abilities more nearly like those of your children to share their experiences to help provide models and examples for your children.

- Express appreciation in a special way for the unique talents, gifts and abilities of each one in your family, affirming the contribution each one makes to the smooth running of the family.

- Think and pray together about how the special abilities of father, mother, sister, brother or other household member could be used by God in the home, in the church, in missionary work in the community.

- Recognizing personal talents and abilities, let each family member prepare a simple plan of one or two specific things he or she could do to witness for God. Small children may draw pictures depicting their contributions.

- Ask family members to share on a regular basis how God has prompted them to use their talents and abilities in their everyday activities.

## A FAMILY MISSIONARY PROJECT

- Plan to involve the family's various talents in a special family missionary project. Get suggestions from church leadership on projects that might be helped by your family's involvement.

- Tailor the family's involvement to accommodate various ages of family members, keeping an appropriate balance between the family's personal needs and the need to share with others. Strive toward an experience that has some measurable results and whereby all can feel a sense of success and fulfillment.

- Read the Bible or gospel literature to an elderly or visually impaired person.

- Pay a friendship visit to a shut-in.

- Do grocery shopping for a shut-in.

- Write a letter of encouragement to a bereaved, grieving or discouraged family.

- Visit someone who is sick.

- Provide a no-interest loan to a financially struggling family.

- Bake a loaf of bread for a homeless person.

- Prepare sandwiches for distribution to homeless individuals.

- Offer a food basket regularly to one or more families in need.

- Do grass-mowing, leaf-raking or other yard work for an elderly person.

- Provide once-a-week child care for a single parent.

- Distribute gospel literature home to home regularly in a specific part of town.

- Sing or play musical instruments at a nursing home or retirement center.

- Give a few hours of service on occasion to families needing assistance in child care, home remodeling, financial management.

- Provide foster child care for a young person in need.

- Give new or used clothing to persons in need or donate such items to an appropriate distribution center.

- Go Ingathering as a family.

- Address invitations to evangelistic meetings.

- Enroll neighbors in a Bible correspondence course.

- Distribute invitations to evangelistic meetings.

- Invite younger family members to share toys with children of needy families.

- Use the family car to transport individuals to evangelistic meetings.

- Invite friends to a health fair or cooking school.

- Invite one or two of your children's friends to church and a meal on Sabbath. Provide transportation if needed.

- Have a "help and bless" brainstorming session with your family. What act of Christian helpfulness might your family perform right now for some acquaintance in your extended family, your church, your neighborhood, your community?

- If there are aspects to the missionary project which can be done during family worship, such as preparing mailings, developing Bible studies, then plan for some special worship time which will incorporate these, giving family members time to discuss their feelings about the missionary activity.

## FAMILY STEWARDSHIP

- Plan a special gift for the current thirteenth Sabbath mission offering.

- Plan a family investment project. Ask your Sabbath School investment leader or Sabbath School superintendent for more information and suggestions on how your family can become involved in this plan of raising money for missions.

- Establish a "Lord's Fund" as part of the family budget in addition to regular tithes and offerings. This money may be kept in the family treasury and distributed when family members feel especially impressed by God to assist in some unusual missionary project or some other special need that comes to their attention.

- In addition to regular family tithes, offerings and church commitments, pray about missionary work with which your family might become sacrificially involved.

## THE ART OF EVANGELISTIC VISITING

- Ask an individual successful in visitation to take your family, or members of your family, on a visitation excursion into your neighborhood. Allow this individual to coach you in appropriate manners, conversation and conduct of the visit.

- To provide an opportunity to become acquainted and begin to cultivate friendship, take a "Welcome to the Neighborhood" gift to a family just moving in.

- Take a "Congratulations on your new baby" gift to a family with a newborn.

- Take a "Congratulations on your wedding" gift to a newly wedded couple.

- Take an appropriate expression of sympathy to a family who has experienced some loss.

- Invite your neighbors to church programs, i.e. Vacation Bible School, holiday celebrations, socials, etc., so you will be prepared to invite them to evangelistic meetings and worship services.

- Take a gift of food to a neighbor. Allow your children to have a part in its preparation and its presentation.

- Give gifts that are tailored to perceived interests and tastes of your neighbors, perhaps a potted plant to a neighbor who likes plants, a stamp for a stamp collector, a recipe for one who enjoys cooking.

- Give gifts that will interest and delight your neighbor's children. Christian periodicals with stories, storybooks, or tapes, for example, are gifts that will be appreciated by both adults and children.

- Ask your neighbors for a favor. Show them that you need their friendship and help as a family. This will place you on common ground with them and open the doors for fellowship.

- When visiting homes of friends or acquaintances offer a humble prayer as you part company. Your prayer will be a powerful witness to your belief in God, His care, and the truth in which you believe.

- Invite other families, acquaintances of the family or those with whom you would like to become better acquainted, to your home for family worship. Make the service brief, interesting and full of life. Sing songs that can be easily sung and pray short, simple prayers. Choose cassettes for listening or readings tailored to the age and interest level of those present.

- Invite others to your home for a meal. Offer friendship and modeling about temperance and healthful living through the meal which is served.

- Invite others to join you in a family outing or recreational activity that is typical of the wholesome times your family spends together.

## REACHING OUT TO THE WORLD

- Learn the names and locations of missionaries from your locale or region that are serving in missions. Pray daily as a family for these missionaries.

- Obtain addresses and write regular letters of encouragement to foreign missionaries.

- Take special interest in the projects of the 13th Sabbath Mission offering. Learn more from libraries, magazines, etc. about the country, the people and needs of the area where one of these specific projects is located. Pray for this project and plan as a family to support your prayers with a sacrificial offering on 13th Sabbath.

- Discover from your pastor or church leadership where there are areas unentered by Seventh-day Adventist missions in your country or some other country. Learn all you can about this area and its people. Pray that doors for entrance to this people will be opened.

- Contact your pastor or church leadership about how to make contact with a pen pal from a foreign country. Have family members write to pen pals appropriate to their ages and share with the family what they learn about life in another country.

- Short terms of service are available for adults and young people in a growing number of areas in the world. The doors to service in these areas are open through the General Conference, through educational institutions and private organizations. Inquire of your pastor or church leadership about the possibilities for family members to experience some mission service. If possible, plan to participate in such a missionary experience.

- As the Adventist message circles the globe, more and more workers are needed in foreign fields in a wide variety of professions and occupations. Consult with your pastor or church leadership, pray about and consider as a family whether some of your family members might serve the Lord in full-time mission service.

- Pick a block in your town where there are no Adventists living and consider this your "unentered" area in which to make missionary visits, distribute literature, etc., to win individuals for Christ.

- Make a study as a family of one of the main world religions outside Christianity. Discuss creative ways Adventists might reach these groups with the good news about Jesus. What about their religious beliefs might make them open or closed to such good news?

- Should it be necessary to relocate as a family, pray about and consider moving to a section of the city, country or region where Seventh-day Adventists are few or non-existent so as to provide a witness there.

- As children are growing in the family discuss the blessings and importance of missionary service either at home or abroad and the possibility of settling themselves as adults in parts of the country that need the witnessing presence of Seventh-day Adventists.

Reprinted from Karen and Ron Flowers *Families Reaching Families: A Family Ministries Resource Book*. Department of Family Ministries, General Conference of Seventh-day Adventists, 1992, pp. 63-71.

# Reprinted Articles

# Church *Planting*: Counting the Cost

## by Doug Tilstra

Excitement filled me as I saw 130 enthusiastic people walk through the open doors into our newly planted church. I couldn't have been happier.

But just two and a half years later, I sat outside the room where the Church Board was discussing not only the future of the church but my future as well. The door opened, and a board member, sent to appraise me of the Board's progress, said to me, "You might as well go home, Doug. We're a long way from being done."

On the way home, alone in my car, I fumed, I cried, I kicked myself. How could a mission launched with such great hope and greater fulfillment be about to evaporate into thin air? Hidden in the darkness of the long drive home, I wrestled with questions too painful to ask aloud. Some were the wrong questions, some have not yet been answered, and some have led to deep insights and discoveries . . . discoveries, perhaps, that can help other church planters who find themselves in a similar situation.

## THERE IS A COST

Jesus said, "Suppose one of you wants to build a tower. Will he not first sit down and estimate the cost? . . . Or suppose a king is about to go to war. . . . Will he not first sit down and consider whether he is able?" (Luke 14:28-31).* In anything we do, there is a cost. Church planting is no exception. In one study 80 percent of leaders surveyed in a study of church planters reported a major family crisis (usually marital) within the first five years of the church plant.[1] More than 50 percent said they would not plant again because of the emotional pressure on themselves and their families.[2] The same study showed that "a significant number of pioneers whose church plants 'failed' have left the full-time pastoral ministry. The planting experience was so personally destructive that these pioneers have entered different careers. Some have resigned their ordination and have little to do with their former sending agency."[3]

Carl George, church growth consultant, said that 50 to 75 percent of new church plants will fail within the first five years.[4]

## COUNTING THE COST

Because, to say the least, this sounds daunting and discouraging, it is important for us to count the cost more thoughtfully. The significant way to do this is to redefine success and failure. Jesus said, "My kingdom is not of this world" (John 18:36) and "Watch out! Be on your guard against all kinds of greed; a man's life does not consist in the abundance of his possessions" (Luke 12:15).

"Society teaches us otherwise," contends Wayne Jacobsen, in *Leadership* magazine. "Our management-conscious culture impresses us with flow charts and agendas. . . . No wonder we fall prey to the notion that our ability to carry out our vision depends on the number of people in the orbit of our voice or under our box in the organizational chart."[5]

Unwittingly, I fell into this trap. I recoiled and disagreed when a fellow pastor chided me early in my planting venture, "Admit it, Doug, you just want to make a big enough splash to hit the seminar circuit!" But when a visiting well-wisher from a neighboring church predicted that "In three years this is going to be the largest church in the area," I surprised myself with the secret satisfaction I found in savoring that fantasy.

I was an accident waiting to happen. I had reduced life to a small package. It consisted of performing well as a church planter so that I would succeed at creating a vibrant and rapidly growing congregation. Much of my vision was noble. But gradually the focus shifted. One by one I placed all my "emotional eggs" in the basket of my church-planting success. I desperately needed this project to succeed. I had too much emotionally invested for it to do anything else. And without realizing it, I came to the place where I defined success almost exclusively as the increase of my influence and prestige.

But there is another definition of success. For the church planter, success does not necessarily mean a large, thriving church within two or three years. Success means faithfulness and obedience.

Church planter Richard Erickson said it well: "Jesus is the Lord of the church, not subject to the planter's plan. The pioneer needs to be willing to work hard and smart, and if the effort does not lead to the establishment of a healthy new church, that is God's responsibility. The pioneer needs to continually affirm that the future success of failure of the ministry is not a result of the amount of effort he or she invests, but it is a miracle of God's grace."[6]

A reality check for the church planter is to ask the simple question, "What if everyone here had my experience?" "A student is not above his teacher, but everyone who is fully trained will be like his teacher" (Luke 6:40). It is a sobering thought. What if everyone at this church had the same quality of family life as mine? What if they all had my anxiety level? Or my spiritual life, fatigue level, emotional unrest, or physical health?

Church planters must realize that the most basic tool they bring to the task is wholeness and balance in their own lives. The significance of this factor cannot be overlooked.

## SET CLEAR GOALS

I tackled my church-planting project with a stack of goals and high expectations. Many of those goals gave excellent focus and direction. Yet I learned there is more to goal-setting than challenging myself or the church with neighborhoods to reach, ministries to start, or deadlines to meet. Here are some points:

*Don't make church planting number one in your life.* Only God deserves that spot. "You shall have no other gods before me" (Exod.20:3). "Love the Lord your God with all your heart and with all your soul and with all your mind and with all your strength" (Mark 12:30). Any church work, especially church planting, can grow into a "holy idolatry." Fight the inclination to build your life around the new church plant.

Make major adjustments? Yes! But make it the center of your life? No way!

*Don't start until there are "clear mutual expectations."* Each person involved in the church plant, from the administrative supervisor to the planters' spouse, needs understanding and ownership of the goals and expectations. Together they can discuss: Why is this church being planted? Who is the target audience? How long might it take? What essential preparation work must be in place before opening Sabbath? What does it mean to be a part of the planting team? What organizational structure will be used? How will leadership roles be determined? Who will decide major expenditures and direction? Are the goals realistic? How will accountability be assessed? What do we do if we don't agree on some of these expectations?

*Be clear on the why.* I was amazed to discover how many different motives brought our team together. Some wanted a church closer to home. Some wanted a clone of their previous church. Some wanted to be part of anything new and novel. Some wanted to start a church for the unchurched. Some wanted involvement they hadn't found elsewhere. Each motive carried with it a set of unwritten and largely unconscious expectations for the church, the pastor, and those who attended. It was months before I even realized the vast difference between our official mission statement and mission statements people carried around in their heads and hearts.

*Set goals for the entirety of your life* (and know how church-planting fits into them). The role of church planter is only one role among many that the pastor will fill. First and foremost, you are a child of God. You are also a neighbor, friend, citizen, son or daughter, and possibly a parent or spouse. A little reflection will likely reveal other roles. During the first two or three years the planting role will need a disproportionate priority. But again, the temptation is to make it the only priority. Goal setting for the other areas of your life will lessen that danger. It might be well to set goals first as an individual then with your spouse and children. Write the goals on paper but not in stone!

## ASSIGNING AND ATTAINING GOALS

Make sure that the forces assigned can attain the goals. The first "assigned force" is you, the church planter. Prioritizing your own fitness is anything but selfish. Airline attendants instruct parents traveling with small children to always put on their own oxygen masks first in an emergency. Why? You won't be much help to another if you are unconscious. "What good will it be for a man if he gains the whole world, yet forfeits his soul?" (Matt. 16:26).

For spiritual fitness, church planters need a hunger for God, not just a hunger for God to make them better church planters! Take a fresh look at classic spiritual disciplines and decide how you will practice them even while church planting. Perhaps Sabbath rest is one of the most challenging. Allow the planting process to lead you to new riches in listening deeply to God and hearing Him as He searches your heart for attitudes and motives.

For emotional fitness a frequent self-inventory is helpful. Alice Brawand in *Secrets of Your Family Tree* lists seven common denominators of pastors at emotional risk.[7] Here's an adapted version.

1. **Endless living in the fast lane.** Do I often feel pressured and overcommitted?

2. **Harboring hidden anger.** What is my relationship like with my parents and siblings? Have I "forgotten" old hurts or grudges?

3. **Projecting a superstar syndrome.** Do I try to excel at everything and be all things to all people?

4. **Habitually hiding one's own deep needs.** Do I enjoy others' perception of me as a person who has it all together? Do I feel useless when no one needs my help?

5. **Operating without a personal support system.** What two or three people know my deepest feelings, fears, and dreams and love me anyway? How often do I meet and pray with them?

6. **Establishing only superficial relationships with others.** How close am I to my extended family members? What friends, other than church members, does our family enjoy regularly? How does my spouse feel about our emotional closeness?

7. **Allowing expectations to drive life to exhaustion.** How aware am I of the power of unspoken expectations? What motivates me? Do I allow comments and opinions of others to affect me personally?

If you are married, the second "assigned force" is your spouse. The church planter's spouse feels all the trauma and stress of the project and yet often can do nothing directly about it. His or her only access to effect change is probably through you, the church planter. That can be explosive given certain critical factors! If your spouse will be actively involved in the project, define roles based on your past record. Ask yourselves, Are we easily threatened or defensive when working together? Has one partner built his or her identity around the career and success of the other? If you are unsure of the answers, it might be well to sort out the issues with a professional counselor or a wise and trusted friend or colleague before you hit a crisis.

An additional proposal may further assist a church planter's spouse: Consider establishing another place to worship, fellowship, and be spiritually fed besides the church you are planting. It could be a small group, a nearby midweek service, or even a church that meets at a different time than yours.

The third "assigned force" is the church-planting team and/or parent church. A church-planting

friend once told me, "I'd rather have a handful of loyal soldiers than a whole army shooting me in the back." Nothing could be more vital for the planting team during the first 12 months than developing a clear and mutual vision/mission statement. Find ways to move it from paper to heads and hearts and narrow the team down to those who internalize the vision. Then model the vision in your own life and train the team in the essentials of that vision.

The final "assigned force" is the administrative supervision. Here are nine things a church planter should cover as he or she seeks to clarify crucial issues with church administration:[8]

1. "Please learn enough about church-planting so you can help me with resourcing."

2. "Please be alert to the unique risks to me and my family from church-planting."

3. "Is there any way I could have access to an experienced planter as a mentor?"

4. "Is church-planting a priority for this conference/union? Does budgeting reflect that commitment?"

5. "Can you help me develop a supportive network with other church planters?"

6. "How safe is it to talk with you if I feel I'm just not making it?"

7. "What do you expect of my spouse?"

8. "Can we dialogue about job description, lines of accountability, conference expectations, and then meet regularly for accountability?"

9. "What happens if I really 'hit the wall' or the church does not thrive or even survive? Is there some provision for that?"

## DON'T GET DISTRACTED

Fortunately, despite the ignorance I displayed by not covering these things with my administrators at the outset, they were a step ahead of me. During a pastoral retreat I approached one of them with a terse message, "I'm in trouble and need help." Glaring distress symptoms had finally broken through my denial. Immediately they made referrals and set in motion the wheels to start a long recovering and regrouping journey for me. I did eventually leave the initial church plant project but have returned to church planting with new energy and vision.

Distraction comes in many forms. For some, it is insufficient focus on the task at hand or inadequate support from administrative headquarters. But perhaps the most ironic distraction is the relentless pursuit of a goal that eventually strangles both the goal and the goal setter.

During my journey back, I have rediscovered power and beauty in words I copied years ago into my Bible flyleaf, "As activity increases and men become successful in doing any work for God, there is danger of trusting to human plans and methods. There is a tendency to pray less and to have less faith. Like the disciples, we are in danger of losing sight of our dependence on God and seeking to make a savior of our activity. We need to look constantly to Jesus, realizing that it is His power which does the work. While we are to labor earnestly for the salvation of the lost, we must also take time for meditation, for prayer, and for the study of the word of God. Only the work accomplished with much prayer, and sanctified by the merit of Christ, will in the end prove to have been efficient for good."[9]

[*] All Scripture passages in this article are from the New International Version.

[1] Richard A. Erickson, Protecting, Promoting, and Prospering the Pioneers: Using the Experience of Church Planters to Strengthen Their Support System (Fuller Theological Seminary, Doctor of Ministry Dissertation, 1992), 36, 136, 270.

[2] Ibid., 63.

[3] Ibid., 64.

[4] Carl George, "Perspective On Winning a Continent" in *How to Plant a Church syllabus* (Pasadena, Calif.: Charles E. Fuller Institute of Evangelism and Church Growth, 1985), 5-9.

[5] Wayne Jacobsen, "A Case of Mistaken Ministerial Identity," *Leadership* (Winter 1992): 93, 94.

[6] Erickson, 307.

[7] In Dave Carder, ed., *Secrets of Your Family Tree* (Chicago: Moody Press, 1991), 117-121.

[8] The majority of these ideas are from Erickson, 352-362.

[9] Ellen G. White, *The Desire of Ages* (Nampa, Idaho: Pacific Press® Pub. Assn., 1940), 362.

Reprinted from *Ministry*, December 1998. Used by permission.

end

# The *Corner* of His Eye

by Larry Libby

Surely He needed to focus. Cement His gaze. Shove aside distractions. Marshall His energies.

In a matter of hours, His blood would congeal in the dust. In a matter of hours His collapsing lungs would suck a final, ragged gasp. In a matter of hours He would strive in single combat with the lord of the abyss, the enemy He had prepared to face since the mists of Eden.

If Jerusalem was the finish line, then Jericho was the back stretch. Less than twenty miles away from a collision that would jar the foundations of hell. The mighty gears of wrath and redemption were about to mesh. Earth trembles. The cosmos held its breath.

Such an odd time to talk to a little man in a tree.

He stopped His march toward the hinge of history to peer up into the leafy limb of a sycamore. There, in the crook between two branches, feeling perhaps a little foolish, sat a bantam-sized IRS agent.

*"Zacchaeus, come down immediately. I must stay at your house today"* (Lk. 19:5).

Scripture says nothing at all about the reactions of His disciples toward this maddening distraction. Had their response been recorded, Holy Writ might have said something like, "Then His disciples looked one unto another and saith, 'What next?'"

Would they ever understand His mind and methods? Hadn't He just taken them aside to warn the end was near?

*"We are going up to Jerusalem, and everything that is written by the prophets about the Son of Man will be fulfilled. He will be handed over to the Gentiles. They will mock him, insult him, spit on him, flog him and kill him"* (Lk. 18:31-32).

Pretty ghastly stuff. Something you had to steel yourself to face. Okay. We're going up to Jerusalem. Passing through Jericho on the way. And then the end of the world.

Right. And now we're all craning our necks at some publican sitting in a tree. Now he's climbing down. Now we're on the way to his place for tea.

They should have known. After three-and-a-half years, they should have known. When had they gone anywhere to do anything without those endless distractions? It was always something. A leper. Ten lepers. Some pushy moms and a kaboodle of kids. A guy on a stretcher coming down through the ceiling.

Naked demoniacs running out of the tombs. A Samaritan floozie at the village well. What was one more tax collector dropping out of a tree?

The day must have been well-advanced by the time they finally put Jericho and Zacchaeus behind them. One more closed chapter in an inscrutable biography. Had they reached the final page? What awaited them up that highway, through those hills? Kingdom or martyrdom? Realization of their dreams or the business end of a Roman spear? At least now they could prepare themselves for the ordeal. Rivet their vision to the road ahead. Arm their spirits for whatever . . . .

*"Jesus, Son of David, have mercy on me!"*

Oh *no!* What now?

*"Son of David, have mercy on me!"*

Maybe He would ignore that pitiful, nasal voice from somewhere back in the crowd. Maybe this time He would press ahead and . . . but no, of course He wouldn't. He had already stopped. His eyes were already searching the side of the road.

*Jesus stopped and said, "Call him."*

So they called to the blind man, *"Cheer up! On your feet! He's calling you."* Throwing his cloak aside, he jumped to his feet and came to Jesus.

*"What do you want me to do for you?" Jesus asked him. The blind man said, "Rabbi, I want to see."*

*"Go," said Jesus, "your faith has healed you."* Immediately he received his sight and followed Jesus along the road (Mk. 10:46-52).

People distractions? Yes, certainly. Jesus experienced them from the outset of His ministry. Yet no one was more goal-oriented. No one.

**From the beginning,** his eyes were locked on Calvary. His step never faltered, His purpose never varied. Thousands of years before Messiah even arrived, Isaiah cocked an ear and caught the determined inflection in His voice: *"I have set my face like flint, and I know I will not be put to shame"* (Is. 50:7).

Like a flint. Resolution chiseled in stone.

The long shadow of the cross sent a chill across the brightest moments of His ministry. The frankincense of the magi foreshadowed a funeral. The fragrant nard poured on His feet pictured a waiting grave.

It was ever before Him. A hill. The silhouette of a soldier holding a hammer. Death and worse than death. Hell and worse than hell. A yawning chasm between Him and the Father.

How could He do other than set His face like a flint? How could He not gather up His men and sweep them along to that terrible goal?

Yet somehow, it never seemed that way.

He always seemed to . . . catch a glimpse of someone out of the corner of His eye.

On His way to help a dying child, He stopped to deal with a despairing woman who had merely touched the fringe of His cloak.

On His way to face the blood-lust of a hastily convened kangaroo court, He sought eye contact with a friend who had just betrayed him.

On His way to Golgotha, staggering under the weight of His own cross, He paused to counsel several distraught women at the side of the road.

On His way to securing salvation for the sins of the world, enduring white-hot agonies of body and spirit, He caught a glimpse of His mother below the cross—and appointed a caretaker for her old age.

On His way out of this life, He caught a glimpse of a repentant felon on the cross next door—and issued an invitation to paradise.

For all His relentless sense of mission, there's something about our Lord's peripheral vision that merits a moment's pause.

**A person with healthy eyesight** can focus on objects directly ahead and still perceive movement on either side. That's peripheral vision.

Athletes learn to hone this lateral edge of their perception just to stay alive. If you're a quarterback dropping into the pocket, you might focus on your tight-end breaking free in the secondary . . . but out of the corner of your eye you're charting the progress of that linebacker rocketing toward your unprotected ribs. If you're intent on keeping your basketball opponent scoreless, you might focus on your man driving into the key, but you'd better be aware of the six-ten center—all 280 pounds of him—who's just set a pick on your right. It would be kinder to run full-stride into a freeway pillar.

Ophthalmologists use a process called perimetry to chart this key element of vision. By this method, they are able to discern blind spots. The onset of diseases like glaucoma kill nerve fibers within the eye responsible for transmitting peripheral vision.

They have a name for that condition. It's called tunnel vision.

Funny thing about eye diseases. They come on a person so slowly you hardly even notice a narrowing field of vision. Before you have time to be concerned, you find yourself staring down a tunnel stretching out in front of your nose.

**What are you seeing these days** . . . out of the corner of your eye?

Any faces on the edge of the crowd? Any tentative hands touching the edge of your coat?

"Ah," you say. "I'm looking up ahead. This is the critical decade—the dawn of a new millennium. I'm mission-driven. Task-oriented. Aimed on target. Pressing toward the mark. I've done my strategic planning in one-, five-, and twenty-year increments. I have a personal mission statement in my Day-Timer that breaks down priorities into achievable, measurable, monthly objectives and daily priorities. Frankly, it doesn't allow for many distractions.

Fine. But now and then it wouldn't hurt to check in with the Great Physician for a vision test. The exam might turn up a blind spot or two.

. . . Maybe a little boy who's been trying awfully hard to get your attention—and has just about given up.

. . . Maybe an old lady in a downstairs apartment who sits at the same window every morning as you hurry through the parking lot to your car.

. . . Maybe a coworker down the hall who used to smile and laugh—but doesn't anymore.

. . . Maybe a neighbor two houses down who suffered a stroke last year and can't seem to take care of the weeds along the sidewalk.

. . . Maybe a hungry Filipino toddler staring up at you from the photograph on an appeal letter.

. . . Maybe a spouse who has been quietly, desperately sending you signals for weeks—but can't break through.

Distractions. Time-sapping diversions.

If you're bothered by such as these, you probably wouldn't have noticed Zacchaeus—out of sight, up a tree. Just a forgettable little man with a hungry heart.

Most likely you would have missed blind Bartimaeus—sitting in the litter on the shoulder of the Jerusalem expressway. Just one more victim of the enemy, trying to cope with darkness.

What this pair had in common was proximity to Jesus of Nazareth. The One who had every right to focus on a goal so hugh time couldn't contain it . . . the One who had every right to ignore the broken men and women in the corner of His eye—but didn't.

Setting aside Heaven's cosmic agenda. He reached through their emptiness with a warm human hand.

Then again, maybe that is Heaven's agenda. And ours.

**Larry Libby is a senior editor at Multnomah Publishers in Sisters, Oregon. Used by permission.**

# *Voices* On The **F**ringe

**by Dorothy Grace**

*The love and unity you enjoy at home should extend to your wider church family if God's kingdom is going to mean anything to your neighbours . . .*

## UNATTACHED

I stand on the outside looking in.

Those on the inside looking out view me as an unknown quantity, best avoided.

The preacher says the church is a family.

A family usually has some single members. In fact they are often in the majority. They are objects of love, care and concern. I am not odd, nor weird. Not maladjusted, nor gay.

I choose not to marry. I left all to follow Him and often He is all I have!

But why?

The Apostle Paul applauded the single state. Why then is the church afraid of it?

Jesus, though approving of marriage, did not choose that path. Church members relate to Him. Why not to His single followers?

## ELDERLY

I stand on the outside looking in.

Those on the inside view me as an appendage from a bygone age. How could I possibly understand current trends and impulses? Yet the church is a family, and most families have grandparents who they love and entertain from time to time.

Like them I can look back on years of experience. I know the successes, the dangers, the pitfalls.

I could give the church the benefit of my experience, but they don't want it.

They don't want me.

It hurts to be considered of no further use.

It would be nice to be included occasionally but they prefer to leave me to my loneliness. I suppose I can pray for them. I've more than enough time on my hands for that!

## CARER

I stand on the outside looking in.

Those on the inside view me as a shadow, lacking in colour, useless where church commitments are concerned.

All my energies are spent to the limit of total exhaustion, caring alone for an aged, disabled parent.

Yet the church is a family. Do families not share the burdens of their members? Do they not care, encourage, listen and help each other?

No-one comes to my aid. No-one stands in for me so I can go shopping or have a cup of tea with a neighbour. They just look at me with pity – when what I need is help!

## TEENAGER

I stand on the outside looking in.

Those on the inside view me as my parents' child. But I'm a person in my own right.

I am ready, eager and willing to serve God. If only they would let me!

I could give my youth, my zeal, my enthusiasm to help carry the church forward onto the 'street'.

The church is a family. Families recognize that their teenagers need responsibility to help them grow.

Yes, there may be growing pains. But if I can't develop I shall wither away. Perhaps I should look elsewhere for the chance to express myself. Jesus understood. He even used a young person to illustrate the kingdom.

## MOTHER

I stand on the outside looking in.

Those on the inside view me as someone fit to serve coffee but not to give an opinion.

I am worthy to arrange the flowers but not to plan church matters.

I can direct a children's nativity play but not lead adults in anything.

I am useful where there's work to do, but not where there are matters to discuss or decisions to be made.

The church is a family. In the family the mother does have some say.

I should like to use my voice as well as my hands for God. Jesus told Mary, "Touch me not . . . go and tell".

If it was alright with Him, it should be alright with them.

## FATHER

I, too, am on the outside, looking in.

Those on the inside tolerate my words but give no weight to my suggestions.

I am not a business tycoon. I am a humble labourer. So it's assumed that I have nothing of value to offer.

Yet I am the head of my family. I run its affairs – quite successfully. I do have something to offer, if only another point of view.

Did God really want the 'ordinary' men just to make up numbers? Did He really intend his church to be led only by the educated cream? So why did He choose humble fishermen to start it?

## STRANGER

I am on the outside, not bothering to look in.

I wouldn't be welcomed anyway. No-one would invite me into her home or be interested in what I could offer.

Someone might shake hands at the end of a service, but he wouldn't want to know my problems, my ideals, my burdens.

I just might be on drugs or come from the wrong end of town.

As it happens I'm just an ordinary guy, looking for a family.

I thought friendship and faith might be available here. I was mistaken.

Church? No thanks! I'd better stay on the outside, looking out.

## CHURCH LEADER

I am on the inside, looking out. I am so busy dealing with individuals who need constant counseling and support, I do not see the single person standing alone uninvited, nor the elderly prayer-warrior being pushed aside.

I do not notice the work-weary carer on the brink of a breakdown.

Nor the teenager struggling to make a positive individual contribution.

I am not aware of mothers being taken for granted, nor some fathers being patronised.

I spend many hours planning events and services. No-one offers to help. So I see little of my own family.

I do not see the stranger at the door.

I see the crowds at the meetings. I see the church accounts, in need of more giving.

I am grateful that my ministry has so much profile within an exclusive fellowship.

## THE FATHER

This is meant to be my church. Yet I don't see love for the elderly, care for the singles. I don't find help for the carer, encouragement for the young.

There's no welcome for the stranger.

I see people hurt, unloved, losing their way, while my church offers a good time to a few of its select club members.

That was not my blueprint. Not my way. Not my wish.

They were to be my family – strong, united, loving, caring.

As the Dad of the family I told them, *"By this shall all men know you are my disciples if you love one another"*.

It's hard to see where I fit in. Am I also on the fringe?

---

Reprinted from *Christian Family*, August 1991.

# A *Light* in the Community

**Ellen G. White**

## FAR-REACHING INFLUENCE OF THE HOME

**The Christian Home Is an Object Lesson.**
The mission of the home extends beyond its own members. The Christian home is to be an object lesson, illustrating the excellence of the true principles of life. Such an illustration will be a power for good in the world. . . . As the youth go out from such a home, the lessons they have learned are imparted. Nobler principles of life are introduced into other households, and an uplifting influence works in the community. {AH 31.1 "Ministry of Healing", p. 352.}

The home in which the members are polite, courteous Christians exerts a far-reaching influence for good. Other families will mark the results attained by such a home, and will follow the example set, in their turn guarding the home against Satanic influences. The angels of God will often visit the home in which the will of God bears sway. Under the power of divine grace such a home becomes a place of refreshing to worn, weary pilgrims. By watchful guarding, self is kept from asserting itself. Correct habits are formed. There is a careful recognition of the rights of others. The faith that works by love and purifies the soul stands at the helm, presiding over the whole household. Under the hallowed influence of such a home, the principle of brotherhood laid down in the word of God is more widely recognized and obeyed. {AH 31.2 "Letter" 272, 1903.}

**Influence of a Well-ordered Family.** It is no small matter for a family to stand as representatives of Jesus, keeping God's law in an unbelieving community.

32

We are required to be living epistles known and read of all men. This position involves fearful responsibilities. {AH 31.3 "Testimonies for the Church", Vol.4, p. 106.}

One well-ordered, well-disciplined family tells more in behalf of Christianity than all the sermons that can be preached. Such a family gives evidence that the parents have been successful in following God's directions, and that their children will serve Him in the church. Their influence grows; for as they impart, they receive to impart again. The father and mother find helpers in their children, who give to others the instruction received in the home. The neighborhood in which they live is helped, for in it they have become enriched for time and for eternity. The whole family is engaged in the service of the Master; and by their godly example, others are inspired to be faithful and true to God in dealing with His flock, His beautiful flock. {AH 32.1 "Review and Herald", June 6, 1899.}

The greatest evidence of the power of Christianity that can be presented to the world is a well-ordered, well-disciplined family. This will recommend the truth as nothing else can, for it is a living witness of its practical power upon the heart. {AH 32.2 "Testimonies for the Church", Vol.4, p. 304.}

The best test of the Christianity of a home is the type of character begotten by its influence. Actions speak louder than the most positive profession of godliness. {AH 32.3 "Patriarchs and Prophets, p. 579.}

Our business in this world . . . is to see what virtues we can teach our children and our families to possess, that they shall have an influence upon other families, and thus we can be an educating power although we never enter into the desk. A well-ordered, a well-disciplined family in the sight of God is more precious than fine gold, even than the golden wedge of Ophir. {AH 32.4 "Manuscript 12", 1895.}

**Wonderful Possibilities Are Ours.** Our time here is short. We can pass through this world but once; as we

33

pass along, let us make the most of life. The work to which we are called does not require wealth or social position or great ability. It requires a kindly, self-sacrificing spirit and a steadfast purpose. A lamp, however small, if kept steadily burning, may be the means of lighting many other lamps. Our sphere of influence may seem narrow, our ability small, our opportunities few, our acquirements limited; yet wonderful possibilities are ours through a faithful use of the opportunities of our own homes. If we will open our hearts and homes to the divine principles of life, we shall become channels for currents of life-giving power. From our homes will flow streams of healing, bringing life, and beauty, and fruitfulness where now are barrenness and dearth. {AH 32.5 "Ministry of Healing", p. 355.}

God-fearing parents will diffuse an influence from their own home circle to that of others that will act as did the leaven that was hid in three measures of meal. {AH 33.1 "Signs of the Times", Sept. 17, 1894.}

Faithful work done in the home educates others to do the same class of work. The spirit of fidelity to God is like leaven and, when manifested in the church, will have an effect upon others, and will be a recommendation to Christianity everywhere. The work of whole-souled soldiers of Christ is as far-reaching as eternity. Then why is it that there is such a lack of the missionary spirit in our churches? It is because there is a neglect of home piety. {AH 33.2 "Review and Herald", Feb. 19, 1895.}

**Influence of an Ill-regulated Family.** The influence of an ill-regulated family is widespread, and disastrous to all society. It accumulates in a tide of evil that affects families, communities, and governments. {AH 33.3 "Patriarchs and Prophets, p. 579.}

It is impossible for any of us to live in such a way that we shall not cast an influence in the world. No member of the family can enclose himself within himself, where other members of the family shall not feel his influence and

34

spirit. The very expression of the countenance has an influence for good or evil. His spirit, his words, his actions, his attitude toward others, are unmistakable. If he is living in selfishness, he surrounds his soul with a malarious atmosphere; while if he is filled with the love of Christ, he will manifest courtesy, kindness, tender regard for the feelings of others and will communicate to his associates, by his acts of love, a tender, grateful, happy feeling. It will be made manifest that he is living for Jesus and daily learning lessons at His feet, receiving His light and His peace. He will be able to say to the Lord, "Thy gentleness hath made me great." {AH 33.4 "The Youth's Instructor", June 22, 1893.}

35

# A POWERFUL CHRISTIAN WITNESS

**Best Missionaries Come From Christian Homes.** Missionaries for the Master are best prepared for work abroad in the Christian household, where God is

feared, where God is loved, where God is worshiped, where faithfulness has become second nature, where haphazard, careless inattention to home duties is not permitted, where quiet communion with God is looked upon as essential to the faithful performance of daily duties. {AH 35.1 "Manuscript 140", 1897.}

Home duties should be performed with the consciousness that if they are done in the right spirit, they give an experience that will enable us to work for Christ in the most permanent and thorough manner. Oh, what might not a living Christian do in missionary lines by performing faithfully the daily duties, cheerfully lifting the cross, not neglecting any work, however disagreeable to the natural feelings! {AH 35.2 "Signs of the Times", Sept. 1, 1898.}

Our work for Christ is to begin with the family, in the home. . . . There is no missionary field more important than this. . . . {AH 35.3.}

By many this home field has been shamefully neglected, and it is time that divine resources and remedies were presented, that this state of evil may be corrected. {AH 35.4 "Testimonies for the Church", Vol.6, pp. 429, 430.}

The highest duty that devolves upon youth is in their own homes, blessing father and mother, brothers and sisters, by affection and true interest. Here they can show self-denial and self-forgetfulness in caring and doing for others. . . . What an influence a sister may have over brothers! If she is right, she may determine the character of her brothers. Her prayers, her gentleness, and her affection may do much in a household. {AH 35.5 "Id.", Vol. 3, pp. 80, 81.}

36

In the home those who have received Christ are to show what grace has done for them. "As many as received Him, to them gave He power to become the sons of God, even to them that believe on His name." A conscious authority pervades the true believer in Christ, that makes its influence felt throughout the home. This is favorable for the perfection of the characters of all in the home. {AH 36.1 "Manuscript 140", 1897.}

**An Argument That the Infidel Cannot Gainsay.** A well-ordered Christian household is a powerful argument in favor of the reality of the Christian religion--an argument that the infidel cannot gainsay. All can see that there is an influence at work in the family that affects the children, and that the God of Abraham is with them. If the homes of professed Christians had a right religious mold, they would exert a mighty influence for good. They would indeed be the "light of the world." {AH 36.2 "Patriarchs and Prophets", p. 144.}

**Children to Extend Knowledge of Bible Principles.** Children who have been properly educated, who love to be useful, to help father and mother, will extend a knowledge of correct ideas and Bible principles to all with whom they associate. {AH 36.3 "Letter 28", 1890.}

When our own homes are what they should be, our children will not be allowed to grow up in idleness and indifference to the claims of God in behalf of the needy all about them. As the Lord's heritage, they will be qualified to take up the work where they are. A light will shine from such homes which will reveal itself in behalf of the ignorant, leading them to the source of all knowledge. An influence will be exerted that will be a power for God and for His truth. {AH 36.4 "Testimonies for the Church", Vol.6, p. 430.}

Parents who can be approached in no other way are frequently reached through their children. {AH 36.5. "Id.", Vol. 4 p. 70.}

37

**Cheerful Homes Will Be a Light to Neighbors.** We need more sunshiny parents and more sunshiny Christians. We are too much shut up within ourselves. Too often the kindly, encouraging word, the cheery smile, are withheld from our children and from the oppressed and discouraged. {AH 37.1.}

Parents, upon you rests the responsibility of being light-bearers and light-givers. Shine as lights in the home, brightening the path that your children must travel. As you do this, your light will shine to those without. {AH 37.2. "Review and Herald, Jan.29", 1901.}

From every Christian home a holy light should shine forth. Love should be revealed in action. It should flow out in all home intercourse, showing itself in thoughtful kindness, in gentle, unselfish courtesy. There are homes where this principle is carried out--homes where God is worshiped and truest love reigns. From these homes morning and evening prayer ascends to God as sweet incense, and His mercies and blessings descend upon the suppliants like the morning dew. {AH 37.3. "Patriarchs and Prophets", p. 144.}

**Results of Family Unity.** The first work of Christians is to be united in the family. Then the work is to extend to their neighbors nigh and afar off. Those who have received light are to let the light shine forth in clear rays. Their words, fragrant with the love of

Christ, are to be a savor of life unto life. {AH 37.4. "Manuscript 11", 1901.}

The more closely the members of a family are united in their work in the home, the more uplifting and helpful will be the influence that father and mother and sons and daughters will exert outside the home. {AH 37.5 "Letter 189", 1903.}

**Good Men Needed More Than Great Minds.** The happiness of families and churches depends upon home

38

influences. Eternal interests depend upon the proper discharge of the duties of this life. The world is not so much in need of great minds as of good men who will be a blessing in their homes. {AH 37.6. "Testimonies for the Church", Vol. 4, p. 522.}

**Avoid Mistakes That May Close Doors.** When religion is manifested in the home, its influence will be felt in the church and in the neighborhood. But some who profess to be Christians talk with their neighbors concerning their home difficulties. They relate their grievances in such a way as to call forth sympathy for themselves; but it is a great mistake to pour our trouble into the ears of others, especially when many of our grievances are manufactured and exist because of our irreligious life and defective character. Those who go forth to lay their private grievances before others might better remain at home to pray, to surrender their perverse will to God, to fall on the Rock and be broken, to die to self that Jesus may make them vessels unto honor. {AH 38.1 "Signs of the Times", Nov. 14, 1892.}

A lack of courtesy, a moment of petulance, a single rough, thoughtless word, will mar your reputation, and may close the door to hearts so that you can never reach them. {AH 38.2 "Testimonies for the Church", Vol.5, p.335.}

**Christianity in the Home Shines Abroad.** The effort to make the home what it should be--a symbol of the home in heaven--prepares us for work in a larger sphere. The education received by showing a tender regard for each other enables us to know how to reach hearts that need to be taught the principles of true religion. The church needs all the cultivated spiritual force which can be obtained, that all, and especially the younger members of the Lord's family, may be carefully guarded. The truth lived at home makes itself felt in

39

disinterested labor abroad. He who lives Christianity in the home will be a bright and shining light everywhere. {AH 38.3 "Signs of the Times", Sept. 1, 1898.}

---

Reprinted from *The Adventist Home,* pp. 31-39 in The Complete Published Ellen G. White Writings (CD Rom). The Ellen G. White Estate, Inc., 1998.

# BOOK REVIEW

# 10 Christian Values Every Kid Should Know: A How-to Guide for Families

**by Donna J. Habenicht**
**Hagerstown, MD: Review & Herald, 2000.**
**272 pages.**

**Reviewed by Kathy S. (Potts) Russell**

*10 Christian Values Every Kid Should Know* is a resource bursting with wonderful information and ideas. It is must reading for those who would promote the development of good character and family values. Inspiration for the book grew out of a graduate course in character development that the author took from the late Ruth Murdoch, a well-known Adventist educator. Since then, Dr. Habenicht has continued to study and teach about values and character development at the graduate level and at family workshops. For her ideas and illustrations, she draws on the experience of her own family as well as the families of her students and friends.

Every tree is known by its fruit (cf. Luke 6:44). We cannot have good "fruit" (values lived by our children) unless we have a strong "tree" (methods for teaching those values). The first section of this two-part book has nine chapters on strategies for teaching values to children. Each chapter begins with a Bible text highlighting the subject of the chapter, followed by thought-provoking illustrations and valuable instruction. As a parent and teacher, I loved the practical suggestions for encouraging positive family values that were offered in the Family Activities sections. The key thoughts and witty quotes at the end of the chapters serve to drive the main points home. Also helpful are the informative charts scattered throughout the chapters showing: how to celebrate a value each month relating to holidays, tangible ways to share values with your child, the differences between the messages conveyed by God and the media, how to protect your family from the influence of the media, child development, communication and decision-making skills, and ideas for strengthening family ties.

The ten chapters in the second part highlight several key values: faith in God, respect, responsibility, kindness and compassion, honesty and integrity, humility, self-control, patience and perseverance, contentment and thankfulness, and loyalty and commitment—all of which find their basis in love (1 Cor. 13). For each value Dr. Habenicht shares Bible texts and guidelines on how to teach it and how to deal with challenges of teaching the value. Family activities, quotes, nature illustrations, how to take advantage of daily opportunities to teach values, and key thoughts flesh out each chapter.

I appreciated the emphasis the author placed on God as the foundation of all good values, the basis of these in His love for us, and His desire to have a relationship with us that will help us to live those values before our children. Living and teaching good values to children while they are young and in a way that they can understand will better equip them for facing future moral challenges. Building families with strong Christian characters is the greatest gift we can share with our world. Reading this book will help families go about this kind of sharing.

Kathy S. (Potts) Russell is a homemaker in Charlotte, North Carolina.

end

## BOOK REVIEW

# How to Help Your Child Really Love Jesus

**by Donna Habenicht**
**Hagerstown, MD: Review and Herald, 1994.**
**224 pages.**

**Reviewed by Linda Mei Lin Koh**

As the title suggests, this is a "how to" book. Not just another "how to" book, but much more. *How to Help Your Child Really Love Jesus* skillfully weaves together the psychology of child development with biblical teachings. Each chapter begins with counsel from the Bible which is followed by examples and developmental theories, and finally ends with the practical "how to's." Parents will find the "Faith Development Tasks," "Temperament Traits in Children," and the "Spiritual Development Chart" very helpful in giving them some insights into understanding their children and their spiritual growth. Moreover, the author's personal experiences throughout the book are a plus because many parents can identify with many of the child behaviors—innocent or belligerent—she illustrates.

I am intrigued by the word "really" in the title. This little word signifies the in-depth spirituality we want our children to develop. We don't want our children to merely practice the rites and rituals of religion—going to church, attending church schools, etc. Instead, we hope to raise children who truly and genuinely love Jesus and want to be His friend. The author has provided practical steps and suggestions to help parents lead their children to such a meaningful, loving relationship with Jesus. Suggestions for strengthening the family bond in the home, conducting effective family worships, developing good consciences, and disciplining with love are in abundance throughout the chapters of the book. In addition, the "Sabbath Activities" chapter provides an excellent list of suggested activities that families can use to stimulate their children's interest in nature, outreach, fellowship and Bible instructional activities. In fact, the list of activities presented in these pages is greater than any family would likely ever complete.

The author is well qualified to write this book by her professional training in psychology and education. Her vast experience in teaching and presenting workshops, as well as her years of directing child evangelism work on the local conference and union levels of the church adds authority to what she says. Her style is simple and clear, understandable by lay people everywhere.

This is an excellent source book for everyone who loves children, and I want to recommend it to parents in particular. As parents take seriously their responsibility to provide spiritual guidance to our children, they will not want to miss reading this book.

---

Linda Koh is the Director of Children's Ministries at the General Conference of the Seventh-day Adventist Church.

## BOOK REVIEW

# Out of the Saltshaker and into the World: Evangelism as a Way of Life

**2nd Edition**
**by Rebecca Manley Pippert**
**Downers Grove, IL: Inter-Varsity Press**
**(IVP), 1999. 288 pages.**

**Reviewed by Valerie Fidelia**

Author Rebecca Manley Pippert is first and foremost a disciple of Jesus Christ. Her love for Him shines throughout this book. Since her days of working with students through the Inter-Varsity Christian Fellowship (IVCF) she has become a recognised authority on evangelism. Married, with two children, Pippert is an internationally known writer and sought-after speaker. Other books on the topic include *A Heart Like His: The Shaping of Character in the Choices of Life* (Crossway, 1996) and *Evangelism: A Way of Life* (InterVarsity, 2000), 12 studies for individuals or groups, which she co-authored with Ruth Siemens.

Arising from the Pippert's personal experience and her ministry with students through IVCF, *Out of the Saltshaker* was first published in 1979 and became an international best seller. In the late 1990's, IVP asked Pippert to do a revision for the twentieth anniversary of the book. With the difference twenty years makes in an ever-changing world, Pippert realized she would need to rewrite major portions of the book and add new material if it was to be relevant to today's world. The revision contains excellent material on personal evangelism.

The book is written in a simple, straightforward style that is easy to read. This is not to say the content is easy. Pippert constantly challenges us, through her marvellous gift of story-telling, to get out there and get busy. I enjoyed her use of pithy one-liners to get her points across, e.g. "Evangelism is God's business from start to finish"; "We do not simply give the gospel, we are the gospel." Throughout the book Pippert argues that Evangelism should be a way of life, and not a project. She has a deep-seated conviction that" much of our evangelism is ineffective because we depend too much on technique and strategy. Evangelism has slipped into the sales

department" pp 10. She urges us to look at Jesus, and the quality of life He calls us to, as a model for what to believe and how to reach out to others. Pippert brings evangelism alive. The people in her book are real people and her suggestions for addressing our reluctance to personalise our evangelism are workable. The principles she lays down are universal; applicable in any setting and any culture. Her illustrations come from all over the world, therefore are not confined to one people group.

Pippert has a passion for people, all people, and a burning desire to introduce them to a Jesus who cares and who is relevant in the twenty-first century. If there is one text that sums up Pippert's approach to Evangelism I believe it is 1 Thess. 2:8, "We loved you so much that we were delighted to share with you not only the gospel of God but our lives as well."

### THE BOOK:

Pippert asks us to consider Jesus as our model for Evangelism. She explores His humanness and His Lordship; His example of radically identifying with the world whilst being radically different from the world. She argues for a heart change in us before we can share with others. She challenges us to look for Jesus in everyone we meet (Luke 9:48; Matt. 25: 40), and to seek ways of sharing Him with them. I found the section on just being ourselves and finding ways of using our personalities to best advantage to talk about our relationship with Jesus very helpful. So many times we say we can't do it because we fear rejection or can't find the words, but Pippert shows us how our very "weaknesses" as we see them, can actually become our strengths in sharing Christ with others. "The Christian must be the one who loves, cares and listens first. We all can take initiative, whether quietly or openly" (p. 109). She examines some of the reasons why we are reluctant to share, including our fear of not being able to answer a seeker's question. "To refrain from sharing the most glorious news ever announced to humanity because we might be asked a question that stumps us is a tragedy" (p. 118).

Not once in this book does Pippert talk about Evangelism in terms of a project or event. No! For her, Evangelism is a way of life. We can learn to include our relationship with Jesus as part of our normal, everyday conversation – with churched *and* unchurched friends. We must learn to pray before and during each encounter that God will give us insight into that individual's needs and give us the words to speak that will open a door for further discussion. Her chapter on "Developing Conversational Skills" is must reading.

Throughout the book (and particularly in chapters 14 and 17) Pippert makes the point that it is the Holy Spirit who convicts and converts. "We could not convert anyone if our life depended on it" (p. 118). However, we have a role in that work and we should "witness in the confident expectation that God will move and act on our hearers in His way and in His time" (p. 119).

The simple, yet effective approach taught throughout this book is a wonderful way for families to engage in evangelism. If we can help ourselves and our children to be comfortable sharing spiritual experiences with friends and strangers there is no end to the possibilities that friendship evangelism holds out. This book encourages us to wholistic evangelism through sharing our friendship, knowledge, time, finances. Our intimate friendship with Jesus Christ becomes the basis of our intimate sharing of this friendship with others. We may eventually set up a small group but the initial contacts will come from our naturally reaching out to the people we meet in the classroom, on the street, on the bus or subway, on an airplane, in the supermarket check-out, the doctor's waiting room etc. "For a variety of reasons, people are drawn in more often by the warmth of relationship than by the brilliance of apologetics" (p. 234).

However, apologetics are not missing from the book. Chapter 15 deals with answering the "modern" sceptic who shares a common understanding of truth. Chapter 16 offers an approach to "post-moderns" who often care more about whether something is experientially "real," than whether it is true. Chapter 17 includes some very helpful material on witnessing to people involved in the New Age and other alternative forms of spirituality. The final two chapters are devoted to evangelism and the local church with helpful suggestions for evangelism training and modelling.

Pippert not only shares examples of success, but of failure also. Not everyone will accept our loving approaches to them, but Pippert helps us to look beyond those situations. We find ourselves becoming excited as we read the accounts of individuals who have dared for Jesus. We yearn to have similar experiences, and undergo the same spiritual growth. This book shares with us how to "be free to live as salt and light, so that (we) will be Christ's agents of healing and hope in a broken world" (p. 10).

Families are uniquely placed in the community to be the "salt and the light." Should we not be training our families in Evangelism as presented in this book? What a powerful force for Jesus we would unleash.

# *More* Resources

**Fitzgerald, T. (2002).** *Christwise discipleship guide.* **Hagerstown, MD: Review and Herald Publishing Association.**

*Christwise* is a revolutionary new baptismal course. Geared toward a variety of learning styles, it is story-based, Christ-centered, interactive and age tailored at three levels: Ages 9-12, 13-15, and 15-18. It seeks to lead the participant into relationship, then on to friendship, worship, discipleship, leadership, ownership, and finally to mentorship, so that the new disciple becomes involved in making disciples for Christ. More than a baptismal course, this is a curriculum for Christian discipleship. It enables youth to mentor other youth, lead them to Christ, and prepare them for baptism.

**Habada, P. (2000).** *GraceLink Sabbath School lessons.* **Silver Spring, MD: General Conference Sabbath School Department.**

The GraceLink lessons provide a basis for the spiritual nurture and evangelization of children in the home. The lessons are developed age appropriately and encourage daily Bible reading, thoughtful reflection on relevant questions, and sharing what they learn with others.

**Habenicht, D. (1998).** *Come meet Jesus.* **Hagerstown, MD: Review and Herald Publishing Association.**

This kit contains a complete set of 26 children's programs that provide resources for children's programming as part of a public evangelism series. It may also be adapted for use in campmeetings, retreats, weekly children's prayer meeting series, or Vacation Bible School. The kit includes: program guides for ages 4-7 and ages 8-11, a CD of 15 upbeat children's songs, 2 music videos, 6 videos with attention-grabbing segments for each lesson, and a copy of the New King James Version of the Holy Bible with H. M. S. Richards Study Helps.

**Holford, K. (2003).** *100 creative prayer ideas for kids.* **Nampa, ID: Pacific Press Publishing Association.**

This book makes prayer time with Jesus interesting, meaningful, and even fun! A helpful index organizes the various prayer activities by age and other categories. Many of these ideas will work especially well in small group settings, or use them in your own prayer time to put a fresh sparkle into your prayer life! From "Bag of Bits Prayer," and "Blessings Basket," to "Garden Prayers," this book provides a smorgasbord of simple activities that will help kids and adults find new delight in talking to God.

**Hopkins, G. L., & Hopp, J. W. (2002).** *It takes a church.* **Nampa, ID: Pacific Press Publishing Association.**

Drugs, alcohol, sex, school violence, broken homes, and Internet pornography are some of the dangers that put our children at high risk. But the lack of support from a network of caring adults is perhaps the greatest, and least talked about, risk factor of all. In this book the authors place the burden of providing spiritual and moral protection for our children squarely on the shoulders of every church member. Acknowledging the lead role of parents, they invite the larger community of believers to join parents in the fight for the hearts and minds of the youth by forming a hedge of support and nurture around our most vulnerable members.

**Kuzma, K.** *Welcome baby program kit.* **Lincoln, NE: AdventSource.**

The Welcome Baby Program is designed to reach young adults, a population group not easily reached by traditional outreach methods. The newsletters are written for all new parents but will be particularly meaningful to parents having their first baby. Kit includes: complete resource manual, handbook for parents and friends, introductory video, set of newsletters, sample welcome baby card.

For information: http://www.adventsource.org or http://www.kaykuzma.com.

**London, H. B., Jr., & Wiseman, N. B. (2003). *Pastors at greater risk*. Ventura, CA: Regal Books.**

London and Wiseman have updated their very helpful 1993 edition of this book. They bring not only pastoral experience but also interviews with well-known Christian leaders to this work designed to help pastors understand and address the unique dangers of pastoral ministry. Everyone needs someone to confide in — even pastors. Here's real pastor-to-pastor help on today's most pressing issues.

**MacLafferty, D. (release date 2005). *Footprints in the sand I & II*. Lincoln, NE: AdventSource.**

This resource is now being piloted from the Collegedale Kid Center as part of the ministry of the university church at Southern Adventist University. It is a two-part, local-church-based children's discipleship program. *Footprints I* is a set of 12 lessons to disciple parents. *Footprints II* consists of 32 additional lessons for discipling juniors and their families. A training event, *Kid University*, is currently offered in the Spring by the Collegedale Kid Center. It provides hands-on leadership development for pastors and discipleship leaders who wish to bring the children's discipleship program to their church. For more information, go to kidcenter@southern.edu.

**Poe, H. L. (2001). *Christian witness in a postmodern world*. Nashville, TN: Abingdon.**

In this book the author addresses the questions: What happens to evangelism when old assumptions about how to present the gospel no longer work? How do you bear witness to Jesus Christ when rational argument and external authority no longer bear much weight among those to whom you are speaking? In a time when Christianity is struggling to reach a changing world, he offers a proposal for bearing Christian witness in a postmodern age through an emphasis on relationships. It is an approach based on a thorough understanding of post-modernity, and it springs naturally from the questions postmodern persons are asking.

**Pollard, L. N. (Ed.). (2000). *Embracing diversity: How to understand and reach people of all cultures*. Hagerstown, MD: Review and Herald.**

Some techniques that work well in one culture may be offensive in another. Mastering interpersonal skills and conversational subtleties can be difficult. The 15 contributing authors to this book provide a guidebook for understanding and reaching people of all cultures based on a biblical foundation for multicultural unity.

**Scazzero, P. with Bird, W. (2003). *The emotionally healthy church: A strategy for discipleship that actually changes lives*. Grand Rapids, MI: Zondervan.**

This book could easily have been titled *The Emotionally Healthy Pastor*. Peter Scazzero tells his own story as a successful church planter whose wife one day announced, "Pete, I'm leaving the church." While the book is by no means autobiographical, Scazzero clearly draws on the painful lessons that he and eventually his entire leadership team learned in the process of growing into an emotionally healthy church. It is essential reading for every pastor who longs for wholeness in his or her own life, family and church. It defines a fresh approach to discipleship that integrates spiritual and emotional health for congregation and pastor.